D1312700

DAPHNE
BYRNE

DAPHNE

BYRNE

LAURA MARKS WRITER

KELLEY JONES ARTIST

MICHELLE MADSEN COLORIST **ROB LEIGH** LETTERER

PIOTR JABŁOŃSKI COLLECTION COVER ARTIST

DAPHNE BYRNE CREATED BY **LAURA MARKS & KELLEY JONES**

CURATED FOR HILL HOUSE COMICS BY **JOE HILL**

DAPHNE BYRNE

PUBLISHED BY DC COMICS. COMPILATION AND
ALL NEW MATERIAL COPYRIGHT © 2020 LAURA
MARKS AND KELLEY JONES. ALL RIGHTS RESERVED.
ORIGINALLY PUBLISHED IN SINGLE MAGAZINE FORM
IN *DAPHNE BYRNE* 1-6. COPYRIGHT © 2019, 2020
LAURA MARKS AND KELLEY JONES. ALL RIGHTS
RESERVED. ALL CHARACTERS, THEIR DISTINCTIVE
LIKENESSES, AND RELATED ELEMENTS FEATURED
IN THIS PUBLICATION ARE TRADEMARKS OF LAURA
MARKS AND KELLEY JONES. HILL HOUSE COMICS
IS A TRADEMARK OF DC COMICS. THE STORIES,
CHARACTERS, AND INCIDENTS FEATURED IN
THIS PUBLICATION ARE ENTIRELY FICTIONAL. DC
COMICS DOES NOT READ OR ACCEPT UNSOLICITED
SUBMISSIONS OF IDEAS, STORIES, OR ARTWORK.
DC – A WARNERMEDIA COMPANY.

DC COMICS, 2900 WEST ALAMEDA AVE., BURBANK,
CA 91505

PRINTED BY TRANSCONTINENTAL INTERGLOBE,
BEAUCEVILLE, QC, CANADA. 9/25/20. FIRST PRINTING.

ISBN: 978-1-77950-465-4

LIBRARY OF CONGRESS CATALOGING-IN-PUBLICATION
DATA IS AVAILABLE.

PEFC Certified

This product is
from sustainably
managed forests and
controlled sources

PEFC/01-31-106   www.pefc.org

CHRIS CONROY EDITOR – ORIGINAL SERIES
MAGGIE HOWELL ASSISTANT EDITOR – ORIGINAL SERIES
JEB WOODARD GROUP EDITOR – COLLECTED EDITIONS
ROBIN WILDMAN EDITOR – COLLECTED EDITION
STEVE COOK DESIGN DIRECTOR – BOOKS
MEGEN BELLERSEN PUBLICATION DESIGN
SUZANNAH ROWNTREE PUBLICATION PRODUCTION

BOB HARRAS SENIOR VP – EDITOR-IN-CHIEF, DC COMICS
MARK DOYLE EXECUTIVE EDITOR, DC BLACK LABEL

JIM LEE PUBLISHER & CHIEF CREATIVE OFFICER
BOBBIE CHASE VP – GLOBAL PUBLISHING INITIATIVES & DIGITAL STRATEGY
DON FALLETTI VP – MANUFACTURING OPERATIONS & WORKFLOW MANAGEM
LAWRENCE GANEM VP – TALENT SERVICES
ALISON GILL SENIOR VP – MANUFACTURING & OPERATIONS
HANK KANALZ SENIOR VP – PUBLISHING STRATEGY & SUPPORT SERVICES
DAN MIRON VP – PUBLISHING OPERATIONS
NICK J. NAPOLITANO VP – MANUFACTURING ADMINISTRATION & DESIGN
NANCY SPEARS VP – SALES
JONAH WEILAND VP – MARKETING & CREATIVE SERVICES
MICHELE R. WELLS VP & EXECUTIVE EDITOR, YOUNG READER

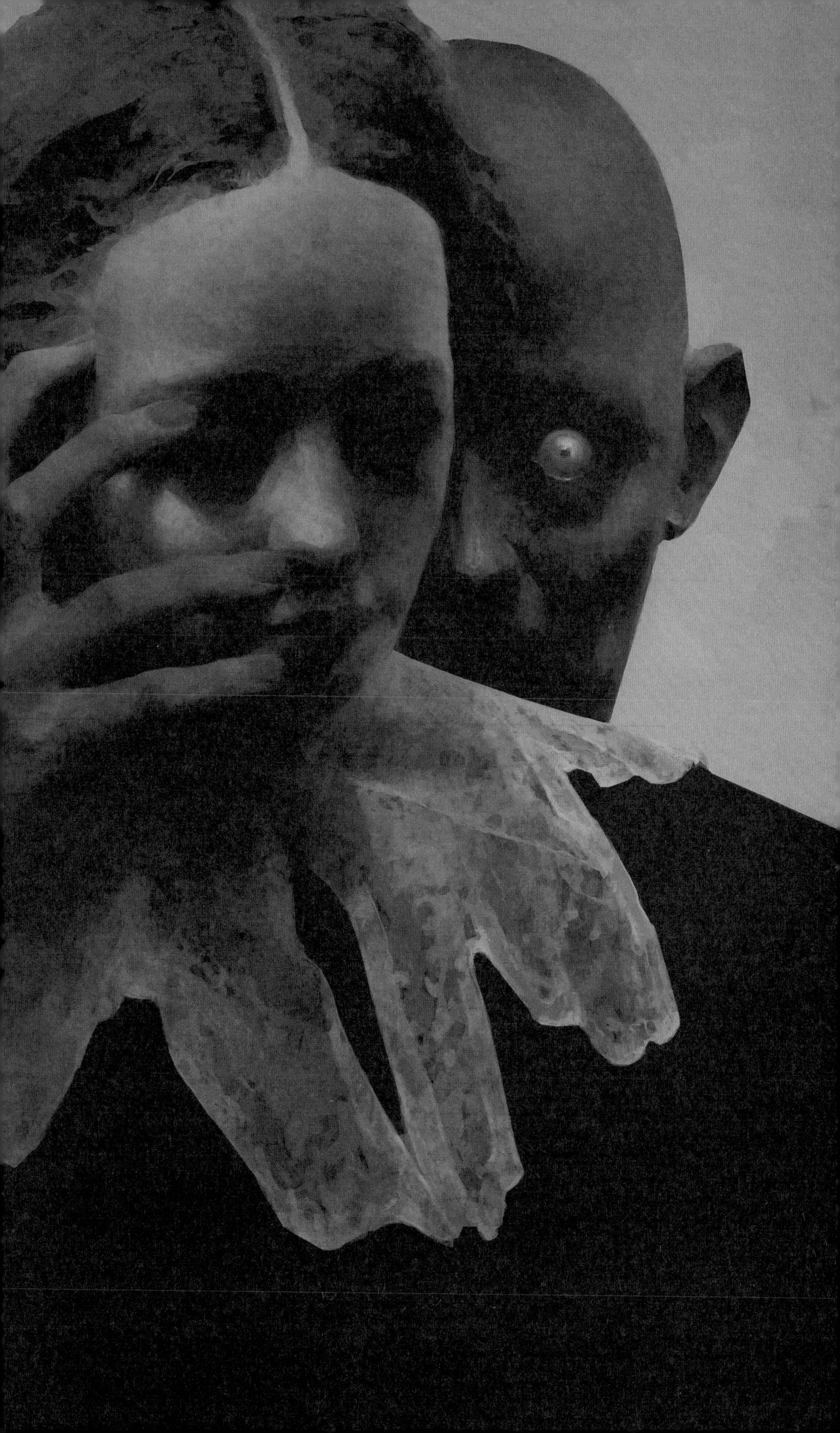

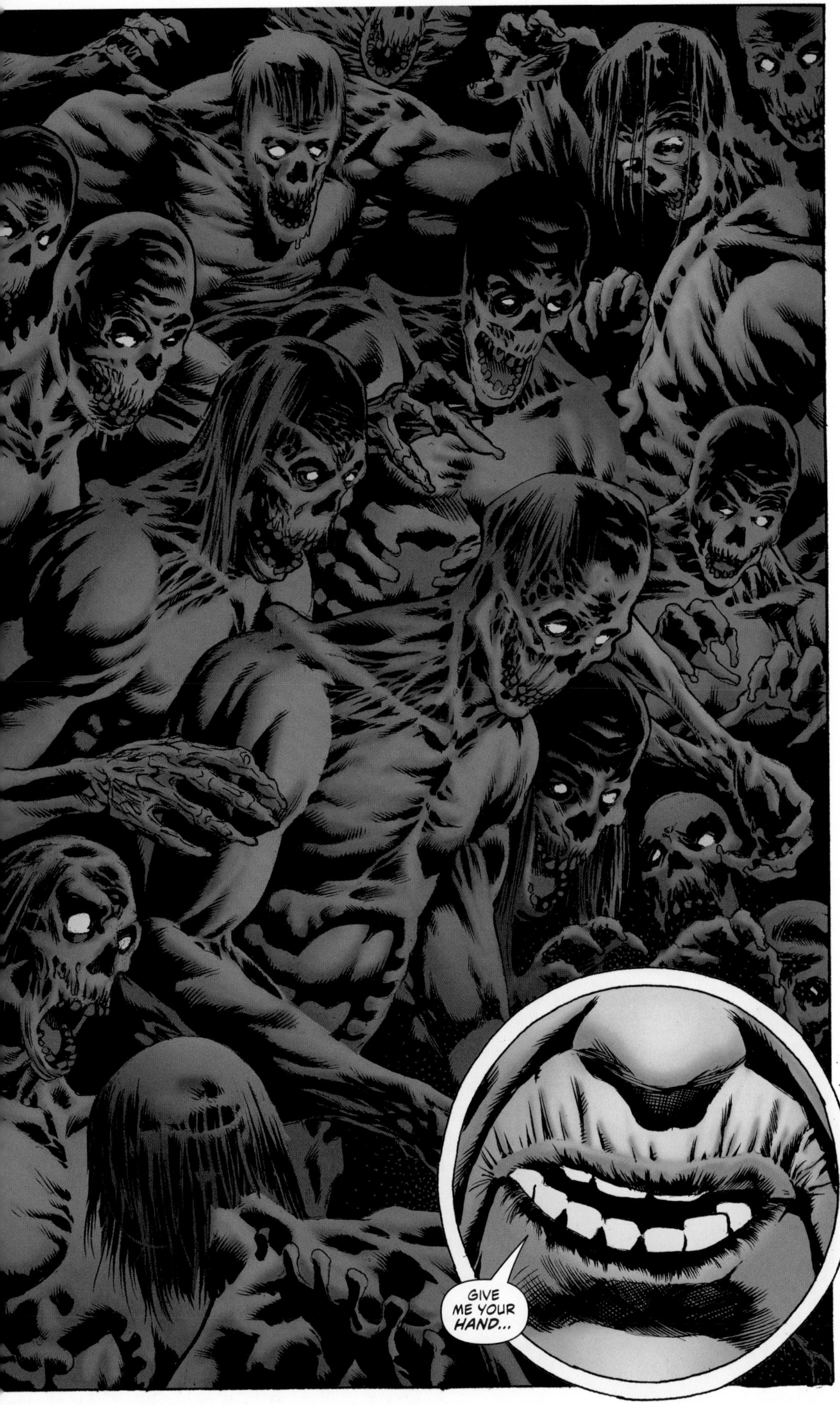
GIVE ME YOUR HAND...

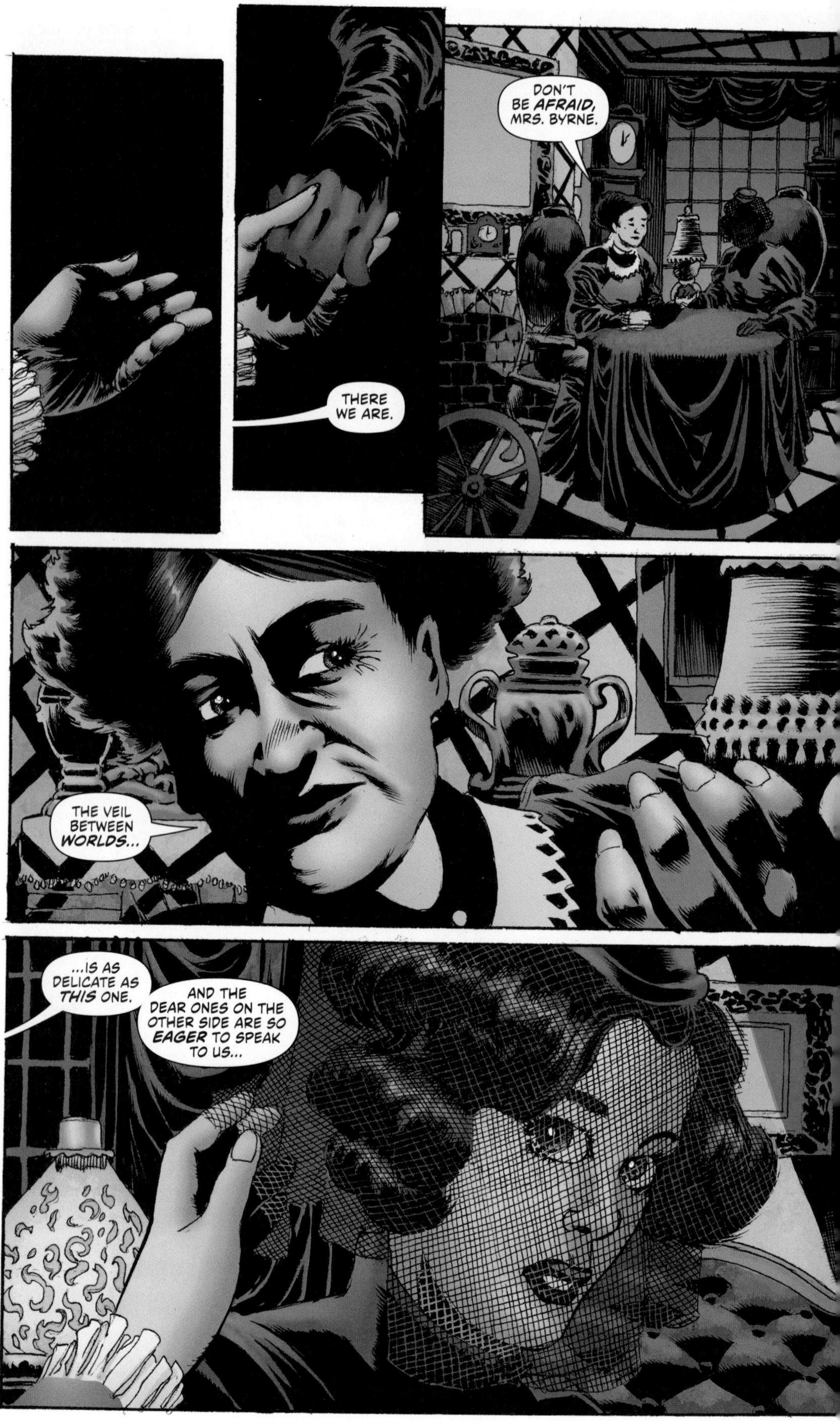
THERE WE ARE.
DON'T BE AFRAID, MRS. BYRNE.
THE VEIL BETWEEN WORLDS...
...IS AS DELICATE AS THIS ONE.
AND THE DEAR ONES ON THE OTHER SIDE ARE SO EAGER TO SPEAK TO US...

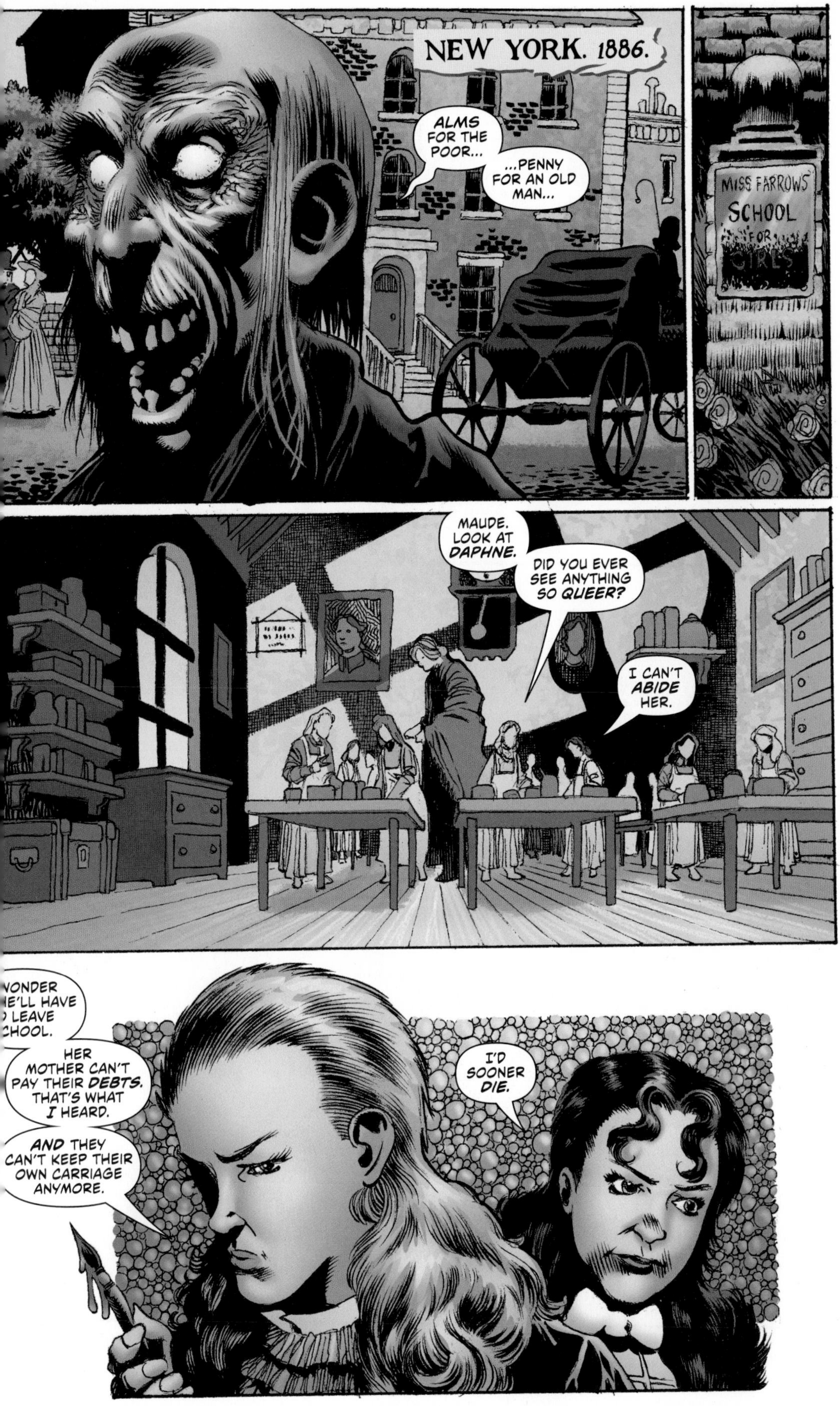
NEW YORK. 1886.
ALMS FOR THE POOR...
...PENNY FOR AN OLD MAN...
MISS FARROWS SCHOOL FOR
MAUDE. LOOK AT DAPHNE.
DID YOU EVER SEE ANYTHING SO QUEER?
I CAN'T ABIDE HER.
VONDER IE'LL HAVE) LEAVE CHOOL.
HER MOTHER CAN'T PAY THEIR DEBTS. THAT'S WHAT I HEARD.
AND THEY CAN'T KEEP THEIR OWN CARRIAGE ANYMORE.
I'D SOONER DIE.

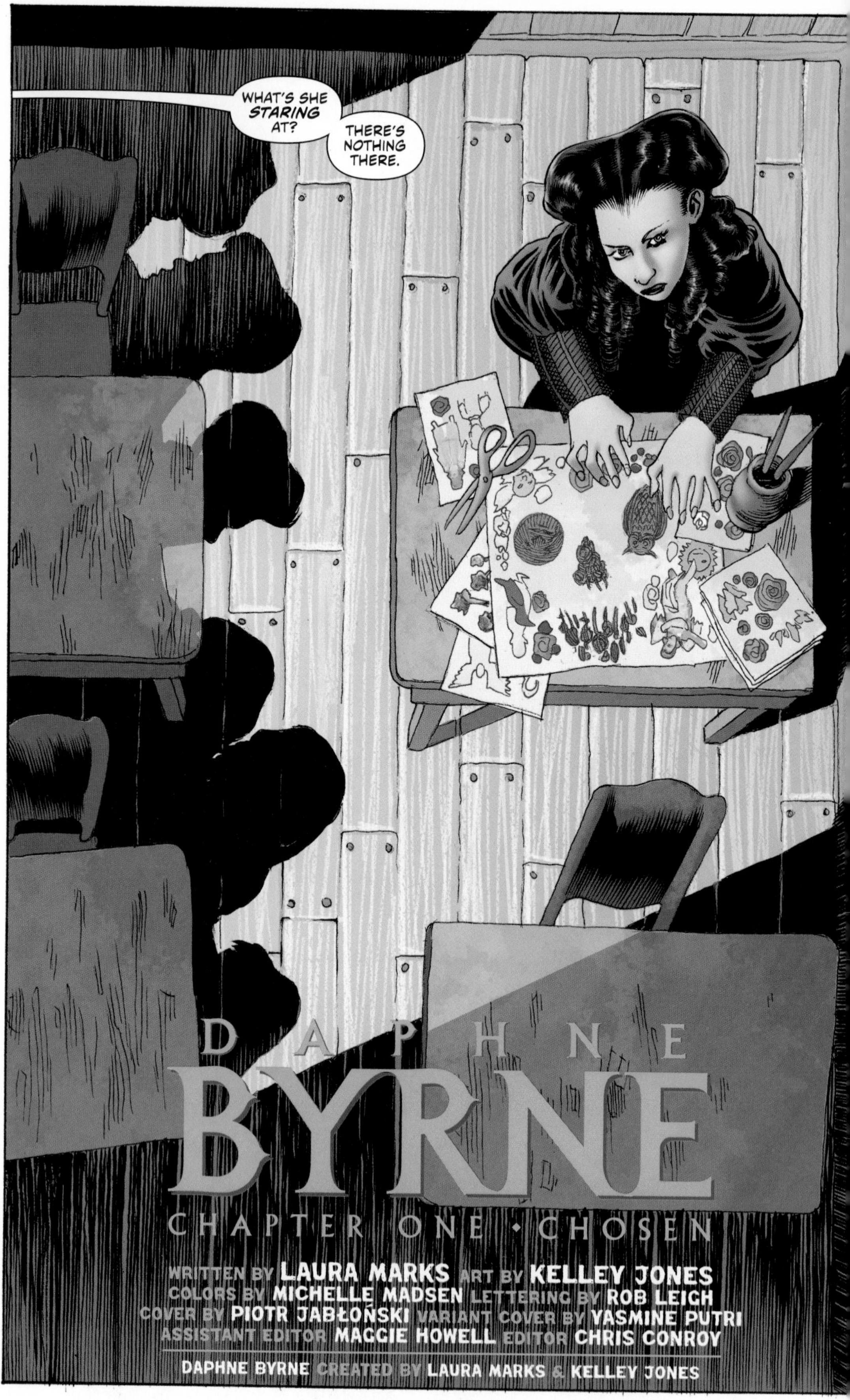

WHAT'S SHE *STARING* AT?
THERE'S NOTHING THERE.
DAPHNE BYRNE
CHAPTER ONE • CHOSEN
WRITTEN BY LAURA MARKS ART BY KELLEY JONES
COLORS BY MICHELLE MADSEN LETTERING BY ROB LEIGH
COVER BY PIOTR JABŁOŃSKI VARIANT COVER BY YASMINE PUTRI
ASSISTANT EDITOR MAGGIE HOWELL EDITOR CHRIS CONROY
DAPHNE BYRNE CREATED BY LAURA MARKS & KELLEY JONES

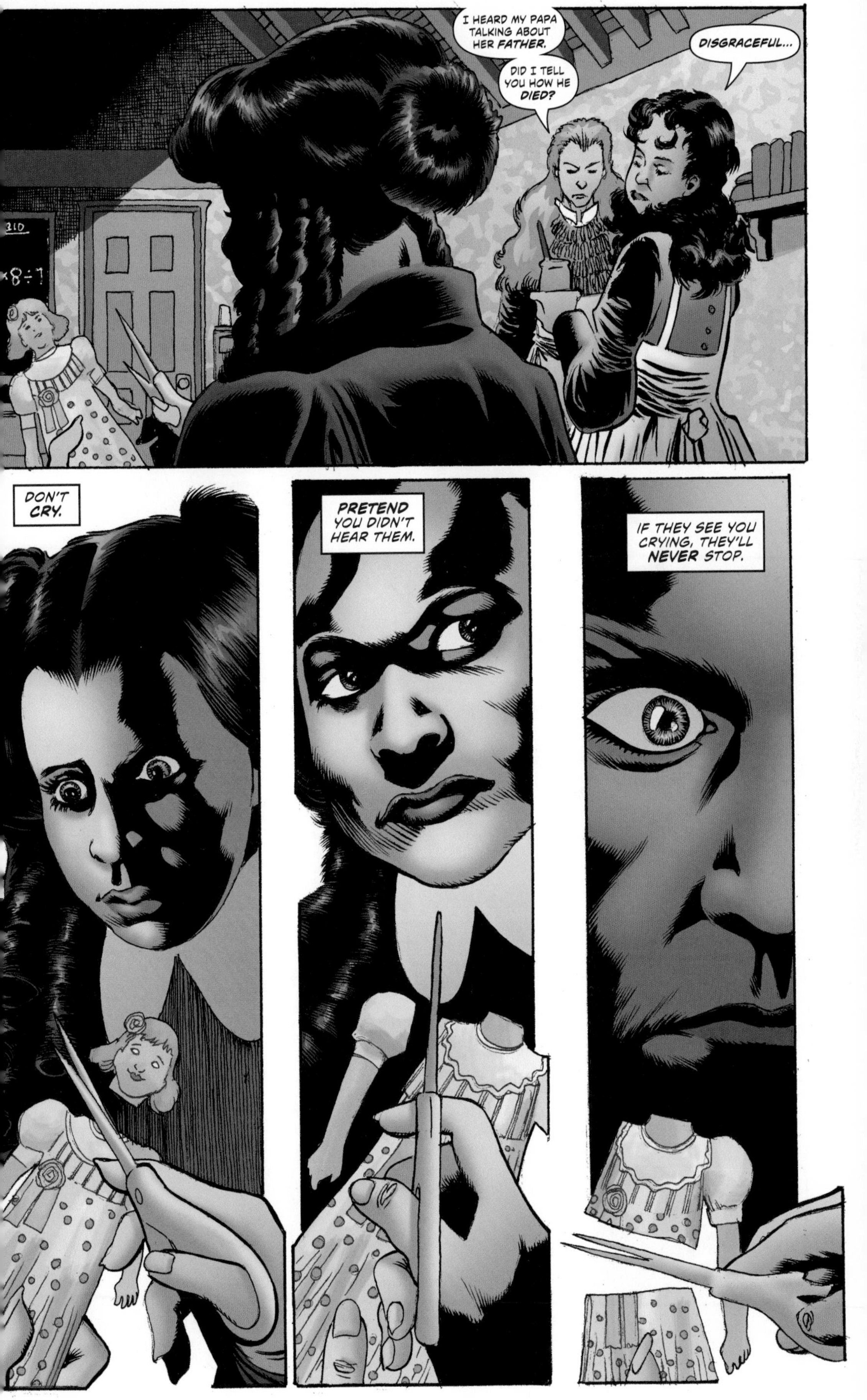
I HEARD MY PAPA TALKING ABOUT HER FATHER.
DID I TELL YOU HOW HE DIED?
DISGRACEFUL...
DON'T CRY.
PRETEND YOU DIDN'T HEAR THEM.
IF THEY SEE YOU CRYING, THEY'LL NEVER STOP.

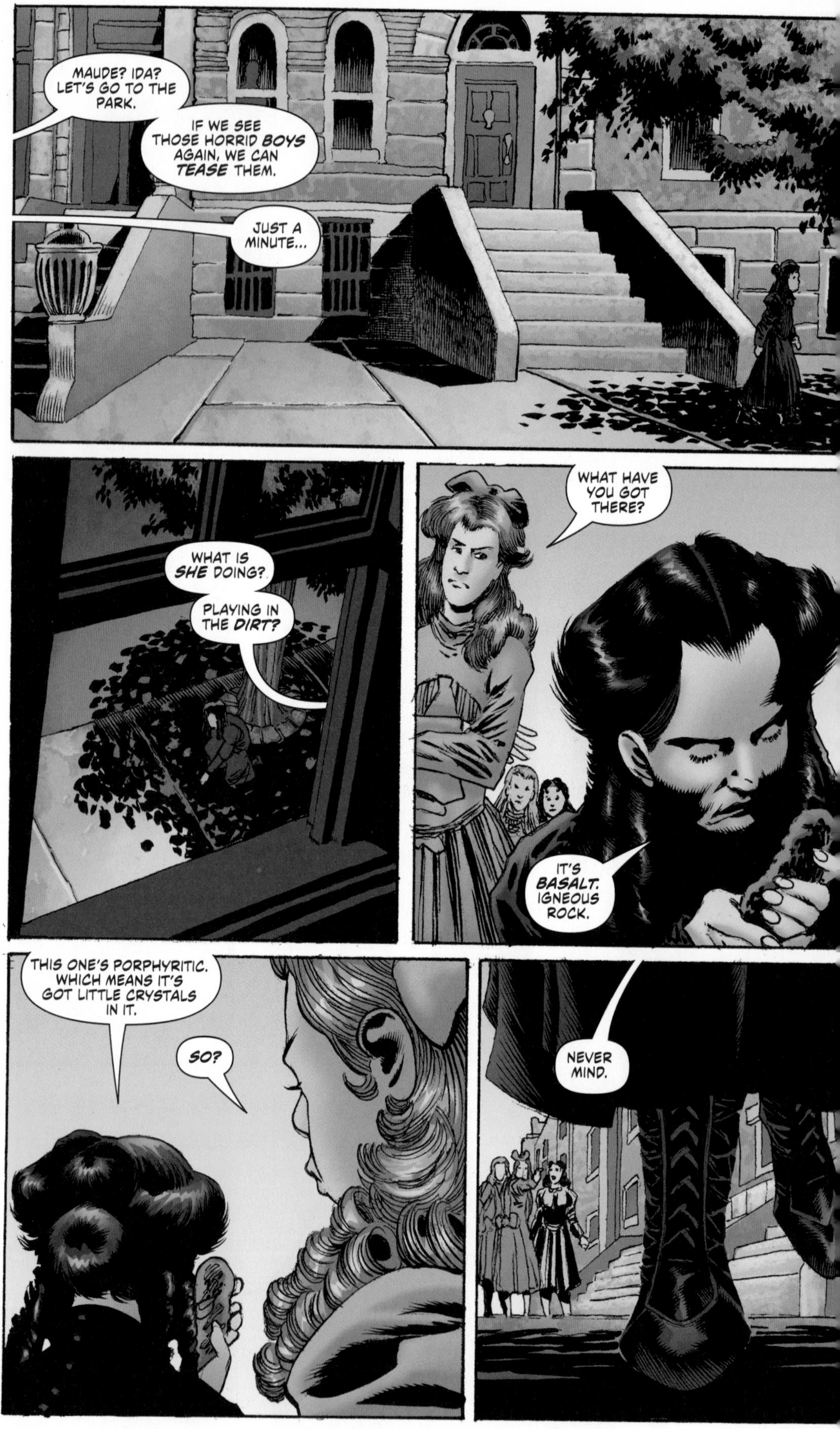
MAUDE? IDA? LET'S GO TO THE PARK.
IF WE SEE THOSE HORRID *BOYS* AGAIN, WE CAN *TEASE* THEM.
JUST A MINUTE...
WHAT IS *SHE* DOING?
PLAYING IN THE *DIRT?*
WHAT HAVE YOU GOT THERE?
IT'S *BASALT.* IGNEOUS ROCK.
THIS ONE'S PORPHYRITIC. WHICH MEANS IT'S GOT LITTLE CRYSTALS IN IT.
SO?
NEVER MIND.

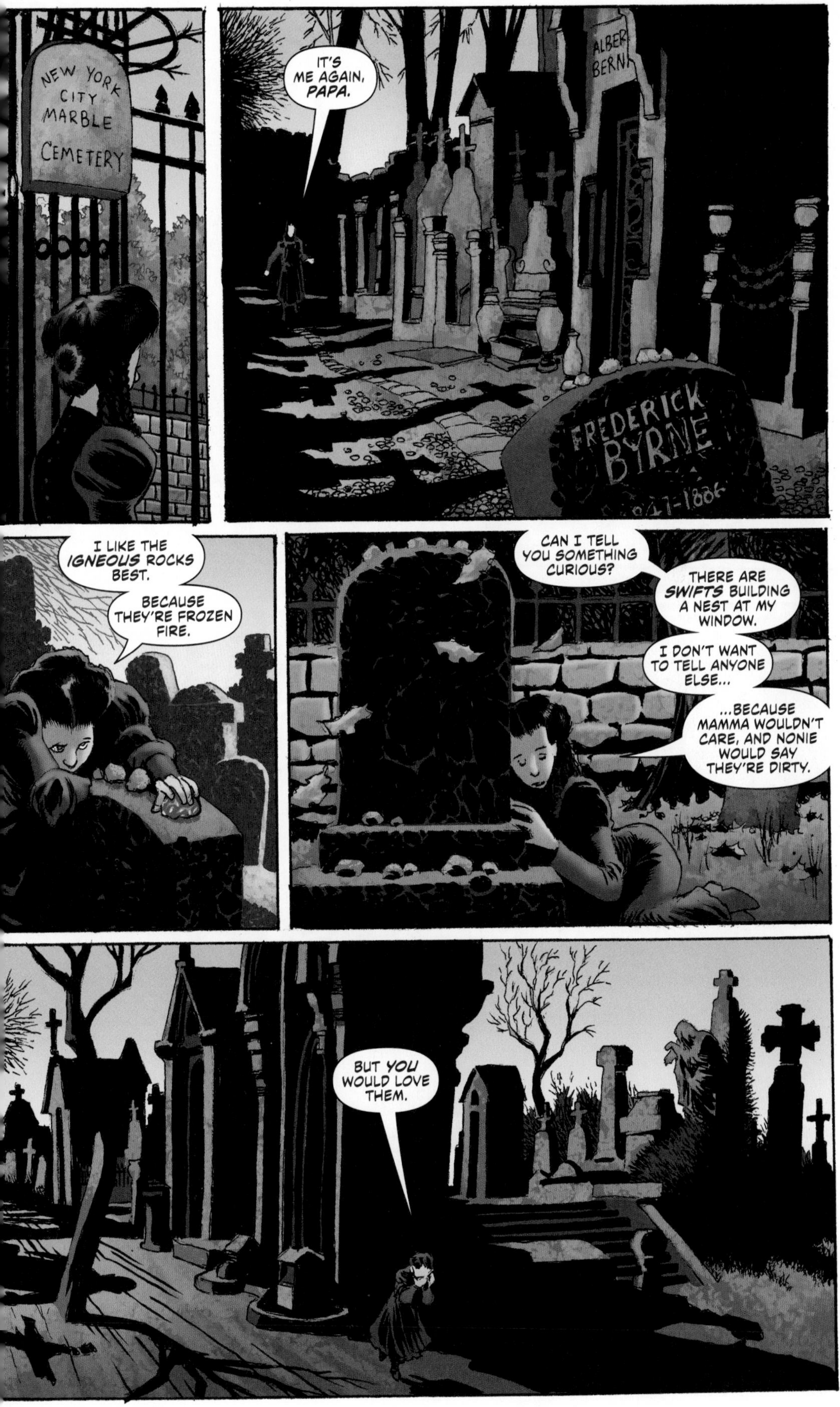
NEW YORK CITY MARBLE CEMETERY
IT'S ME AGAIN, *PAPA.*
FREDERICK BYRNE
I LIKE THE *IGNEOUS* ROCKS BEST.
BECAUSE THEY'RE FROZEN FIRE.
CAN I TELL YOU SOMETHING CURIOUS?
THERE ARE *SWIFTS* BUILDING A NEST AT MY WINDOW.
I DON'T WANT TO TELL ANYONE ELSE...
...BECAUSE MAMMA WOULDN'T CARE, AND NONIE WOULD SAY THEY'RE DIRTY.
BUT *YOU* WOULD LOVE THEM.

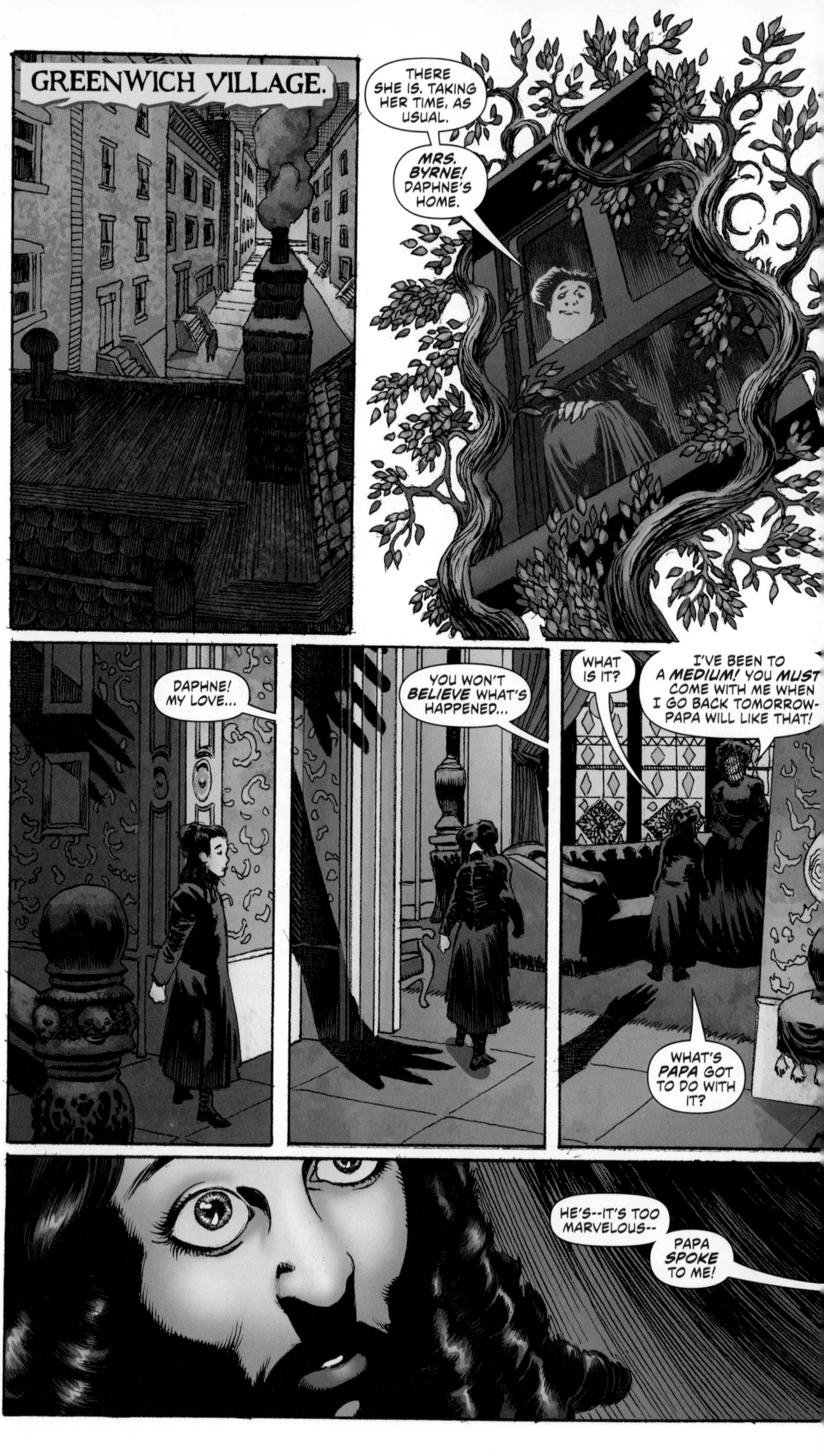
GREENWICH VILLAGE.
THERE SHE IS. TAKING HER TIME, AS USUAL.
MRS. BYRNE! DAPHNE'S HOME.
DAPHNE! MY LOVE...
YOU WON'T BELIEVE WHAT'S HAPPENED...
WHAT IS IT?
I'VE BEEN TO A MEDIUM! YOU MUST COME WITH ME WHEN I GO BACK TOMORROW- PAPA WILL LIKE THAT!
WHAT'S PAPA GOT TO DO WITH IT?
HE'S--IT'S TOO MARVELOUS--
PAPA SPOKE TO ME!

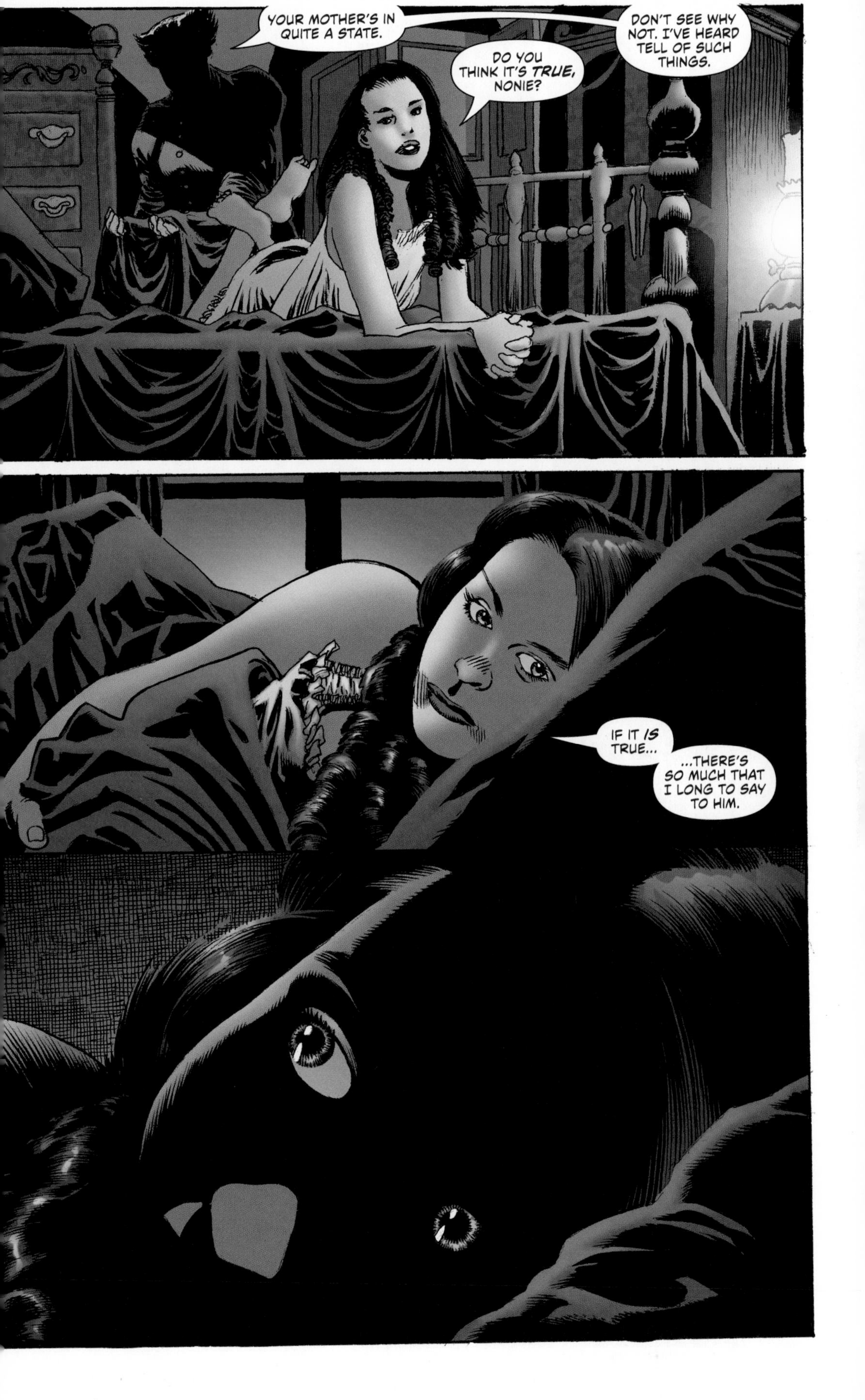
YOUR MOTHER'S IN QUITE A STATE.
DO YOU THINK IT'S *TRUE,* NONIE?
DON'T SEE WHY NOT. I'VE HEARD TELL OF SUCH THINGS.
IF IT *IS* TRUE...
...THERE'S SO MUCH THAT I LONG TO SAY TO HIM.

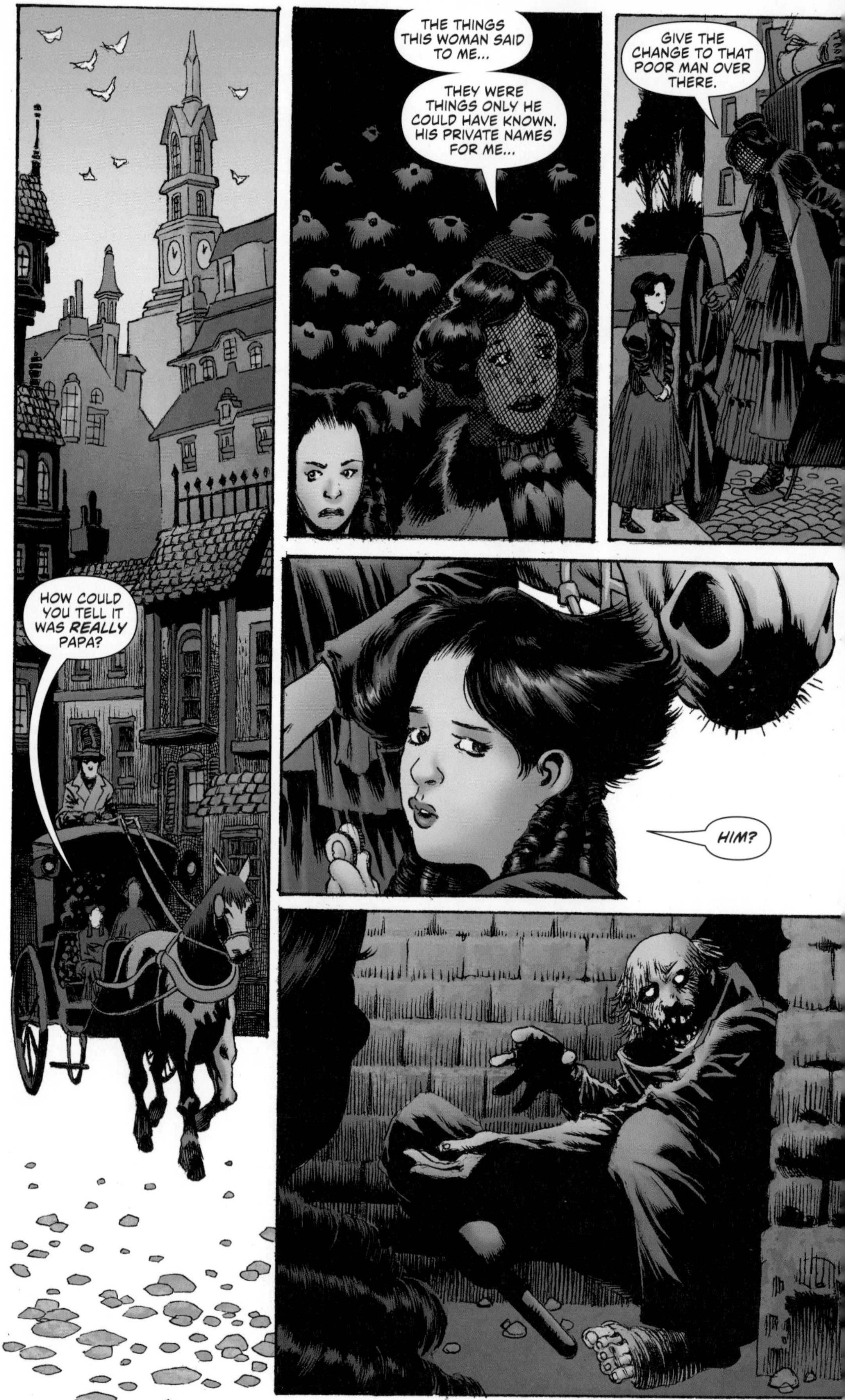
HOW COULD YOU TELL IT WAS *REALLY* PAPA?
THE THINGS THIS WOMAN SAID TO ME...
THEY WERE THINGS ONLY HE COULD HAVE KNOWN. HIS PRIVATE NAMES FOR ME...
GIVE THE CHANGE TO THAT POOR MAN OVER THERE.
HIM?

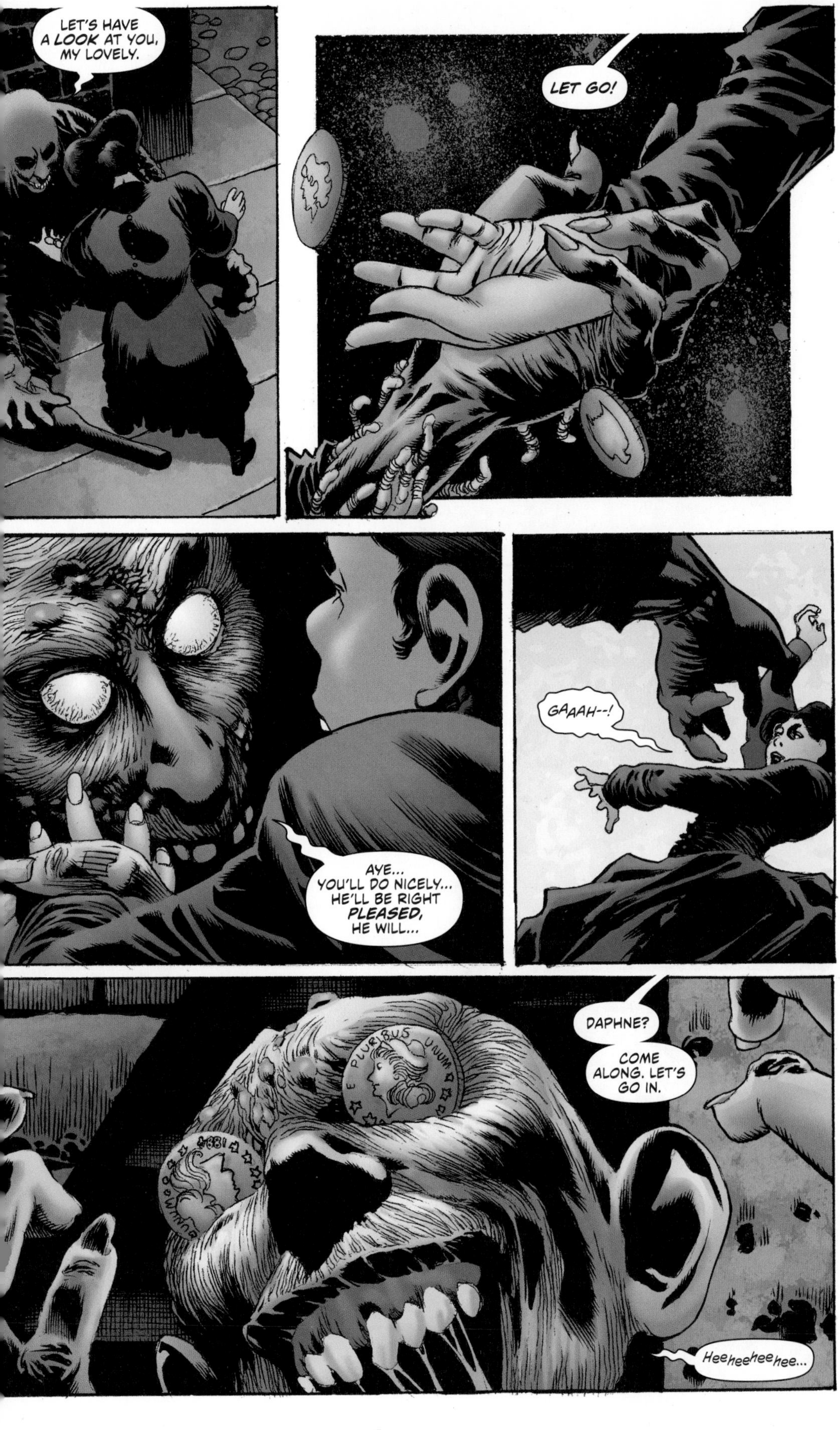
LET'S HAVE A LOOK AT YOU, MY LOVELY.
LET GO!
AYE... YOU'LL DO NICELY... HE'LL BE RIGHT PLEASED, HE WILL...
GAAAH--!
DAPHNE?
COME ALONG. LET'S GO IN.
Heeheeheeheehee...

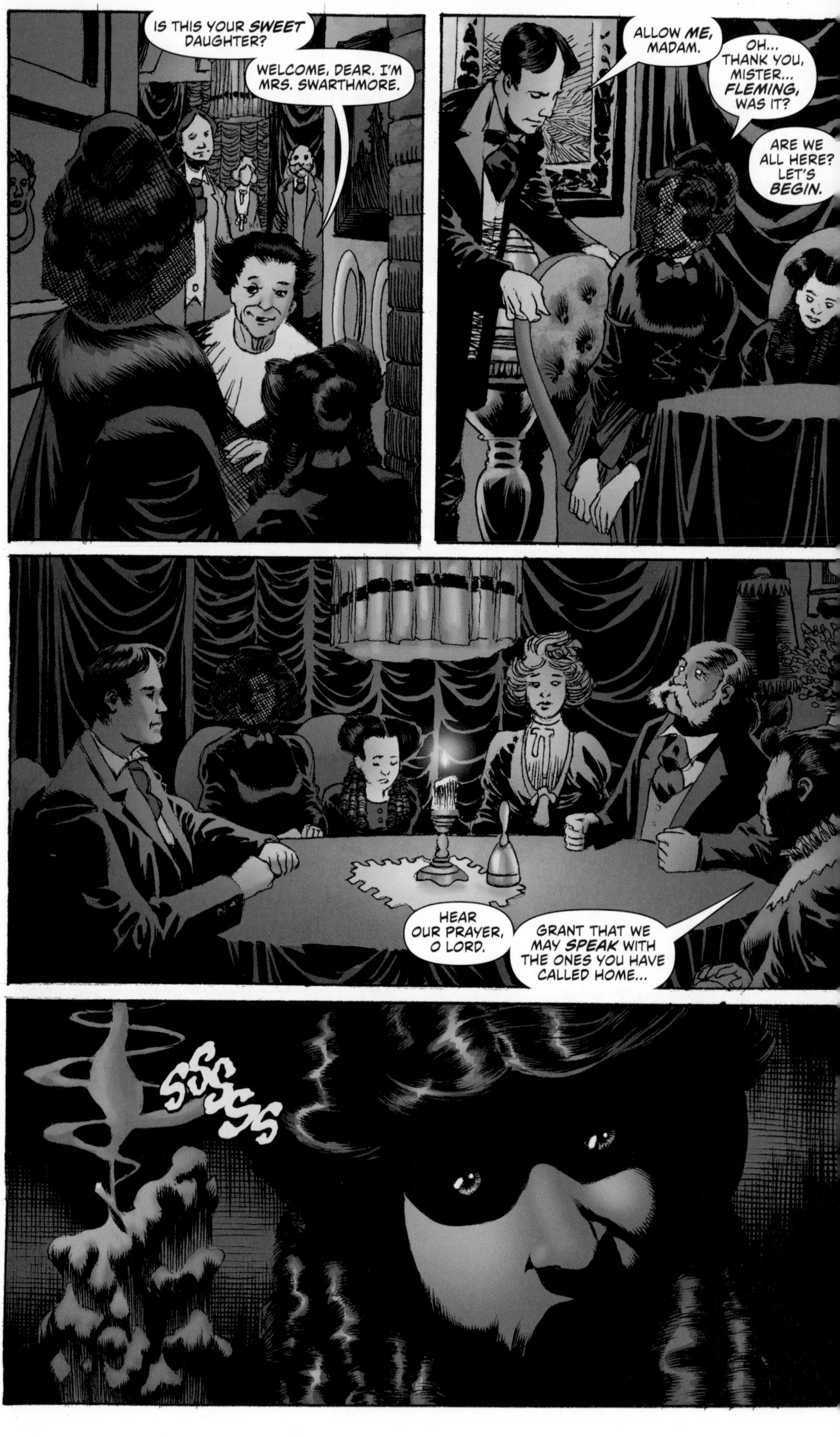
IS THIS YOUR SWEET DAUGHTER?
WELCOME, DEAR. I'M MRS. SWARTHMORE.
ALLOW ME, MADAM.
OH... THANK YOU, MISTER... FLEMING, WAS IT?
ARE WE ALL HERE? LET'S BEGIN.
HEAR OUR PRAYER, O LORD.
GRANT THAT WE MAY SPEAK WITH THE ONES YOU HAVE CALLED HOME...
SSSSSS

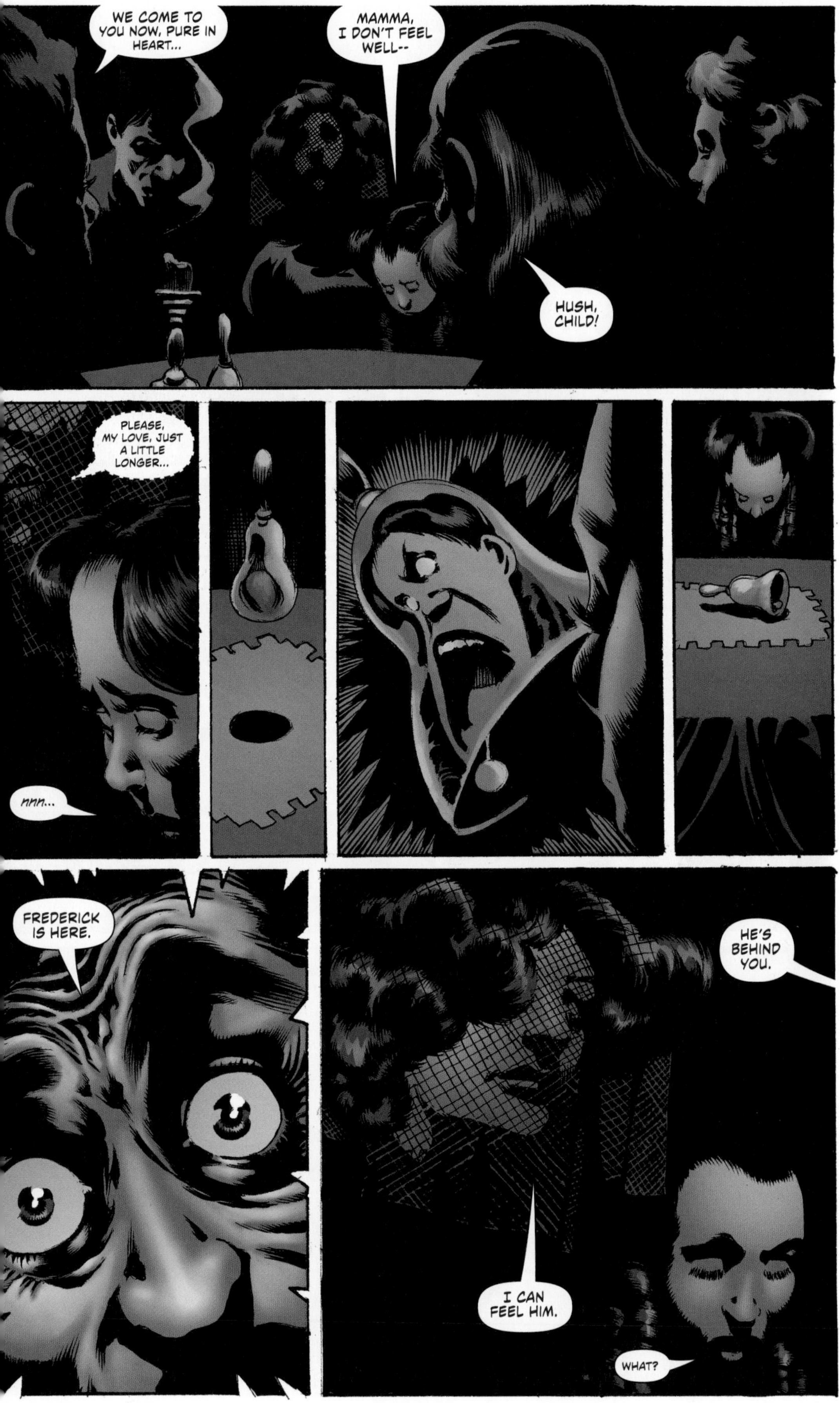
WE COME TO YOU NOW, PURE IN HEART...
MAMMA, I DON'T FEEL WELL--
HUSH, CHILD!
PLEASE, MY LOVE, JUST A LITTLE LONGER...
nnn...
FREDERICK IS HERE.
HE'S BEHIND YOU.
I CAN FEEL HIM.
WHAT?

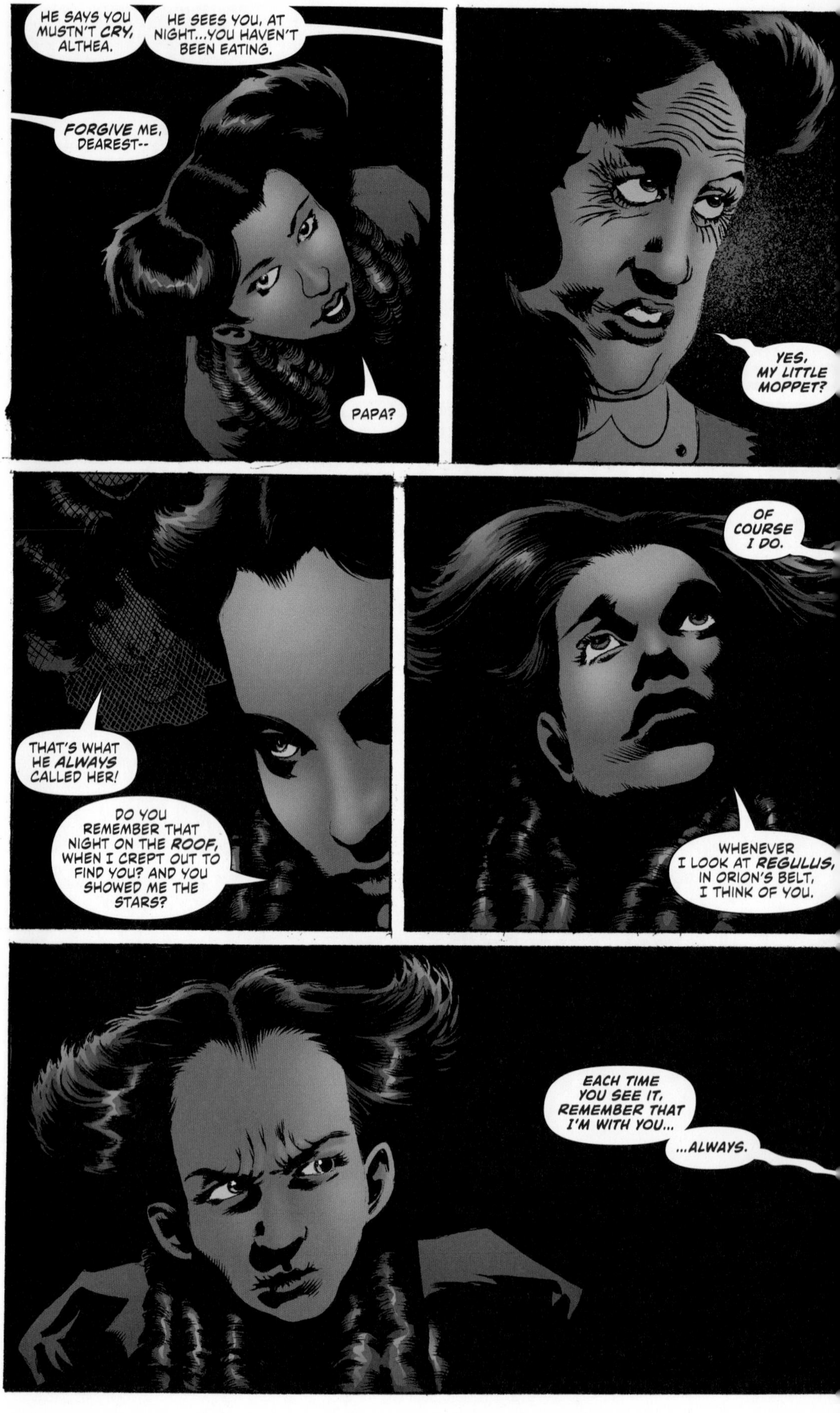
HE SAYS YOU MUSTN'T CRY, ALTHEA.
HE SEES YOU, AT NIGHT...YOU HAVEN'T BEEN EATING.
FORGIVE ME, DEAREST--
PAPA?
YES, MY LITTLE MOPPET?
THAT'S WHAT HE ALWAYS CALLED HER!
DO YOU REMEMBER THAT NIGHT ON THE ROOF, WHEN I CREPT OUT TO FIND YOU? AND YOU SHOWED ME THE STARS?
OF COURSE I DO.
WHENEVER I LOOK AT REGULUS, IN ORION'S BELT, I THINK OF YOU.
EACH TIME YOU SEE IT, REMEMBER THAT I'M WITH YOU...
...ALWAYS.

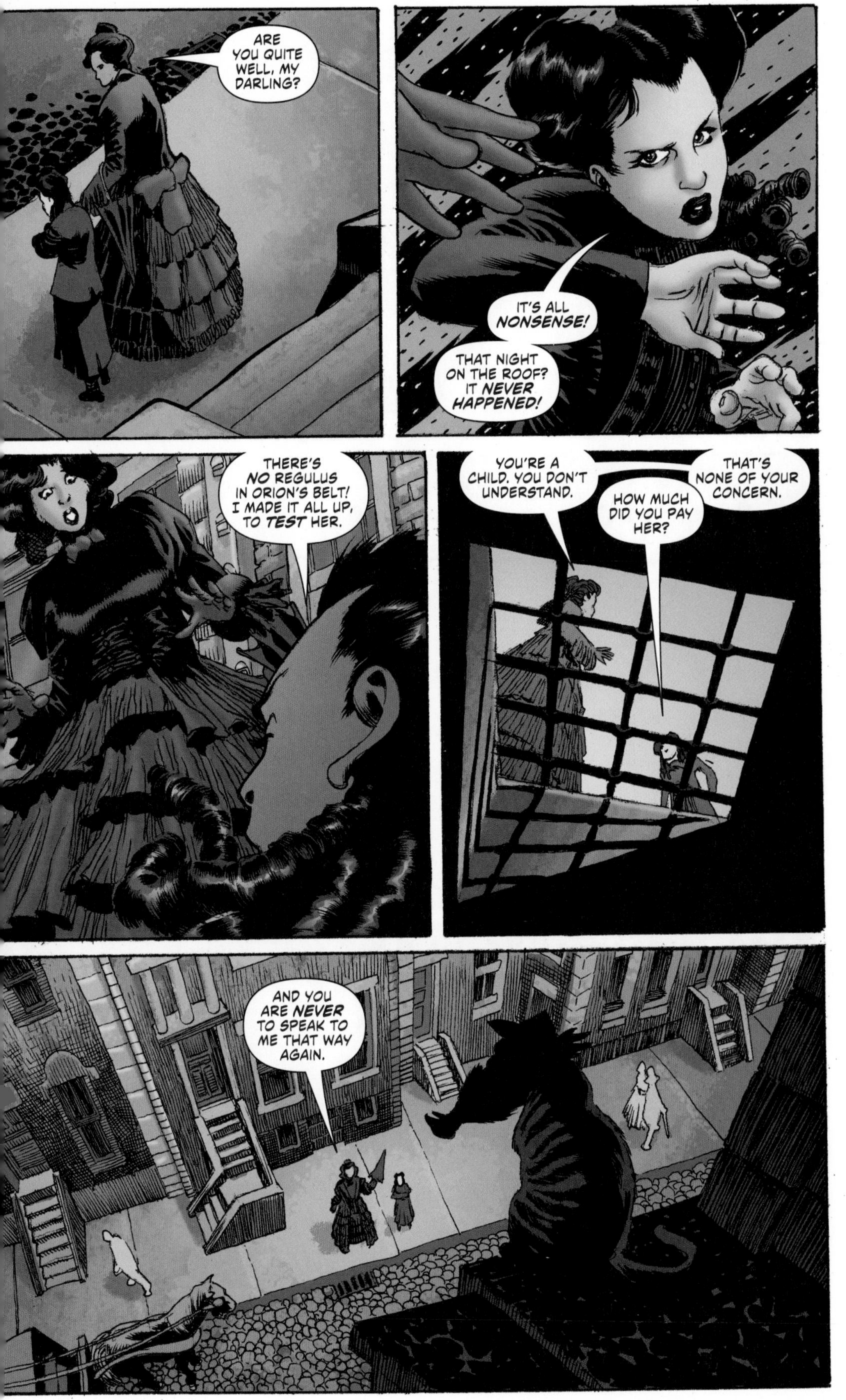
ARE YOU QUITE WELL, MY DARLING?
IT'S ALL NONSENSE!
THAT NIGHT ON THE ROOF? IT NEVER HAPPENED!
THERE'S NO REGULUS IN ORION'S BELT! I MADE IT ALL UP, TO TEST HER.
YOU'RE A CHILD. YOU DON'T UNDERSTAND.
HOW MUCH DID YOU PAY HER?
THAT'S NONE OF YOUR CONCERN.
AND YOU ARE NEVER TO SPEAK TO ME THAT WAY AGAIN.

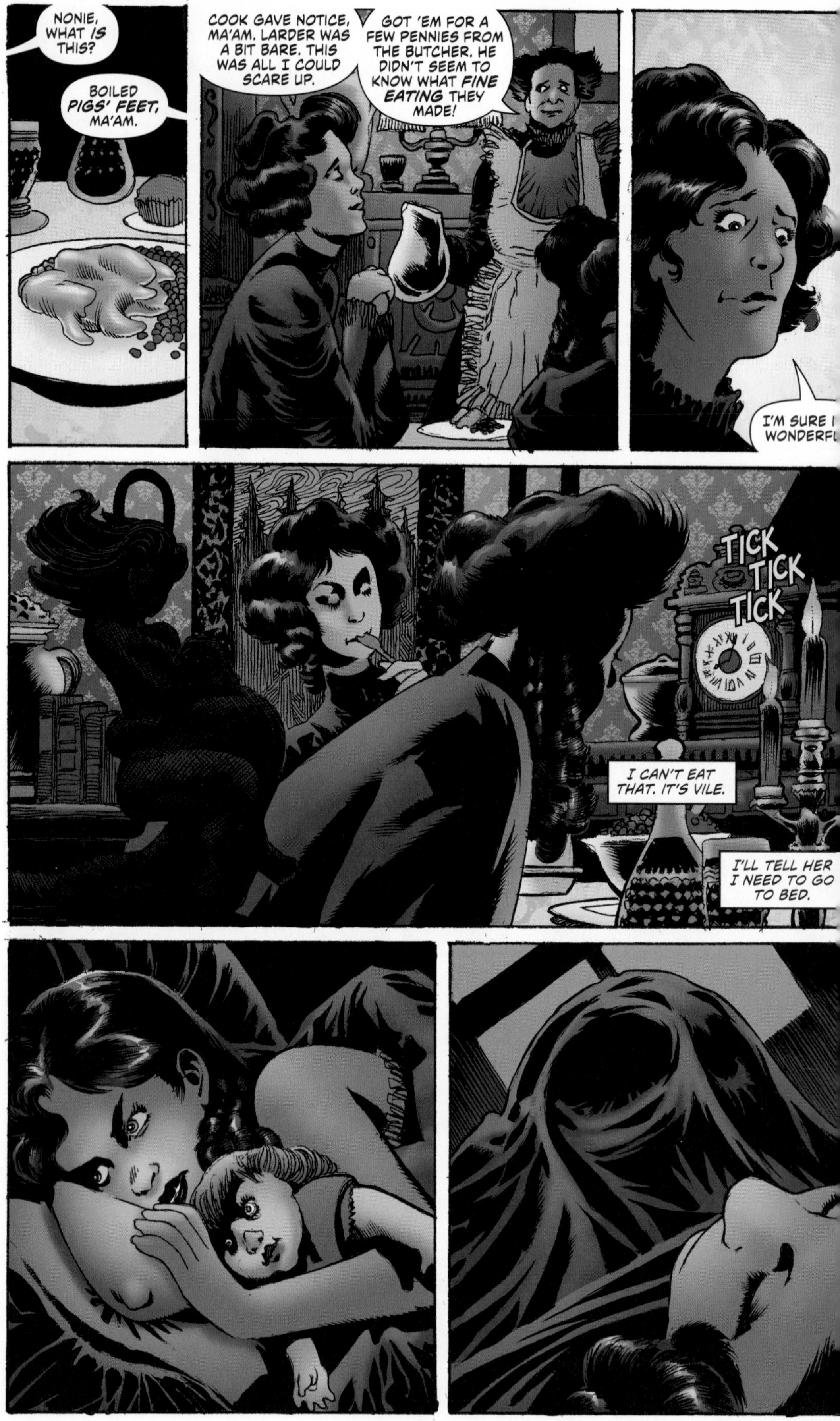
NONIE, WHAT IS THIS?
BOILED PIGS' FEET, MA'AM.
COOK GAVE NOTICE, MA'AM. LARDER WAS A BIT BARE. THIS WAS ALL I COULD SCARE UP.
GOT 'EM FOR A FEW PENNIES FROM THE BUTCHER. HE DIDN'T SEEM TO KNOW WHAT FINE EATING THEY MADE!
I'M SURE I
WONDERF
TICK TICK TICK
I CAN'T EAT THAT. IT'S VILE.
I'LL TELL HER I NEED TO GO TO BED.

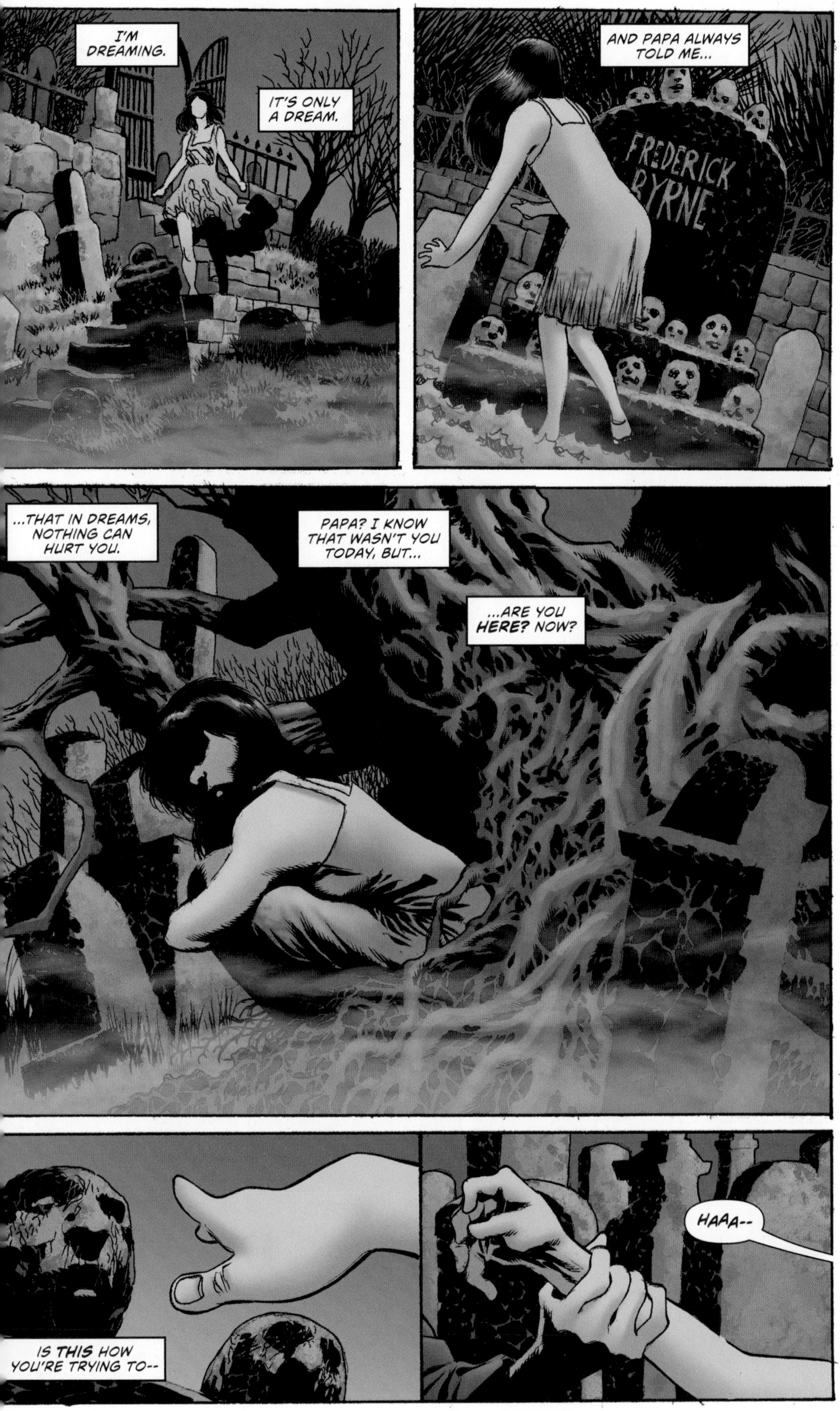
I'M DREAMING.
IT'S ONLY A DREAM.
AND PAPA ALWAYS TOLD ME...
FREDERICK BYRNE
...THAT IN DREAMS, NOTHING CAN HURT YOU.
PAPA? I KNOW THAT WASN'T YOU TODAY, BUT...
...ARE YOU HERE? NOW?
IS THIS HOW YOU'RE TRYING TO--
HAAA--

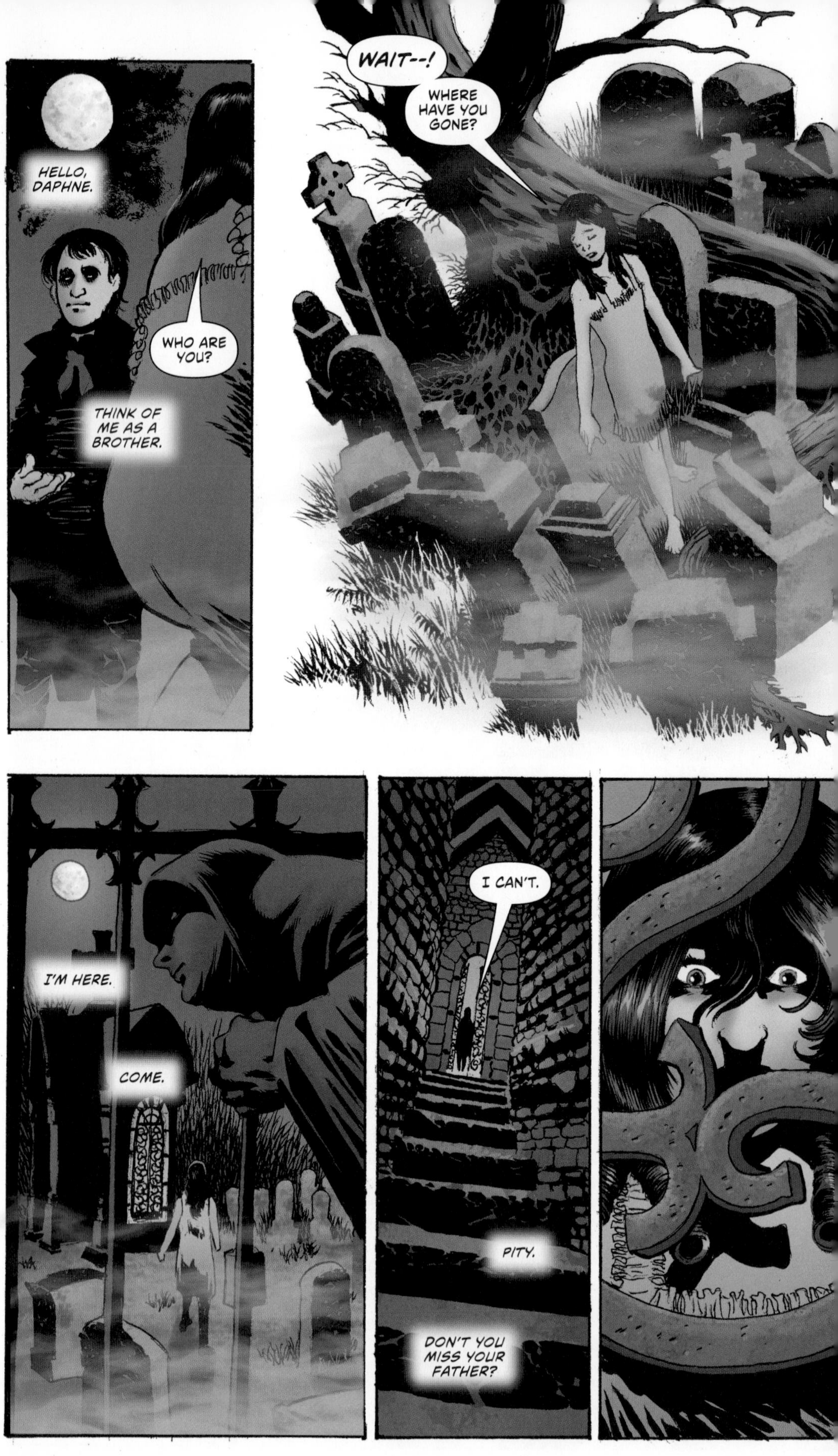
HELLO, DAPHNE.
WHO ARE YOU?
THINK OF ME AS A BROTHER.
WAIT--!
WHERE HAVE YOU GONE?
I'M HERE.
COME.
I CAN'T.
PITY.
DON'T YOU MISS YOUR FATHER?

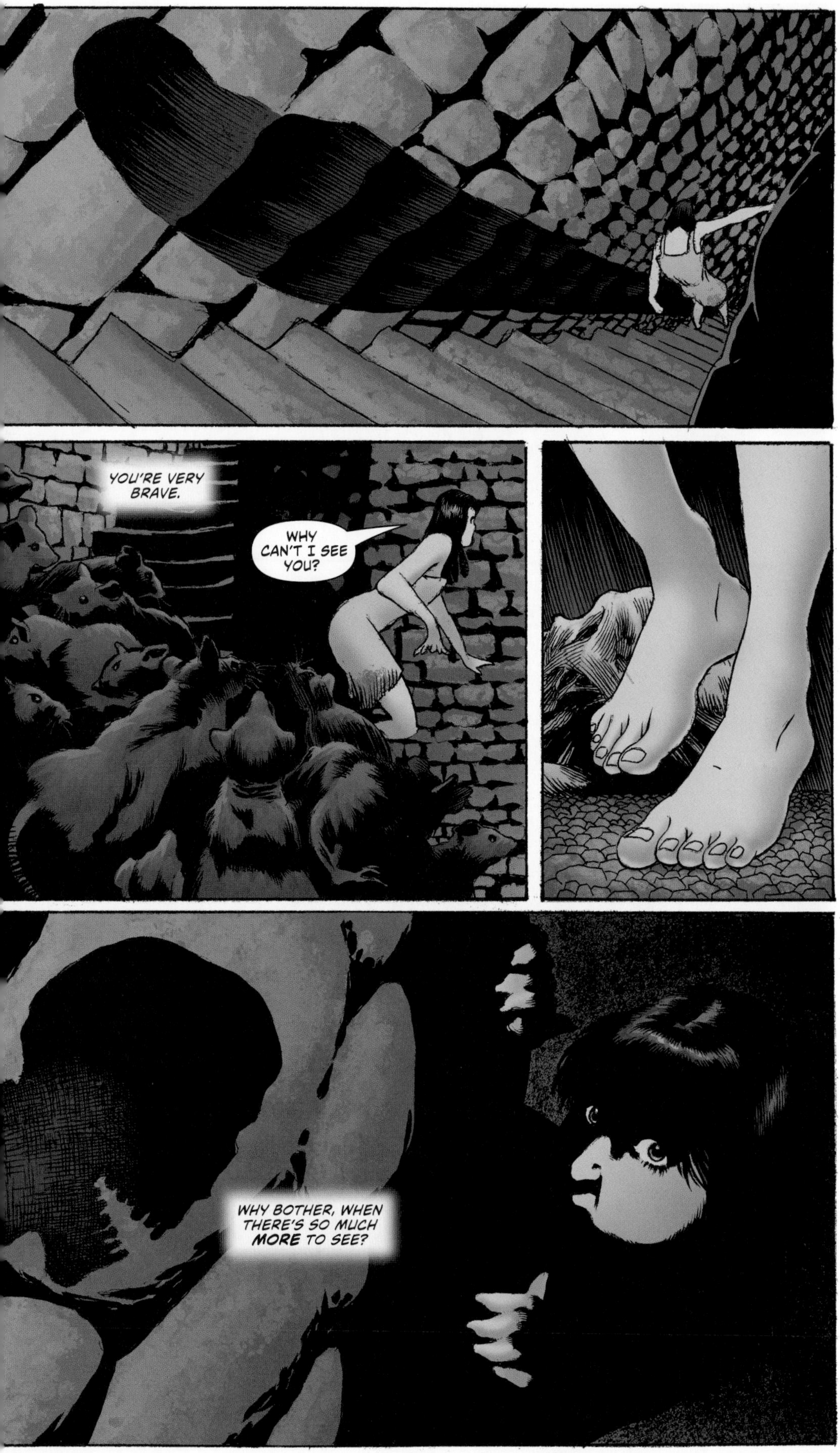
YOU'RE VERY BRAVE.
WHY CAN'T I SEE YOU?
WHY BOTHER, WHEN THERE'S SO MUCH MORE TO SEE?

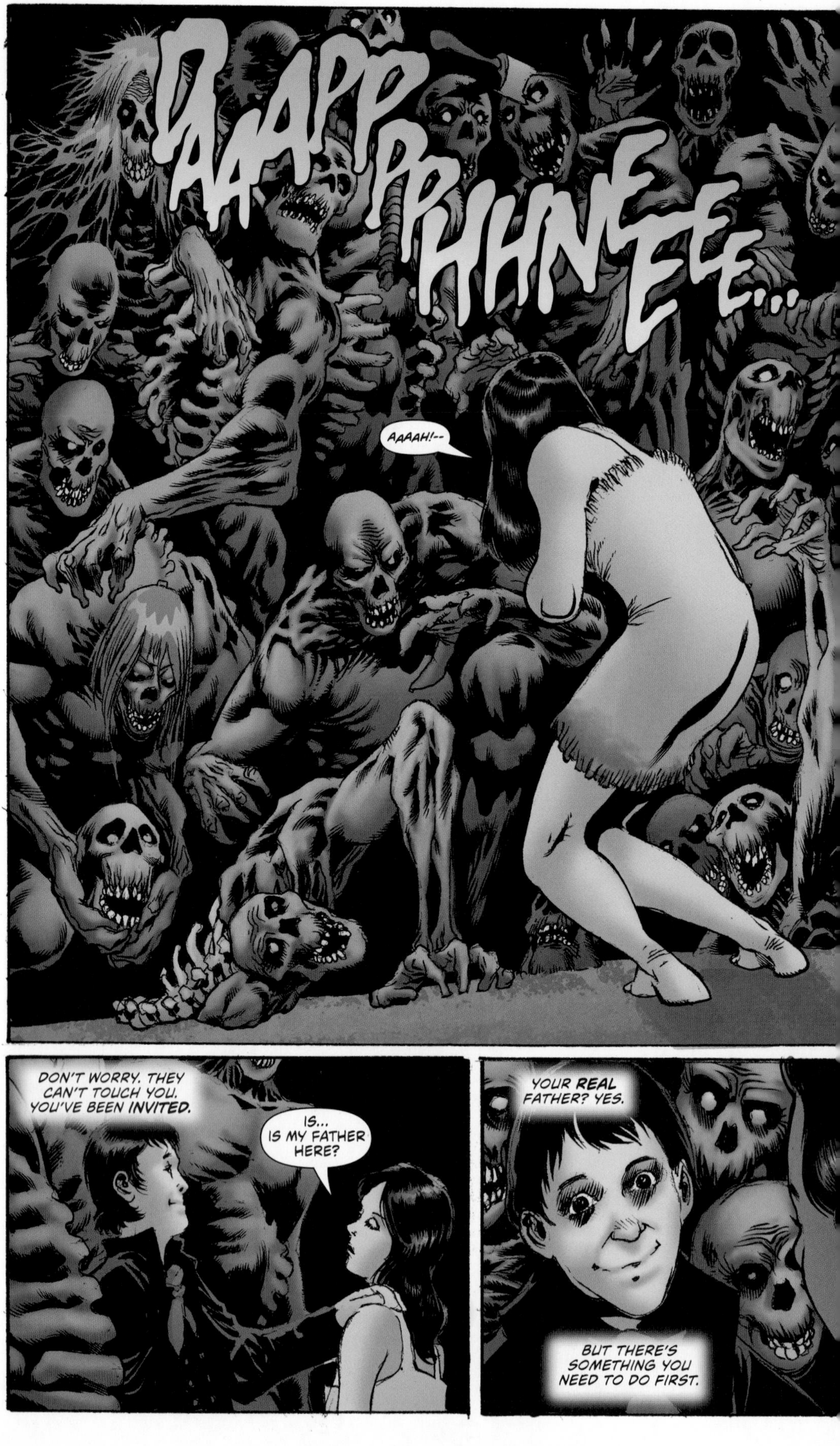
AAAPPPHHNEEE...
AAAAH!--
DON'T WORRY. THEY CAN'T TOUCH YOU. YOU'VE BEEN INVITED.
IS... IS MY FATHER HERE?
YOUR REAL FATHER? YES.
BUT THERE'S SOMETHING YOU NEED TO DO FIRST.

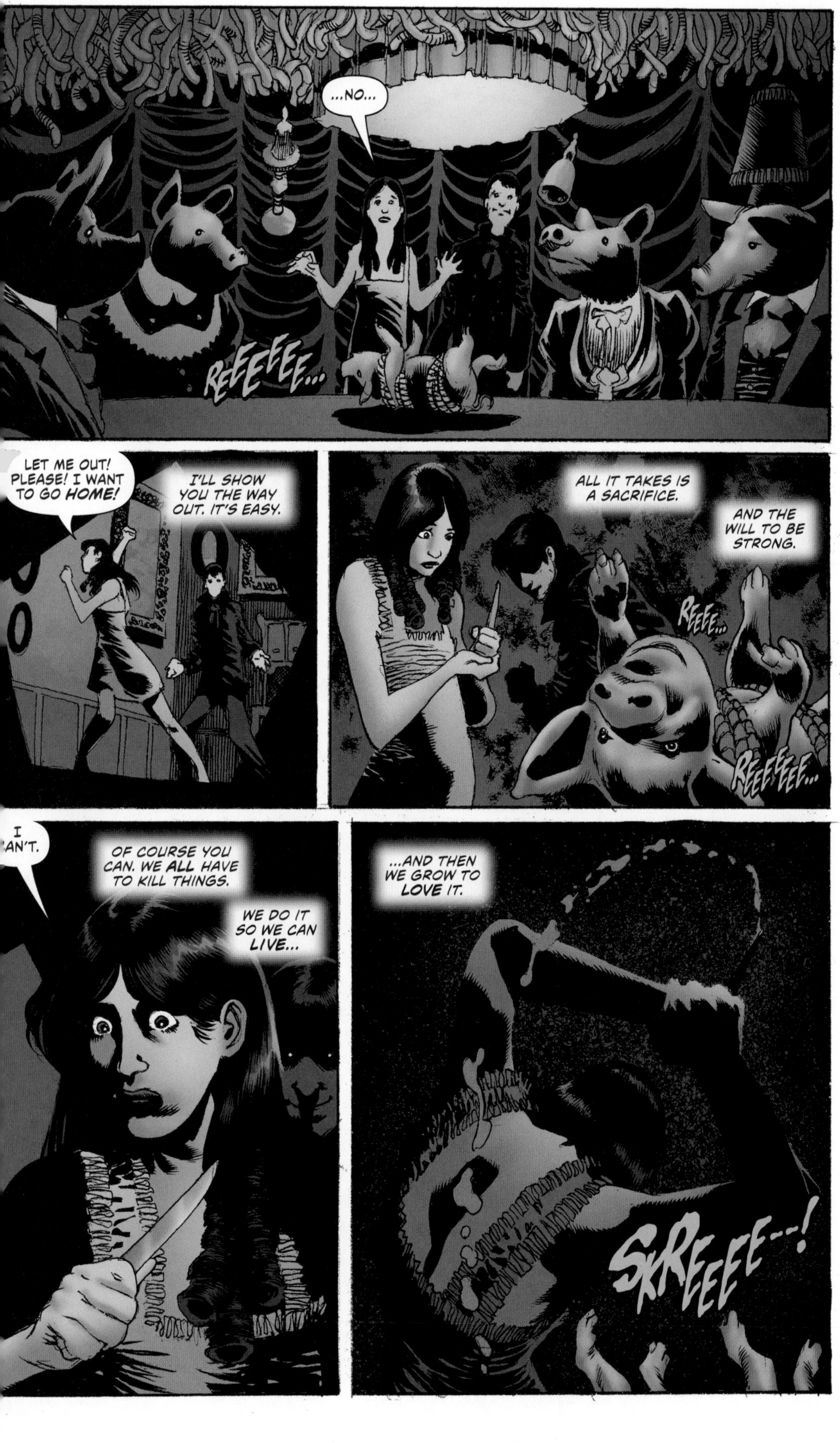
...NO...
REEEEEEE...
LET ME OUT! PLEASE! I WANT TO GO HOME!
I'LL SHOW YOU THE WAY OUT. IT'S EASY.
ALL IT TAKES IS A SACRIFICE.
AND THE WILL TO BE STRONG.
REEEE...
REEEEEEEE...
I CAN'T.
OF COURSE YOU CAN. WE ALL HAVE TO KILL THINGS.
WE DO IT SO WE CAN LIVE...
...AND THEN WE GROW TO LOVE IT.
SKREEEE--!

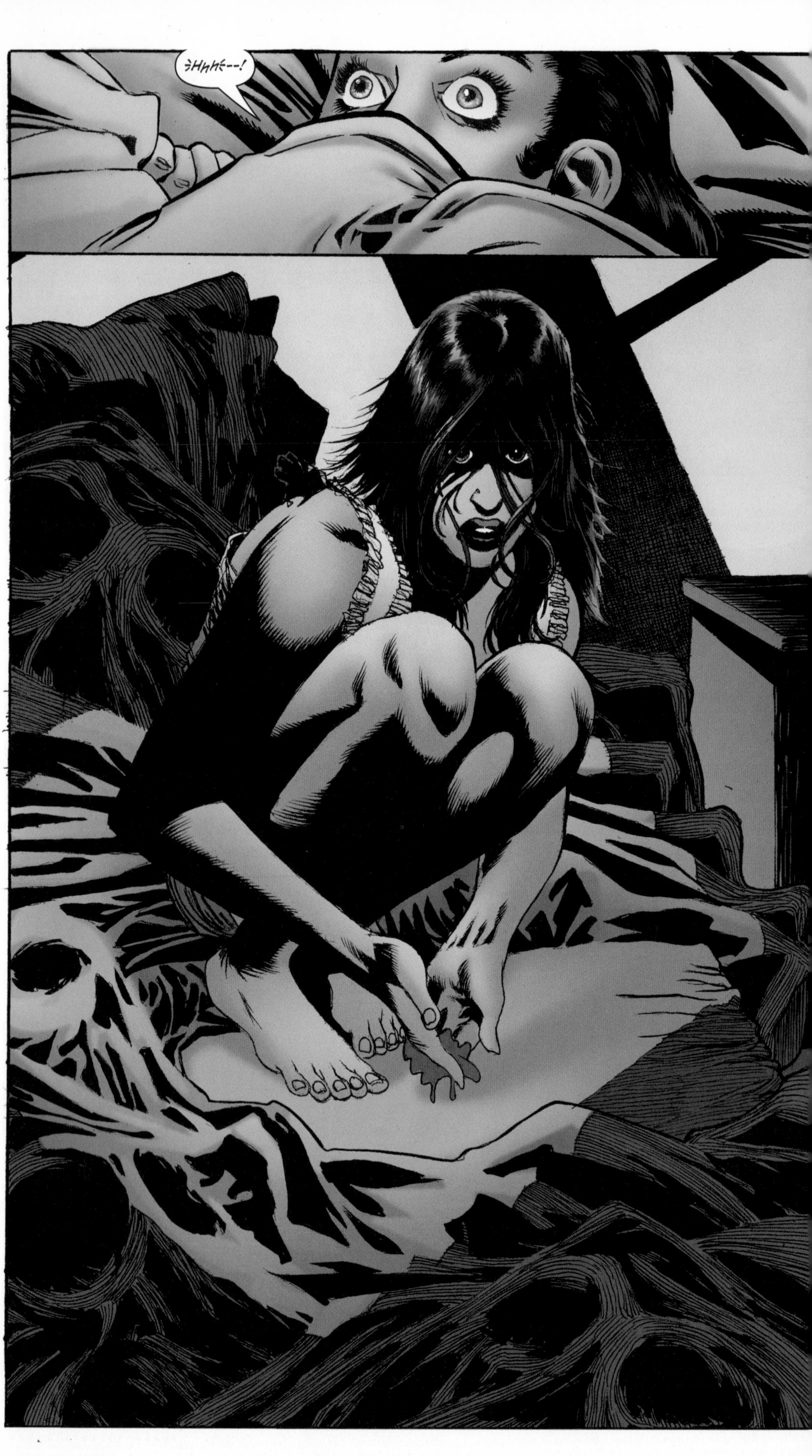
Hhh---!

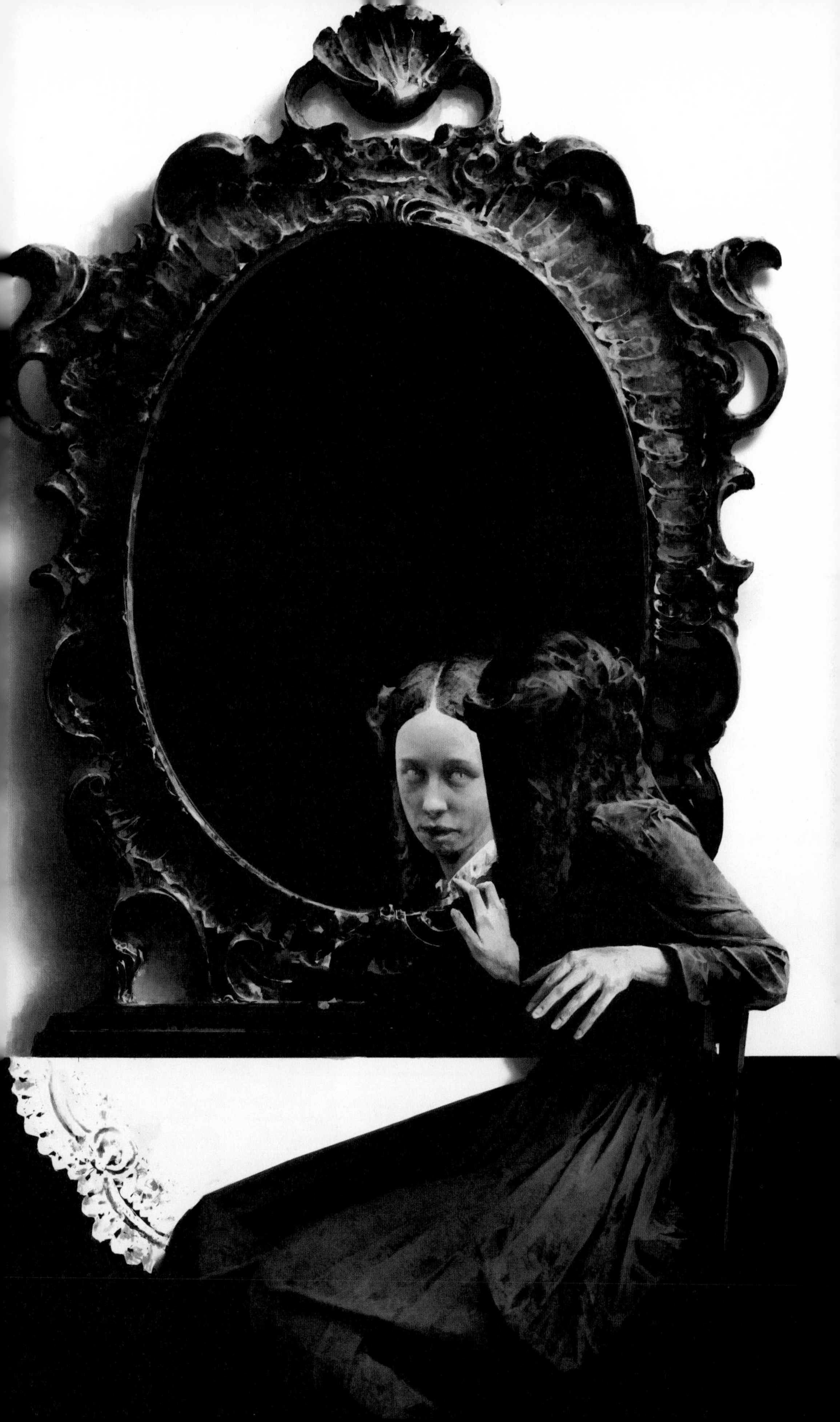

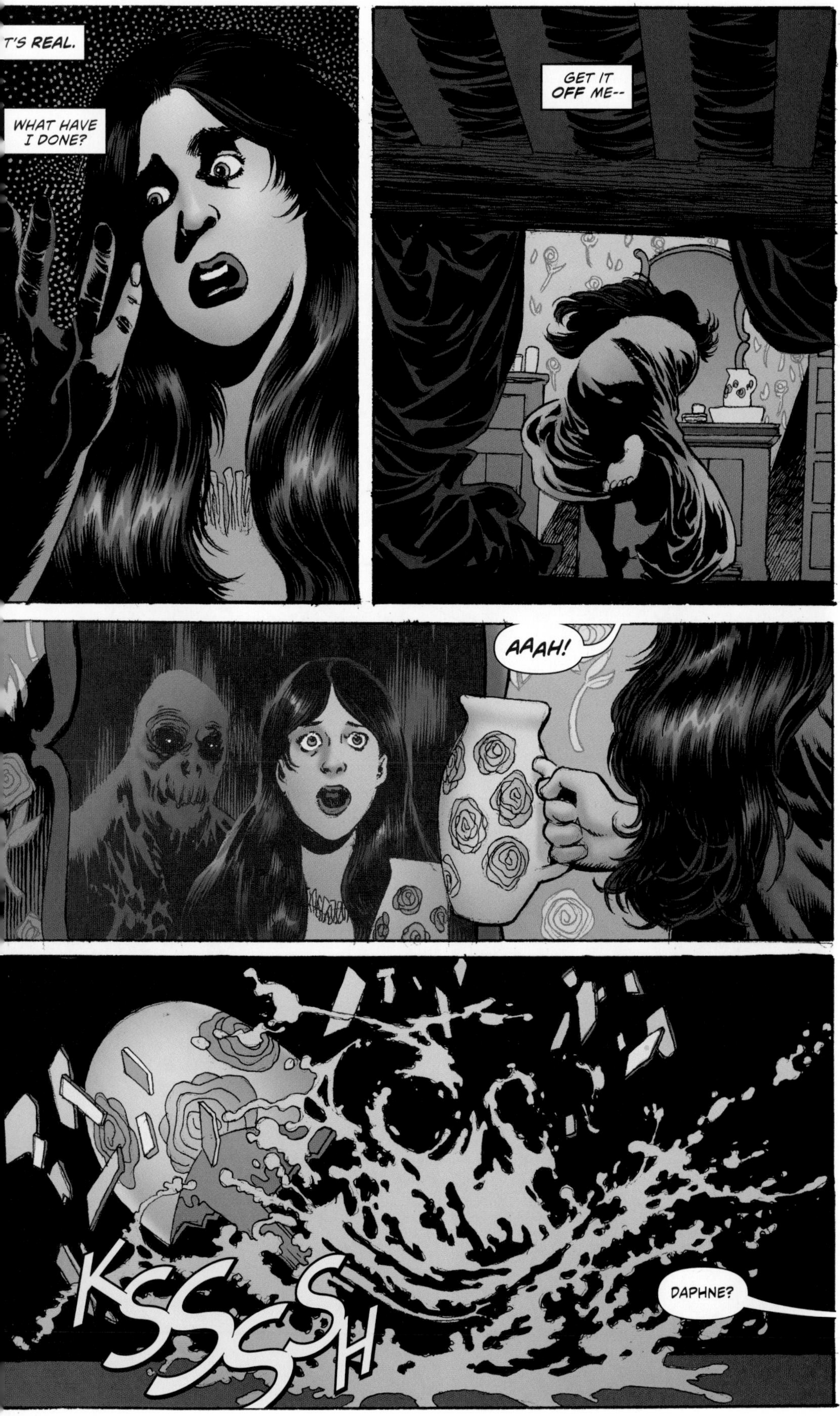

T'S REAL.
WHAT HAVE I DONE?
GET IT OFF ME--
AAAH!
KSSSSH
DAPHNE?

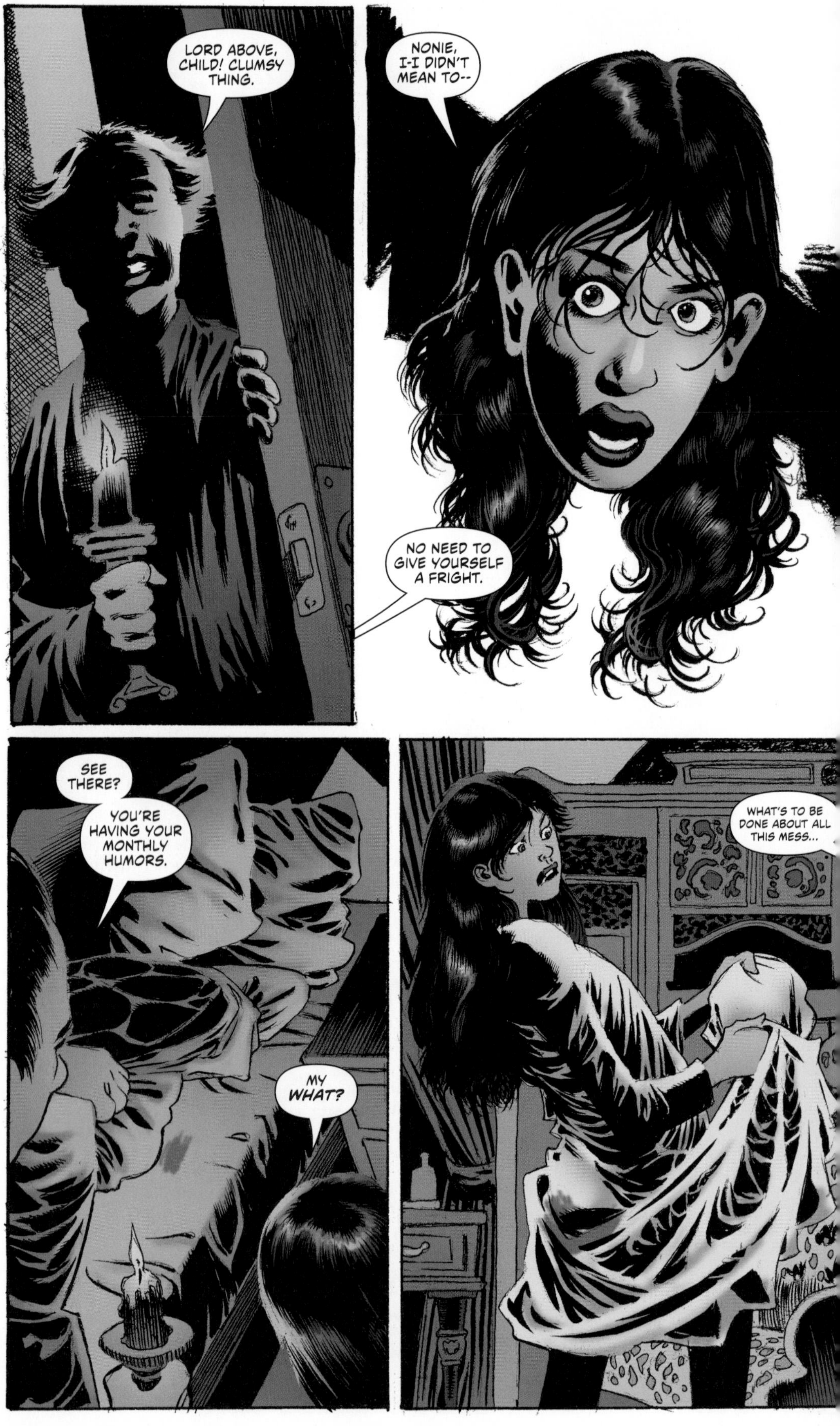
LORD ABOVE, CHILD! CLUMSY THING.
NONIE, I-I DIDN'T MEAN TO--
NO NEED TO GIVE YOURSELF A FRIGHT.
SEE THERE?
YOU'RE HAVING YOUR MONTHLY HUMORS.
MY WHAT?
WHAT'S TO BE DONE ABOUT ALL THIS MESS...

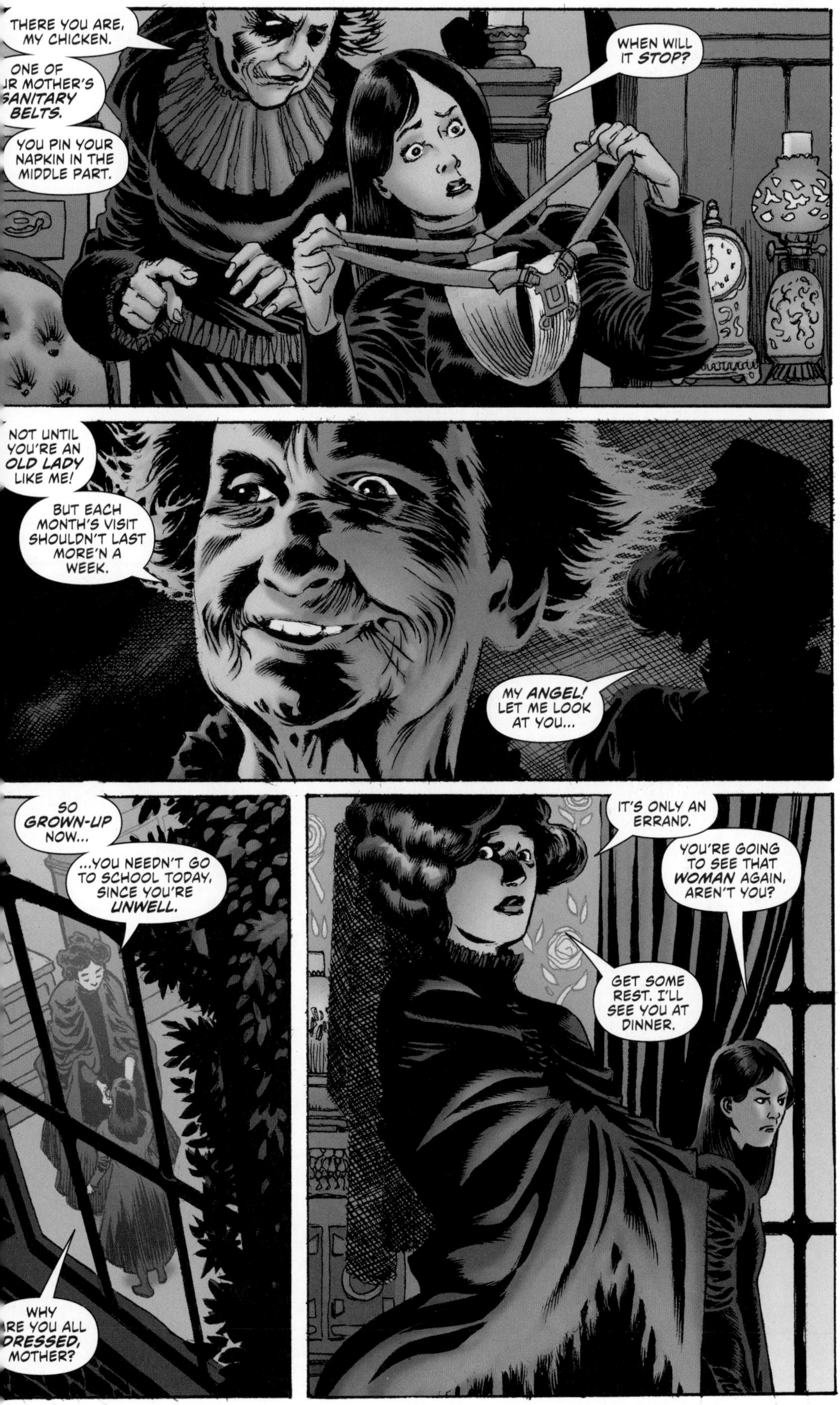
THERE YOU ARE, MY CHICKEN.
ONE OF ...R MOTHER'S ...SANITARY BELTS.
YOU PIN YOUR NAPKIN IN THE MIDDLE PART.
WHEN WILL IT STOP?
NOT UNTIL YOU'RE AN OLD LADY LIKE ME!
BUT EACH MONTH'S VISIT SHOULDN'T LAST MORE'N A WEEK.
MY ANGEL! LET ME LOOK AT YOU...
SO GROWN-UP NOW...
...YOU NEEDN'T GO TO SCHOOL TODAY, SINCE YOU'RE UNWELL.
WHY ...RE YOU ALL ...DRESSED, MOTHER?
IT'S ONLY AN ERRAND.
YOU'RE GOING TO SEE THAT WOMAN AGAIN, AREN'T YOU?
GET SOME REST. I'LL SEE YOU AT DINNER.

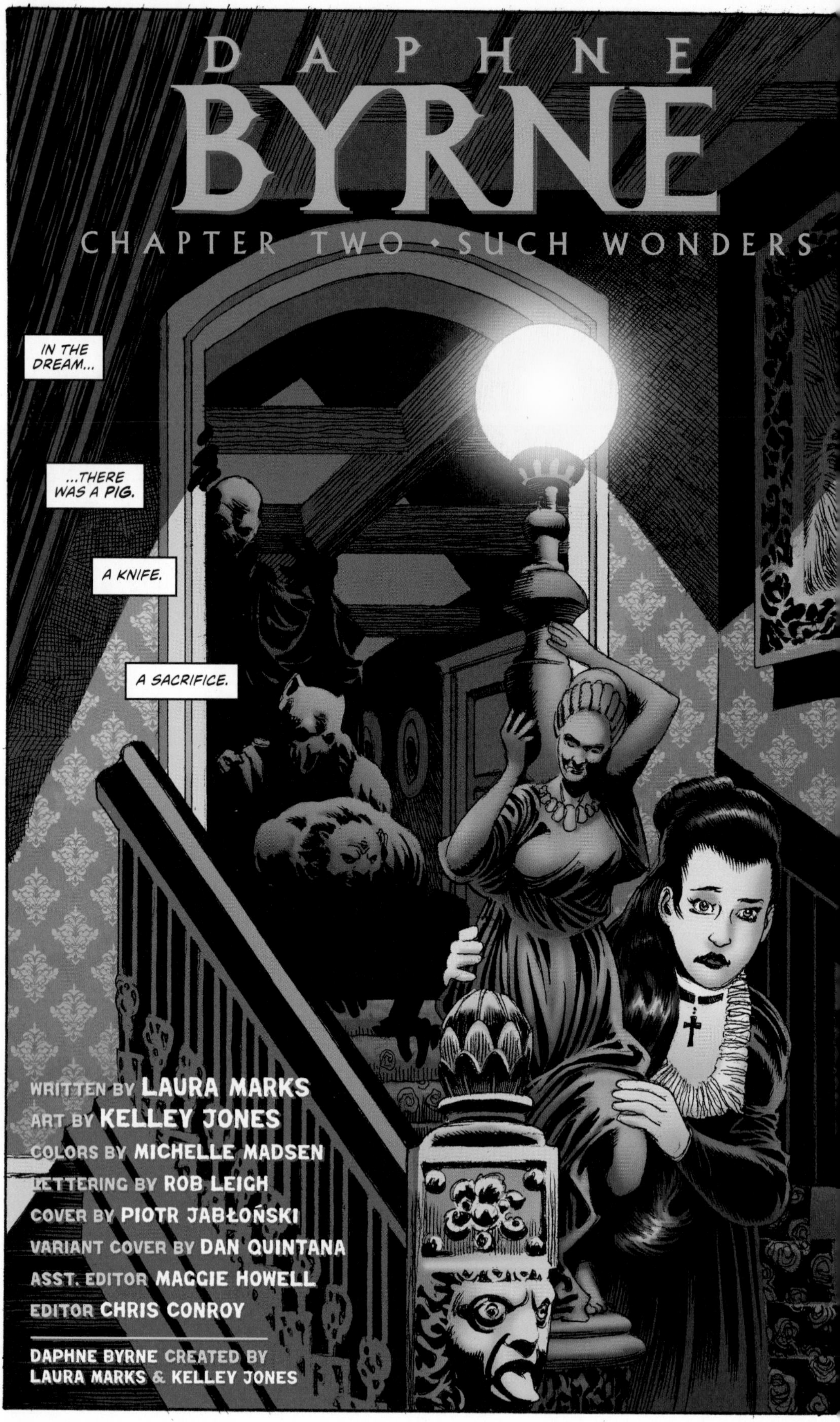
DAPHNE
BYRNE
CHAPTER TWO • SUCH WONDERS
IN THE DREAM...
...THERE WAS A PIG.
A KNIFE.
A SACRIFICE.
WRITTEN BY LAURA MARKS
ART BY KELLEY JONES
COLORS BY MICHELLE MADSEN
LETTERING BY ROB LEIGH
COVER BY PIOTR JABŁOŃSKI
VARIANT COVER BY DAN QUINTANA
ASST. EDITOR MAGGIE HOWELL
EDITOR CHRIS CONROY
DAPHNE BYRNE CREATED BY
LAURA MARKS & KELLEY JONES

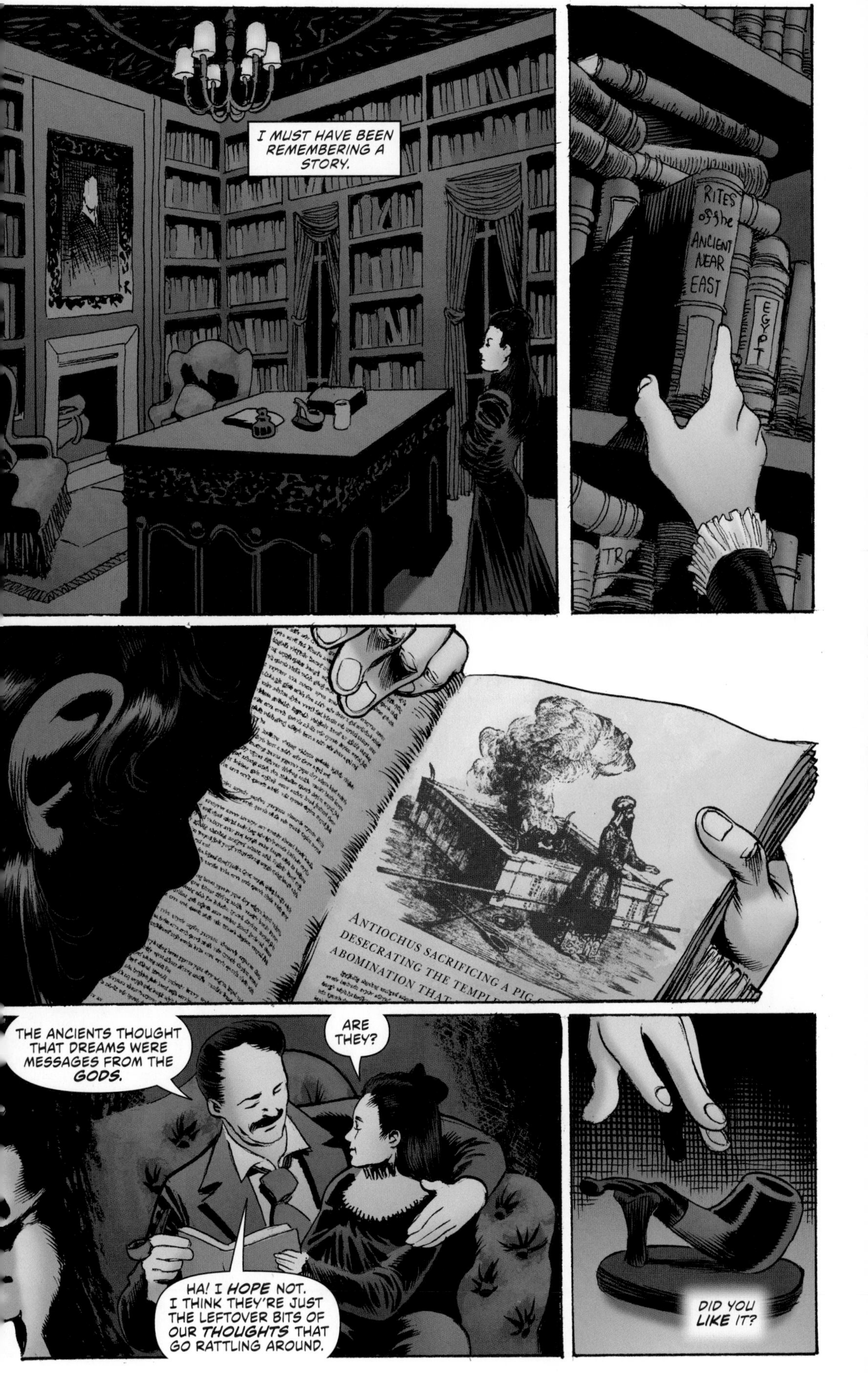
I MUST HAVE BEEN REMEMBERING A STORY.
RITES of the ANCIENT NEAR EAST
EGYPT
ANTIOCHUS SACRIFICING A PIG
DESECRATING THE TEMPL
ABOMINATION THAT
THE ANCIENTS THOUGHT THAT DREAMS WERE MESSAGES FROM THE *GODS.*
ARE THEY?
HA! I *HOPE* NOT. I THINK THEY'RE JUST THE LEFTOVER BITS OF OUR *THOUGHTS* THAT GO RATTLING AROUND.
DID YOU *LIKE* IT?

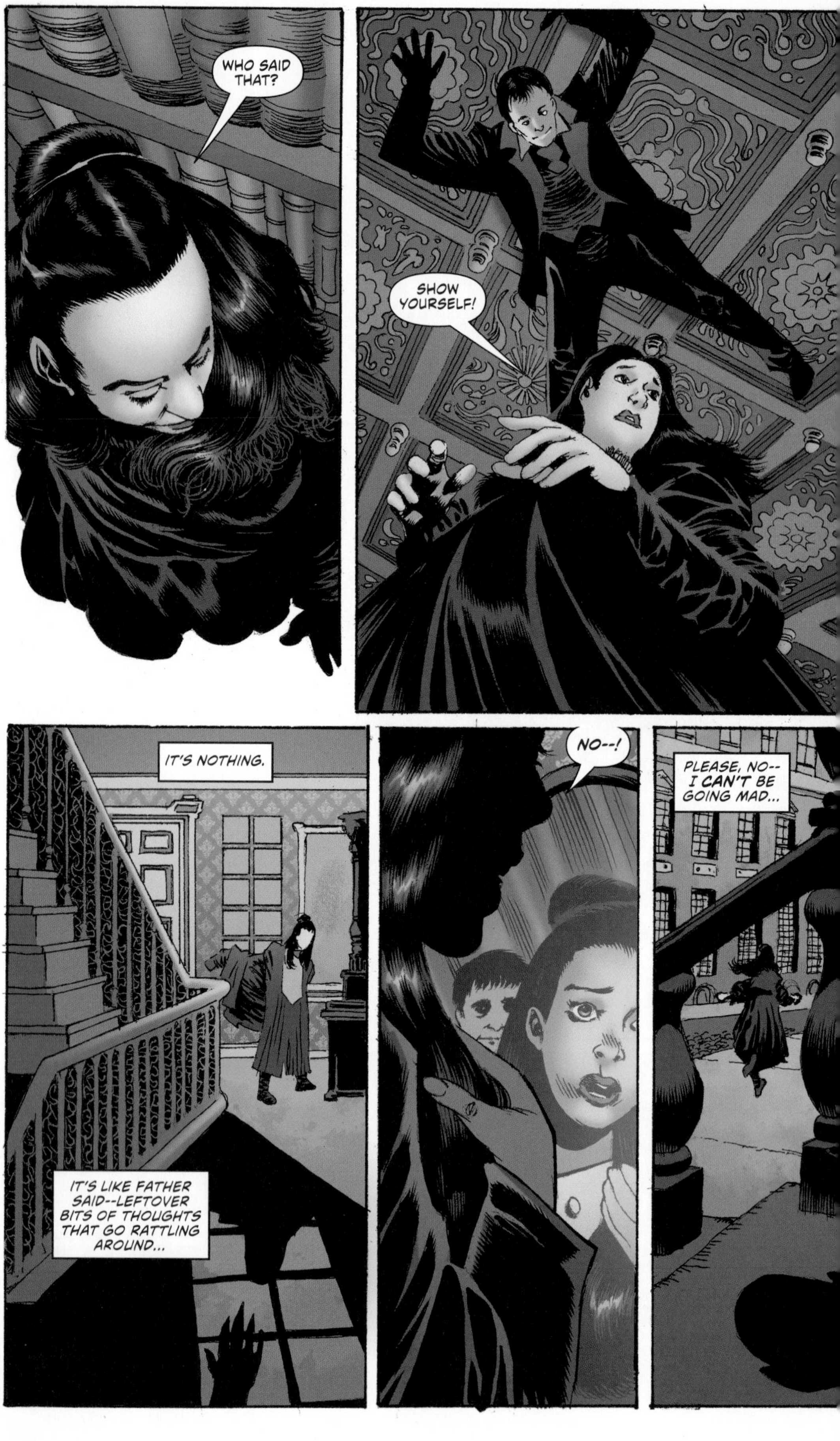
WHO SAID THAT?
SHOW YOURSELF!
IT'S NOTHING.
IT'S LIKE FATHER SAID--LEFTOVER BITS OF THOUGHTS THAT GO RATTLING AROUND...
NO--!
PLEASE, NO-- I CAN'T BE GOING MAD...

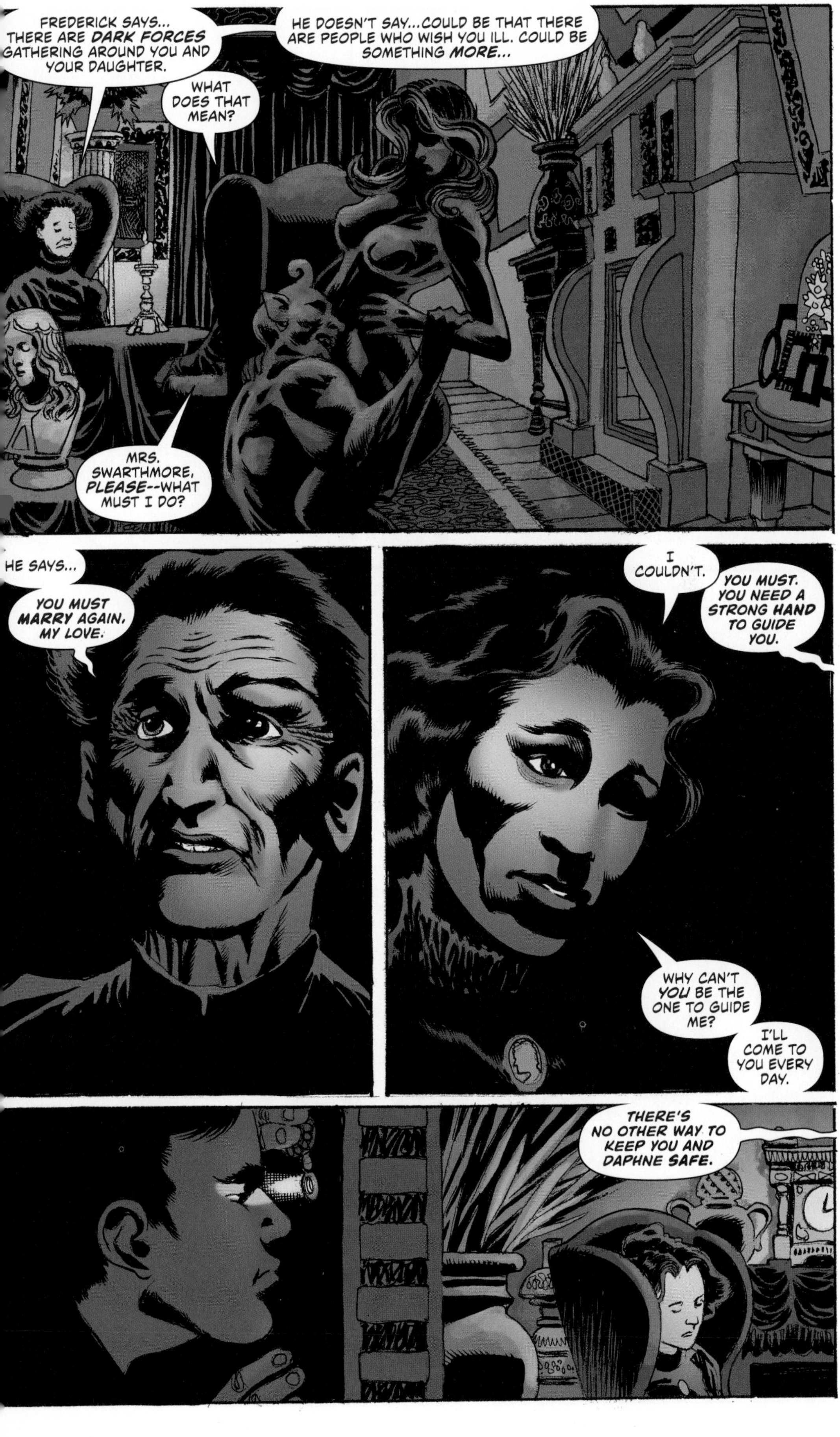
FREDERICK SAYS... THERE ARE DARK FORCES GATHERING AROUND YOU AND YOUR DAUGHTER.
WHAT DOES THAT MEAN?
HE DOESN'T SAY...COULD BE THAT THERE ARE PEOPLE WHO WISH YOU ILL. COULD BE SOMETHING MORE...
MRS. SWARTHMORE, PLEASE--WHAT MUST I DO?
HE SAYS...
YOU MUST MARRY AGAIN, MY LOVE.
I COULDN'T.
YOU MUST. YOU NEED A STRONG HAND TO GUIDE YOU.
WHY CAN'T YOU BE THE ONE TO GUIDE ME?
I'LL COME TO YOU EVERY DAY.
THERE'S NO OTHER WAY TO KEEP YOU AND DAPHNE SAFE.

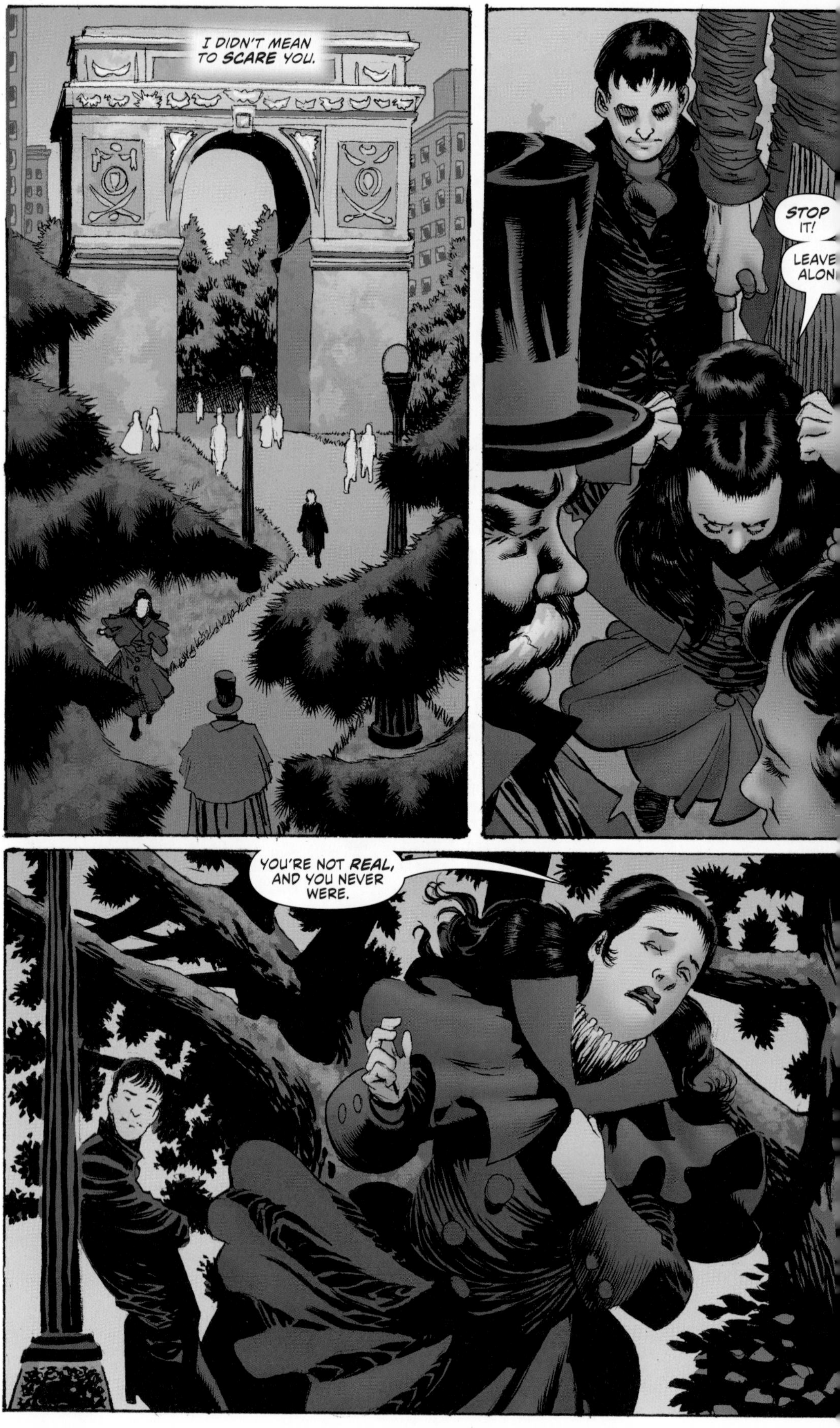
I DIDN'T MEAN TO SCARE YOU.
STOP IT!
LEAVE ALON
YOU'RE NOT REAL, AND YOU NEVER WERE.

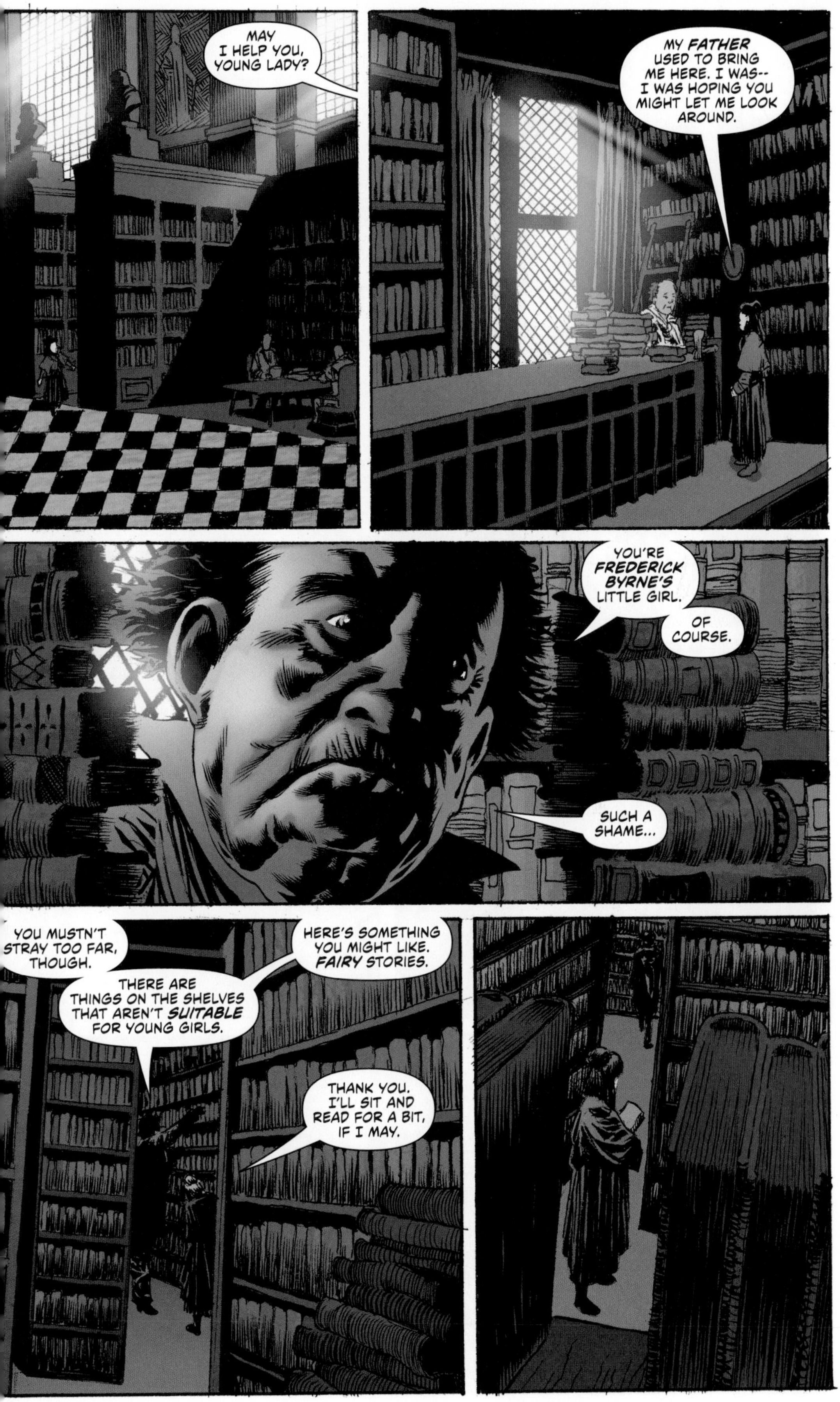
MAY I HELP YOU, YOUNG LADY?
MY *FATHER* USED TO BRING ME HERE. I WAS-- I WAS HOPING YOU MIGHT LET ME LOOK AROUND.
YOU'RE *FREDERICK BYRNE'S* LITTLE GIRL.
OF COURSE.
SUCH A SHAME...
YOU MUSTN'T STRAY TOO FAR, THOUGH.
THERE ARE THINGS ON THE SHELVES THAT AREN'T *SUITABLE* FOR YOUNG GIRLS.
HERE'S SOMETHING YOU MIGHT LIKE. *FAIRY* STORIES.
THANK YOU. I'LL SIT AND READ FOR A BIT, IF I MAY.

Hodgson's Fashionable Dream-Book; or, The Book of Destiny Laid Open.

To dream of an open **grave**, foretells sickness and disappointment...

To dream of **knives** denotes plenty; you will speedily be married, and have a family.

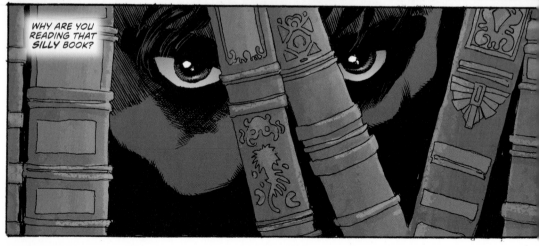

WHY ARE YOU READING THAT SILLY BOOK?

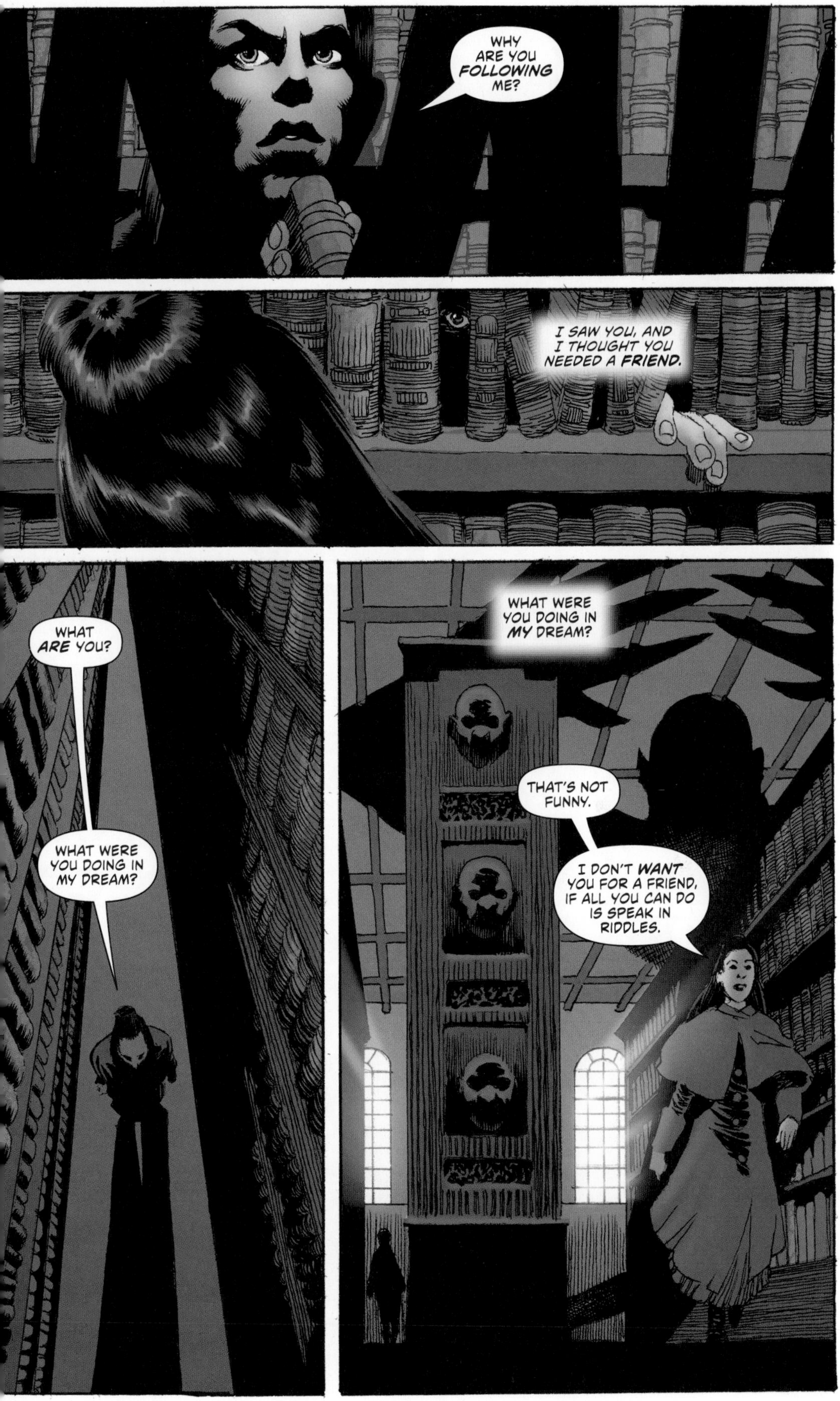

WHY ARE YOU *FOLLOWING* ME?
I SAW YOU, AND I THOUGHT YOU NEEDED A ***FRIEND.***
WHAT *ARE* YOU?
WHAT WERE YOU DOING IN MY DREAM?
WHAT WERE YOU DOING IN *MY* DREAM?
THAT'S NOT FUNNY.
I DON'T *WANT* YOU FOR A FRIEND, IF ALL YOU CAN DO IS SPEAK IN RIDDLES.

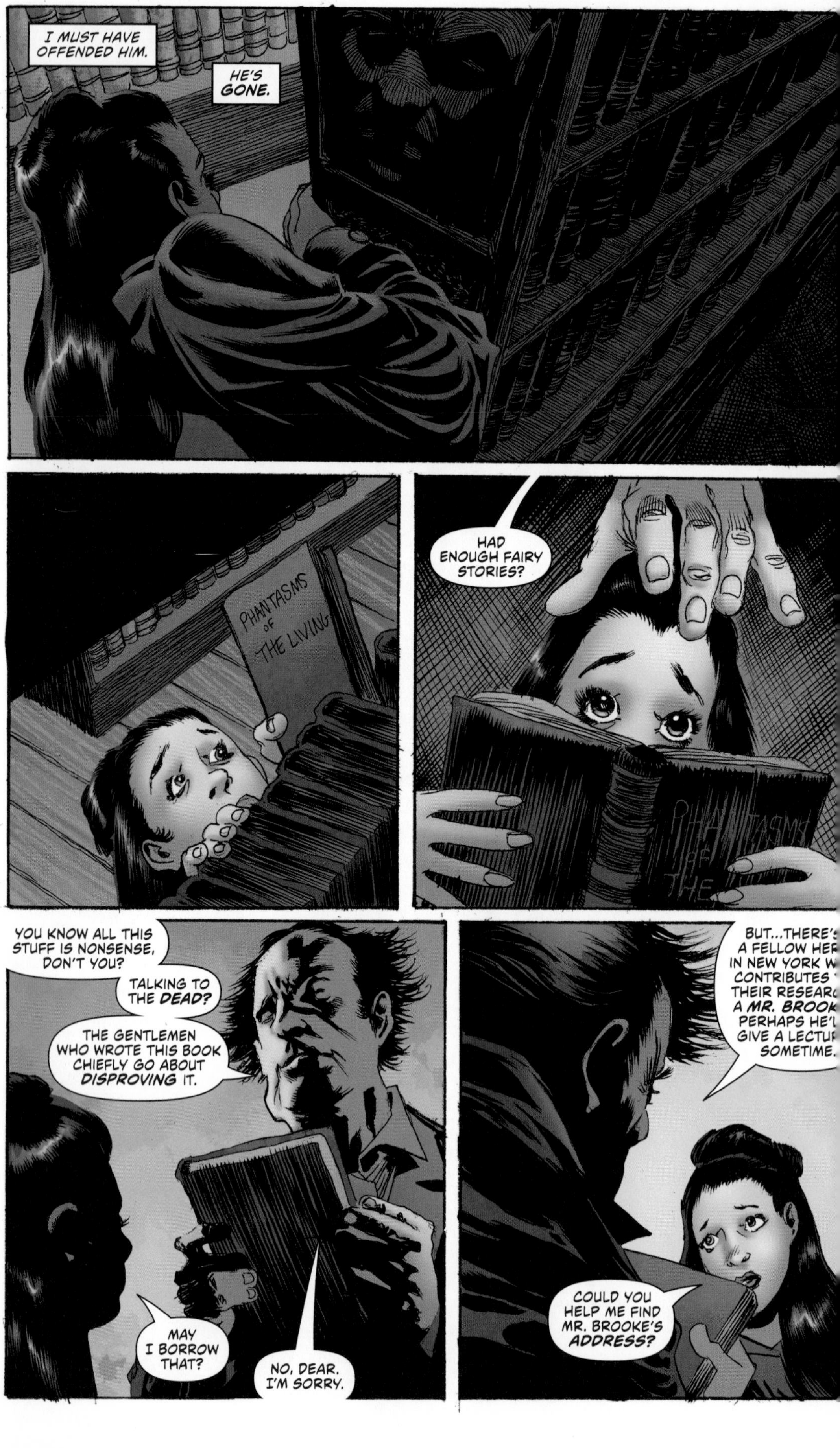
I MUST HAVE OFFENDED HIM.
HE'S GONE.
PHANTASMS OF THE LIVING
HAD ENOUGH FAIRY STORIES?
YOU KNOW ALL THIS STUFF IS NONSENSE, DON'T YOU?
TALKING TO THE DEAD?
THE GENTLEMEN WHO WROTE THIS BOOK CHIEFLY GO ABOUT DISPROVING IT.
MAY I BORROW THAT?
NO, DEAR. I'M SORRY.
BUT...THERE'S A FELLOW HER IN NEW YORK W CONTRIBUTES THEIR RESEARC A MR. BROOK PERHAPS HE'L GIVE A LECTUR SOMETIME.
COULD YOU HELP ME FIND MR. BROOKE'S ADDRESS?

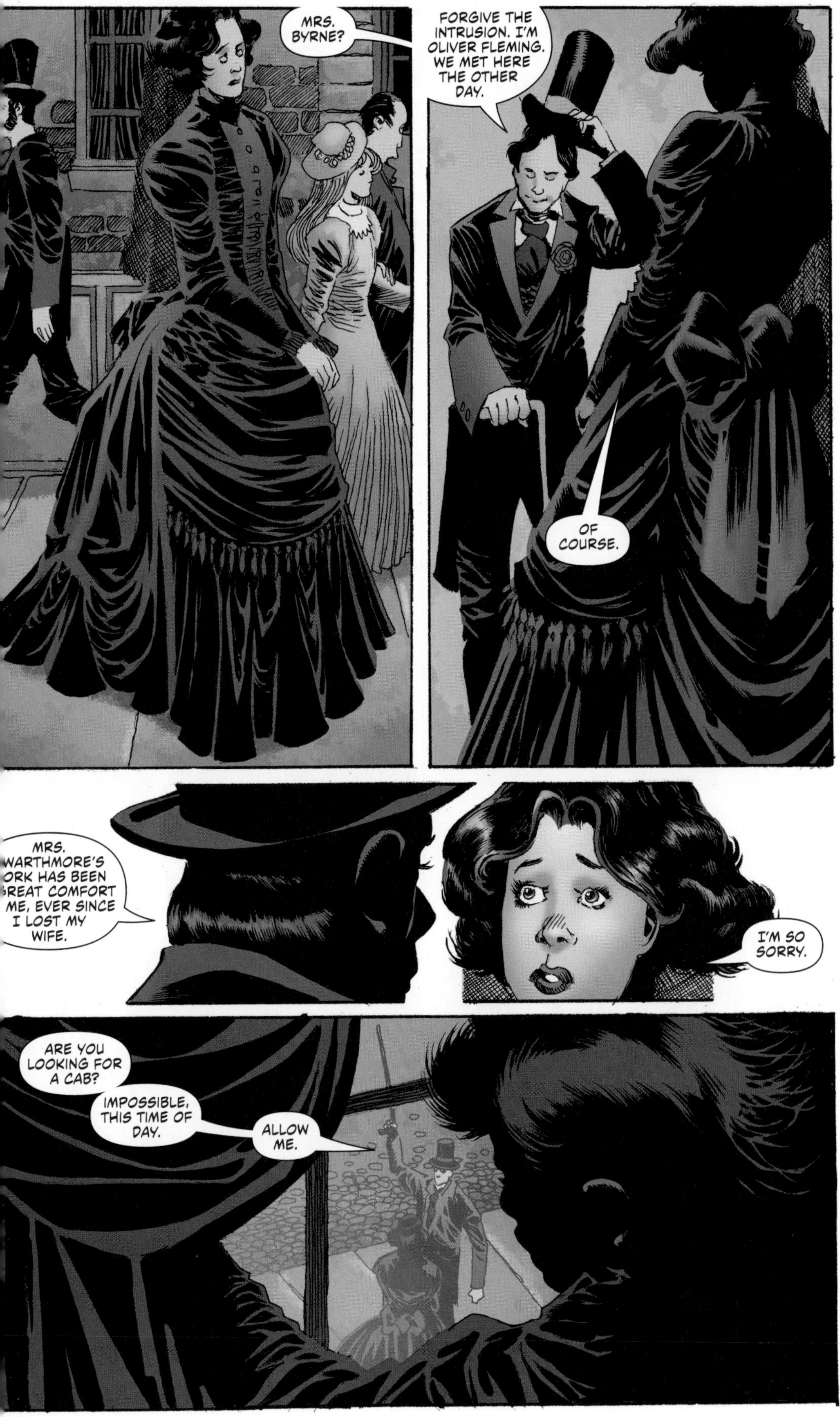
MRS. BYRNE?
FORGIVE THE INTRUSION. I'M OLIVER FLEMING. WE MET HERE THE OTHER DAY.
OF COURSE.
MRS. WARTHMORE'S ORK HAS BEEN REAT COMFORT ME, EVER SINCE I LOST MY WIFE.
I'M SO SORRY.
ARE YOU LOOKING FOR A CAB?
IMPOSSIBLE, THIS TIME OF DAY.
ALLOW ME.

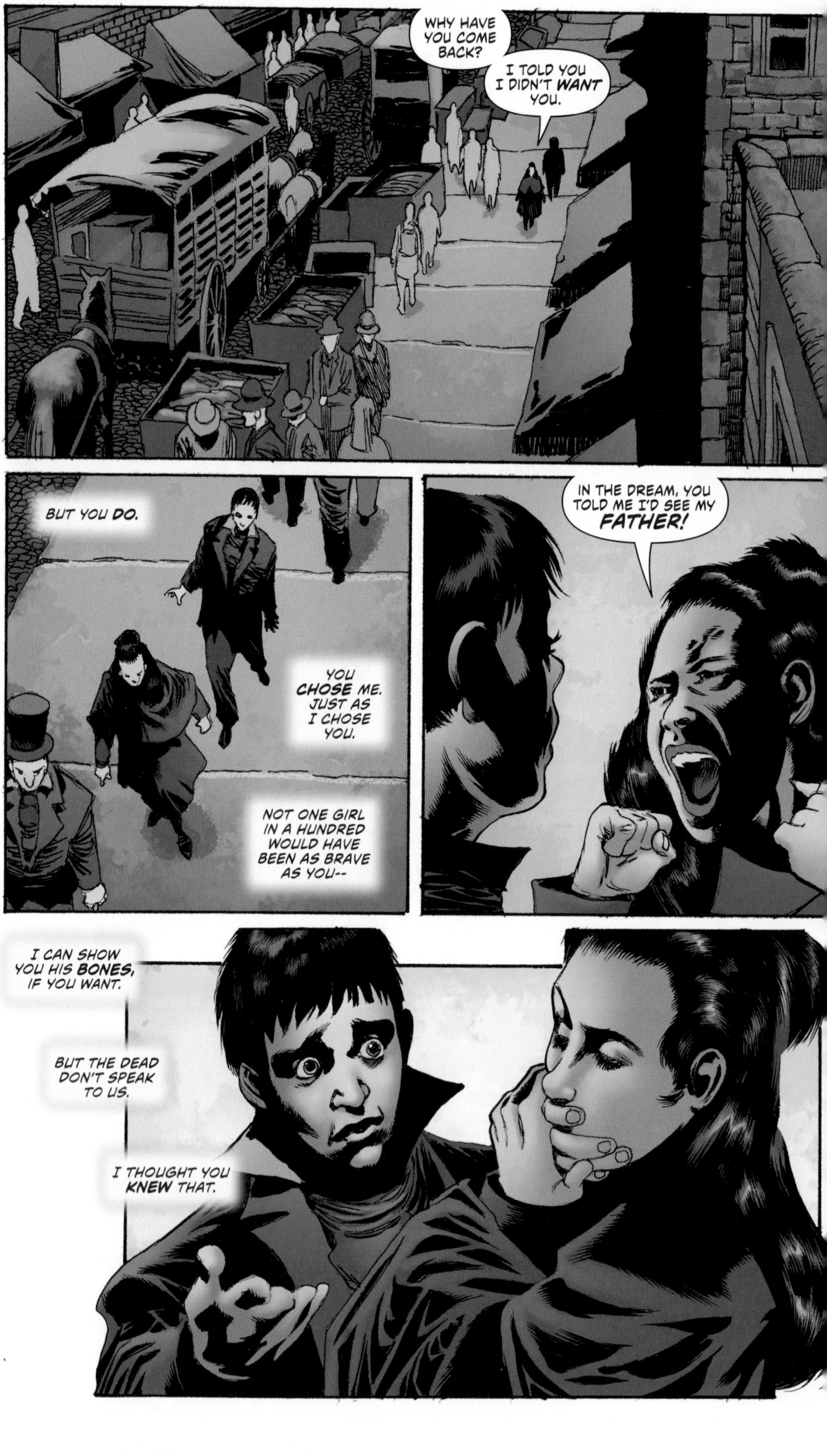
WHY HAVE YOU COME BACK?
I TOLD YOU I DIDN'T **WANT** YOU.
BUT YOU **DO.**
YOU **CHOSE** ME. JUST AS I CHOSE YOU.
NOT ONE GIRL IN A HUNDRED WOULD HAVE BEEN AS BRAVE AS YOU--
IN THE DREAM, YOU TOLD ME I'D SEE MY **FATHER!**
I CAN SHOW YOU HIS **BONES,** IF YOU WANT.
BUT THE DEAD DON'T SPEAK TO US.
I THOUGHT YOU **KNEW** THAT.

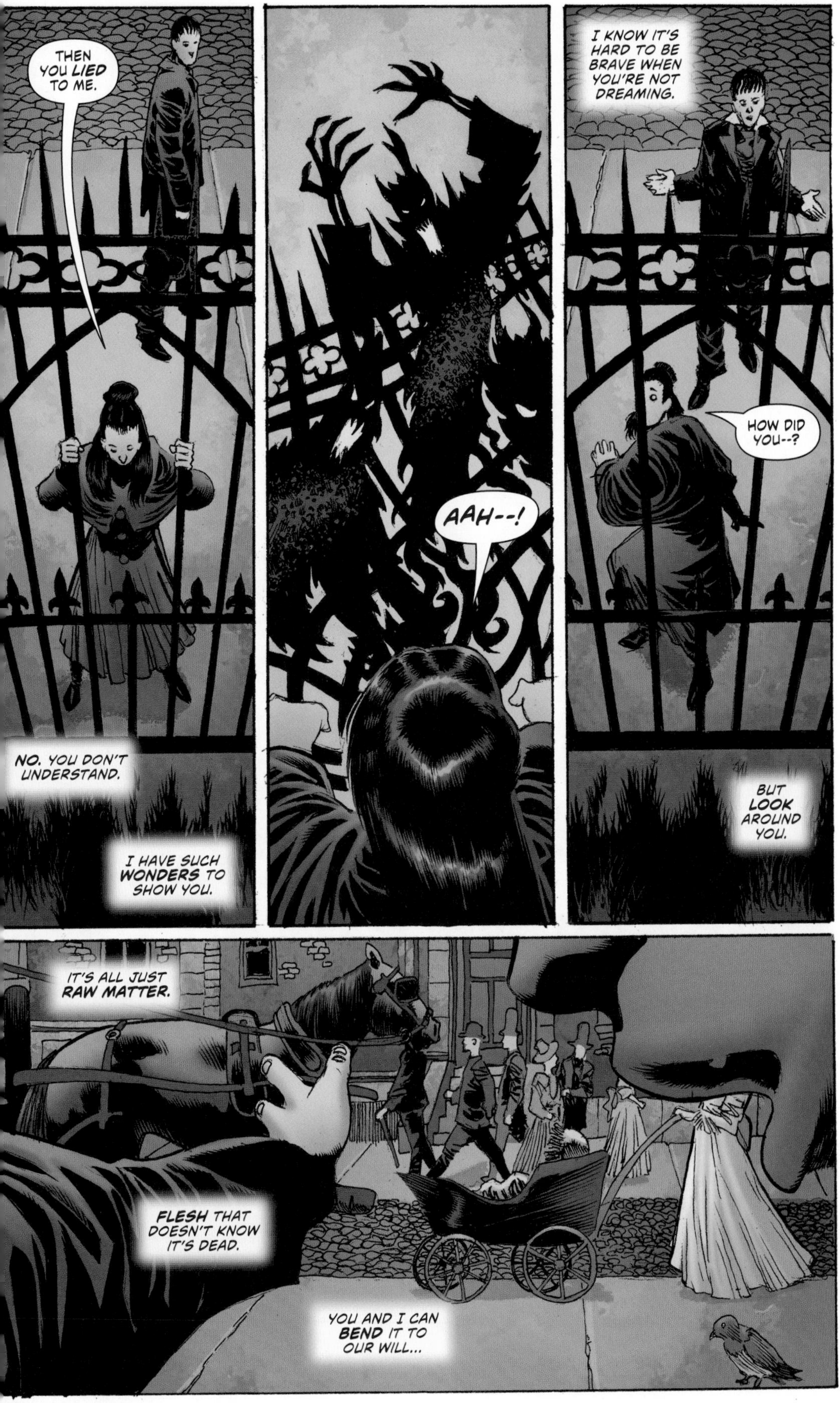
THEN YOU LIED TO ME.
NO. YOU DON'T UNDERSTAND.
I HAVE SUCH WONDERS TO SHOW YOU.
AAH--!
I KNOW IT'S HARD TO BE BRAVE WHEN YOU'RE NOT DREAMING.
HOW DID YOU--?
BUT LOOK AROUND YOU.
IT'S ALL JUST RAW MATTER.
FLESH THAT DOESN'T KNOW IT'S DEAD.
YOU AND I CAN BEND IT TO OUR WILL...

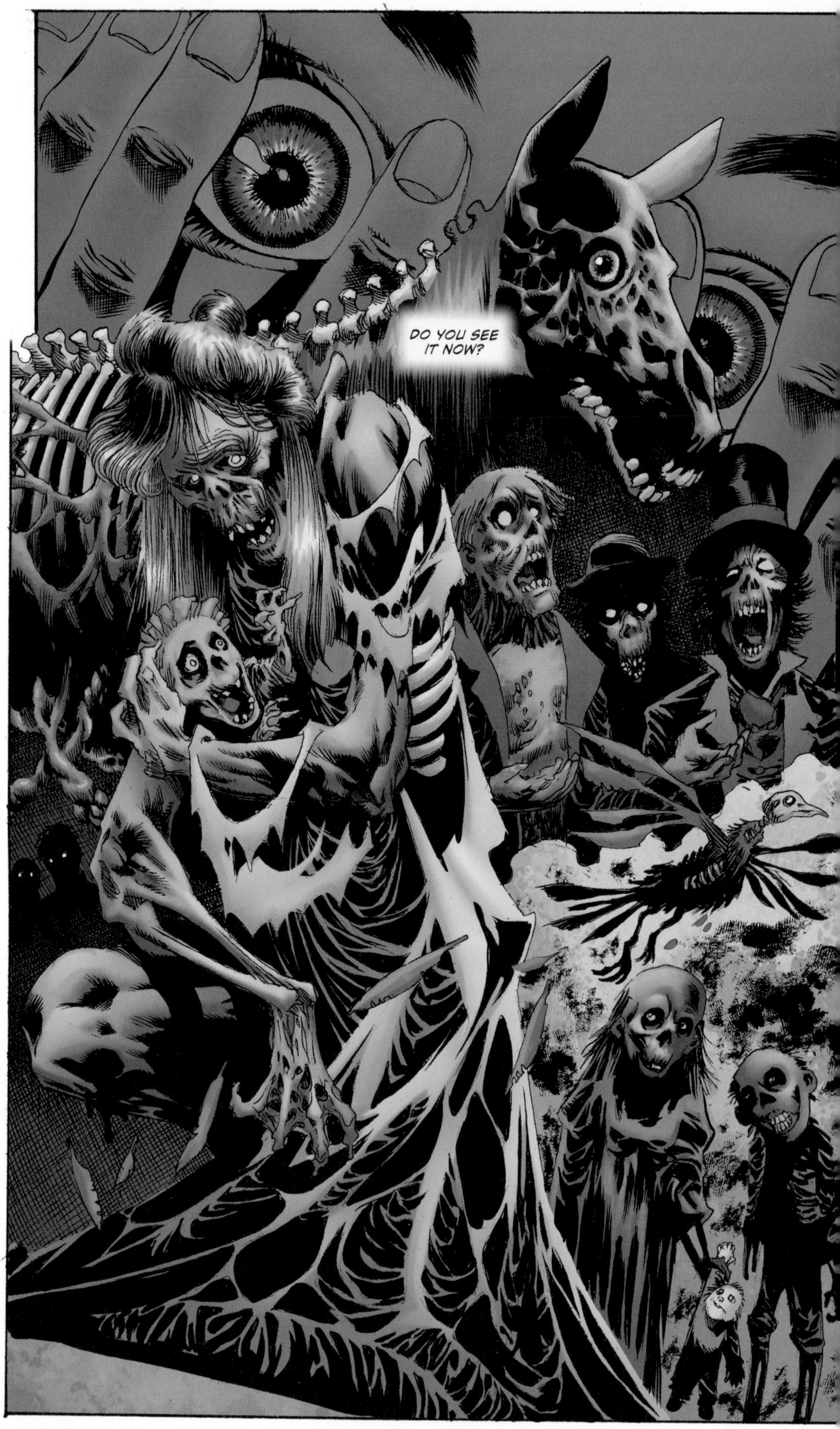
DO YOU SEE IT NOW?

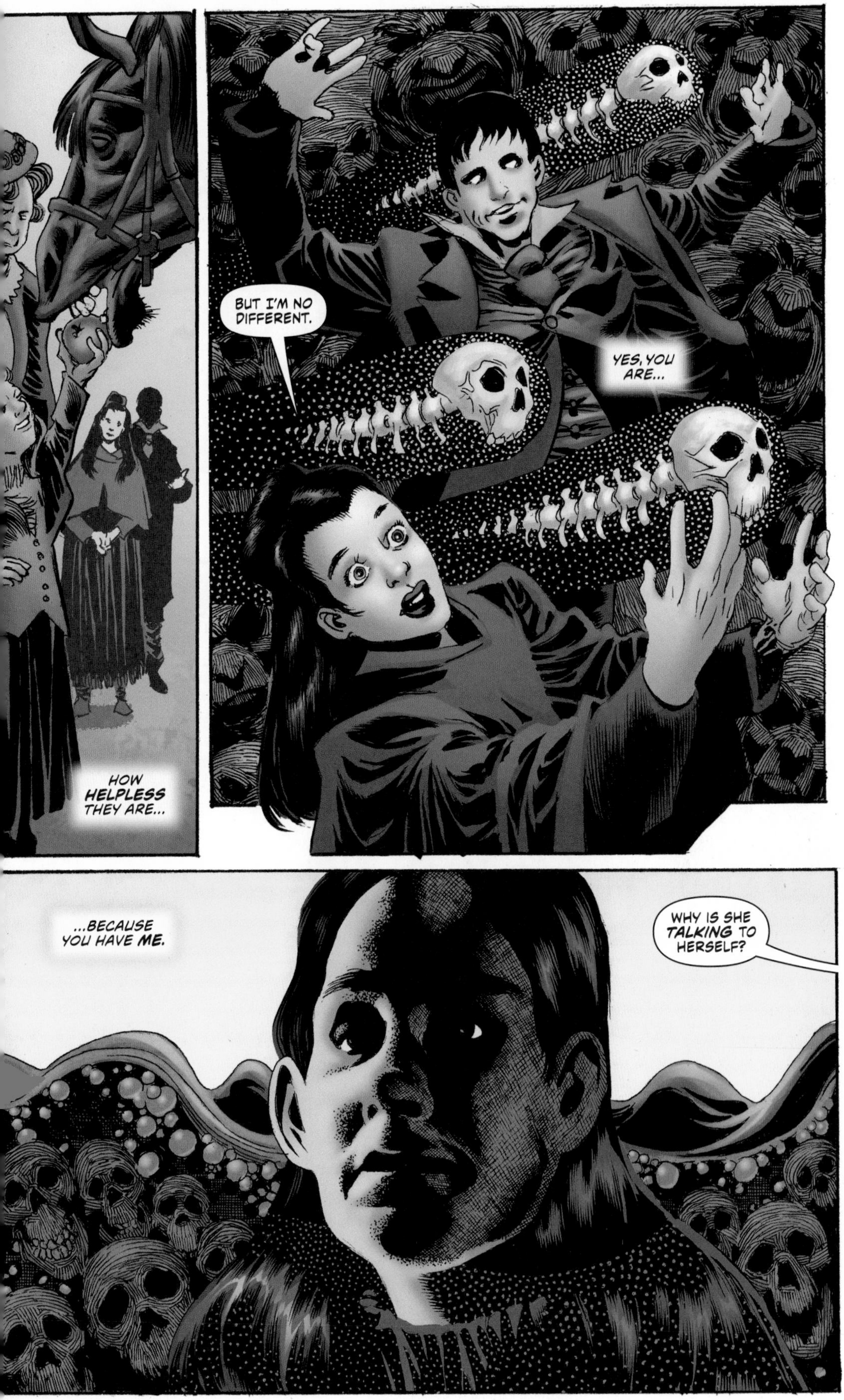

HOW HELPLESS THEY ARE...
BUT I'M NO DIFFERENT.
YES, YOU ARE...
...BECAUSE YOU HAVE ME.
WHY IS SHE TALKING TO HERSELF?

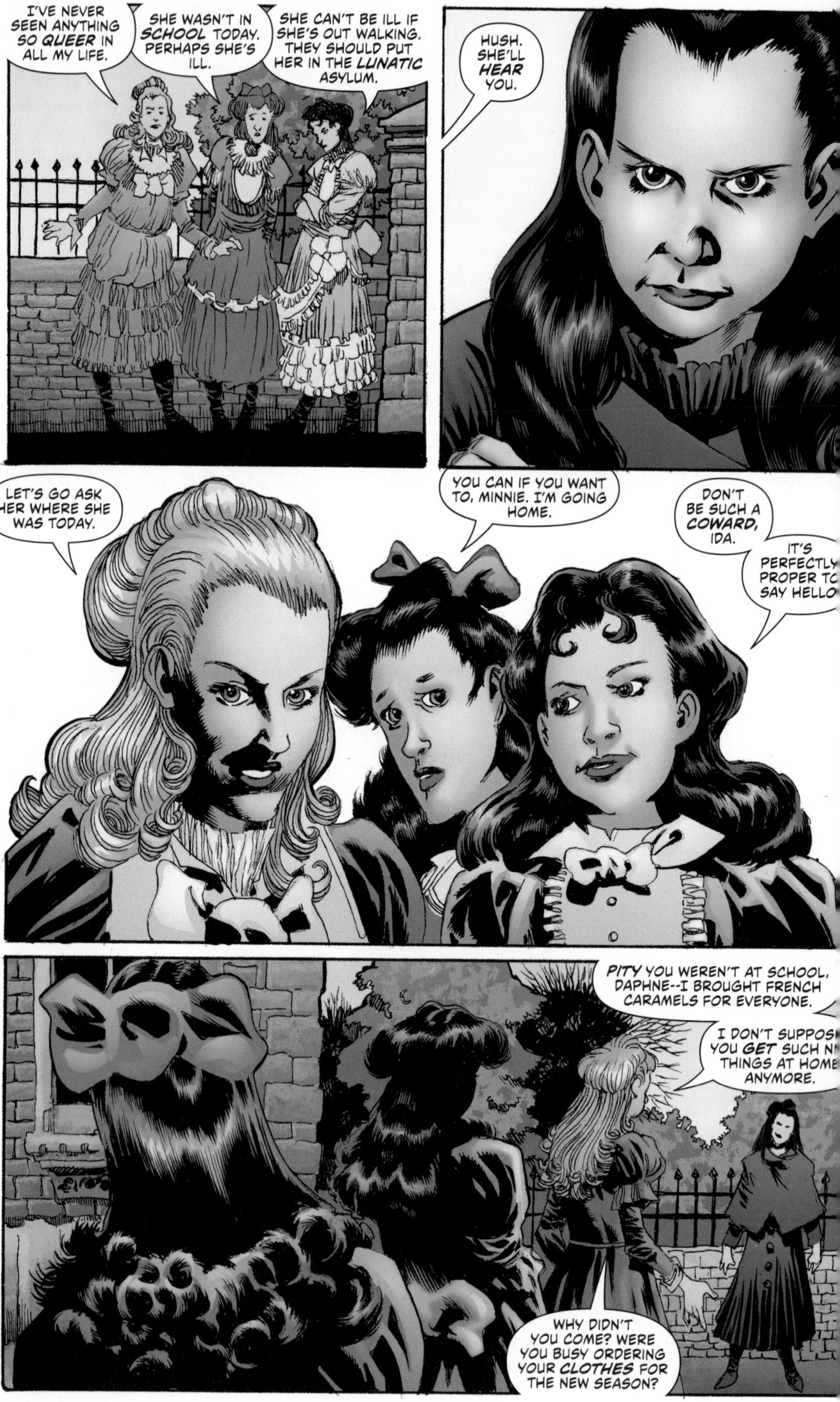
I'VE NEVER SEEN ANYTHING SO *QUEER* IN ALL MY LIFE.
SHE WASN'T IN *SCHOOL* TODAY. PERHAPS SHE'S ILL.
SHE CAN'T BE ILL IF SHE'S OUT WALKING. THEY SHOULD PUT HER IN THE *LUNATIC* ASYLUM.
HUSH. SHE'LL *HEAR* YOU.
LET'S GO ASK HER WHERE SHE WAS TODAY.
YOU CAN IF YOU WANT TO, MINNIE. I'M GOING HOME.
DON'T BE SUCH A *COWARD,* IDA.
PITY YOU WEREN'T AT SCHOOL, DAPHNE--I BROUGHT FRENCH CARAMELS FOR EVERYONE.
WHY DIDN'T YOU COME? WERE YOU BUSY ORDERING YOUR *CLOTHES* FOR THE NEW SEASON?
ANYMORE.

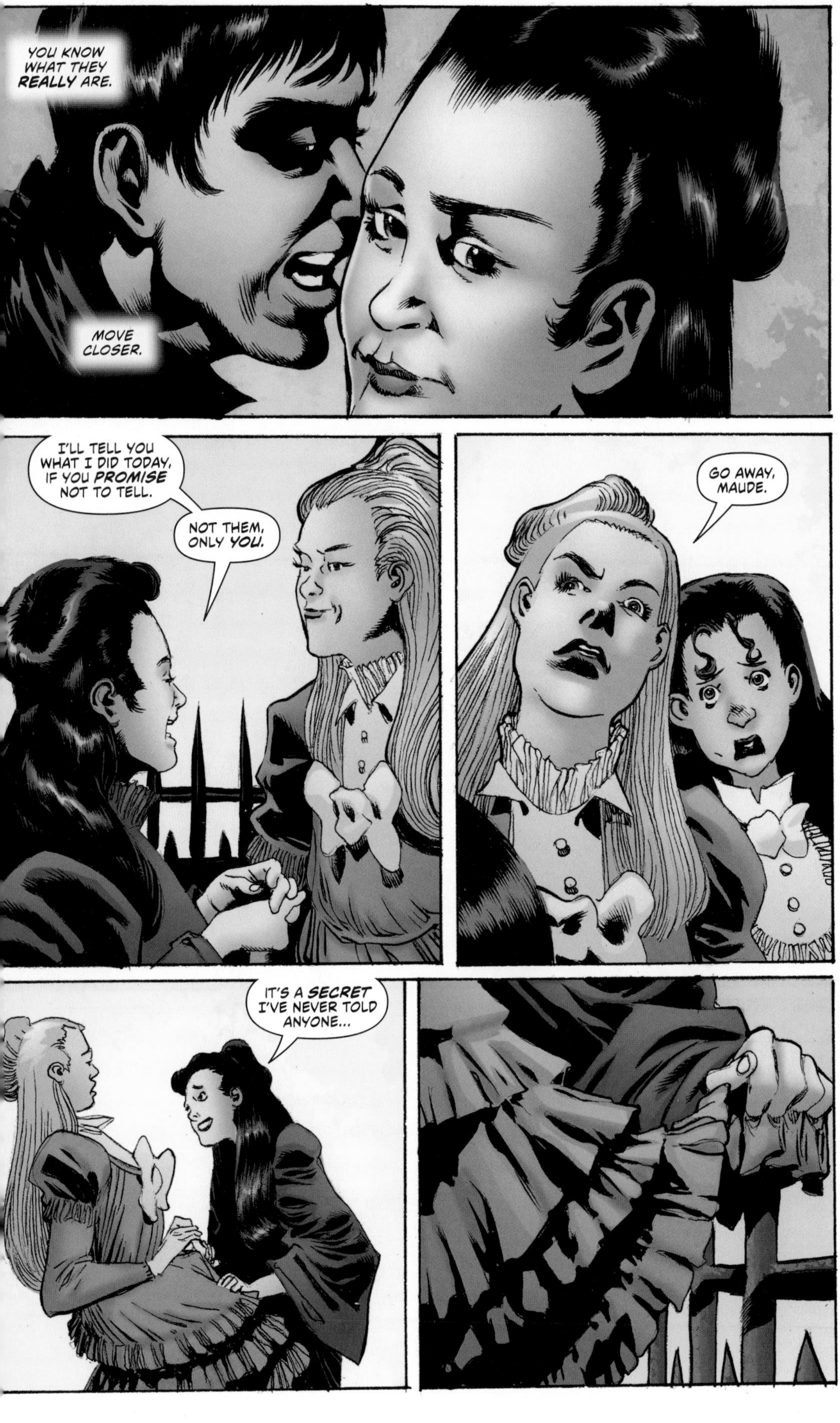

YOU KNOW WHAT THEY REALLY ARE.
MOVE CLOSER.
I'LL TELL YOU WHAT I DID TODAY, IF YOU PROMISE NOT TO TELL.
NOT THEM, ONLY YOU.
GO AWAY, MAUDE.
IT'S A SECRET I'VE NEVER TOLD ANYONE...

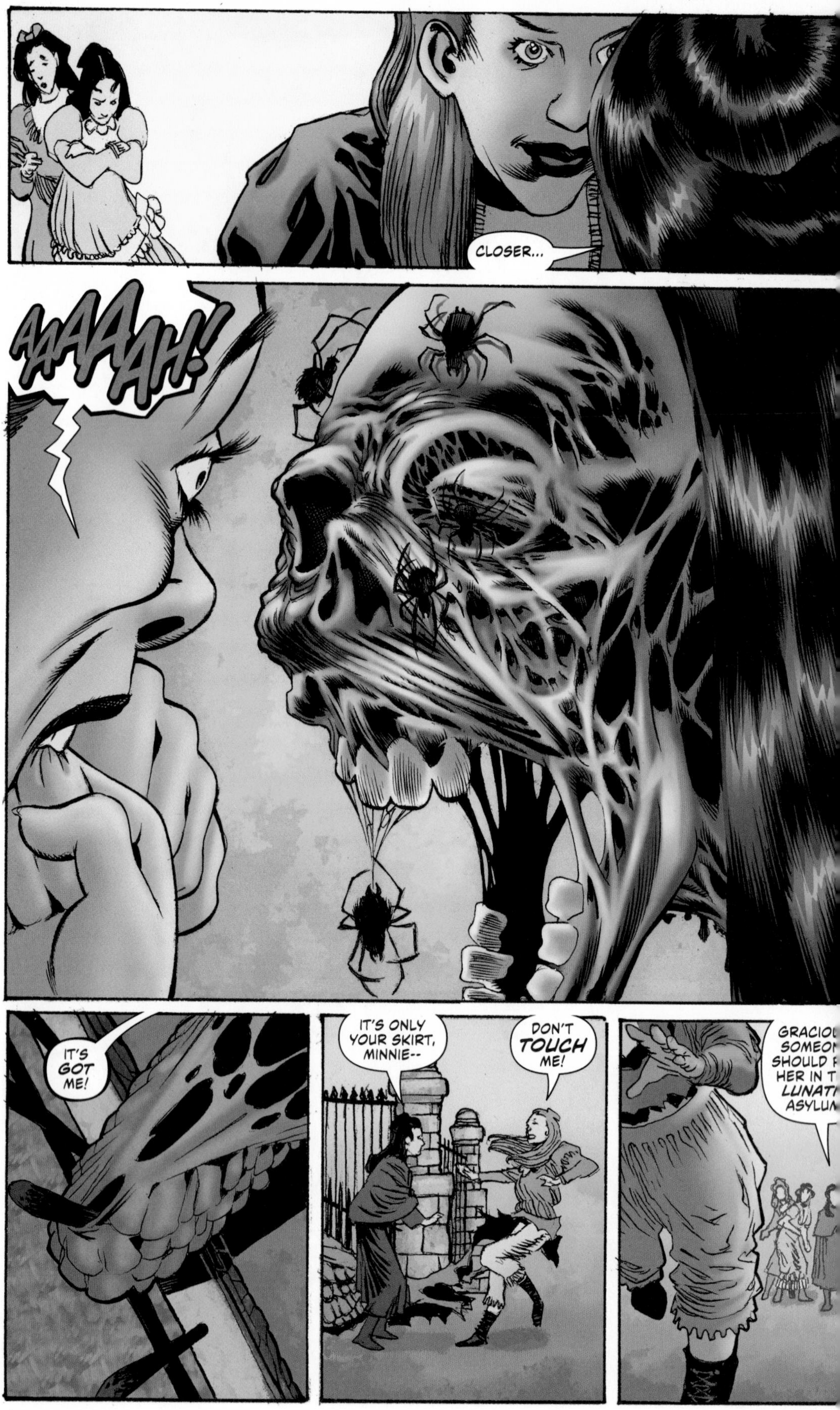
CLOSER...
AAAAAH!
IT'S GOT ME!
IT'S ONLY YOUR SKIRT, MINNIE--
DON'T TOUCH ME!
GRACIOU SOMEON SHOULD HER IN T LUNATI ASYLUM

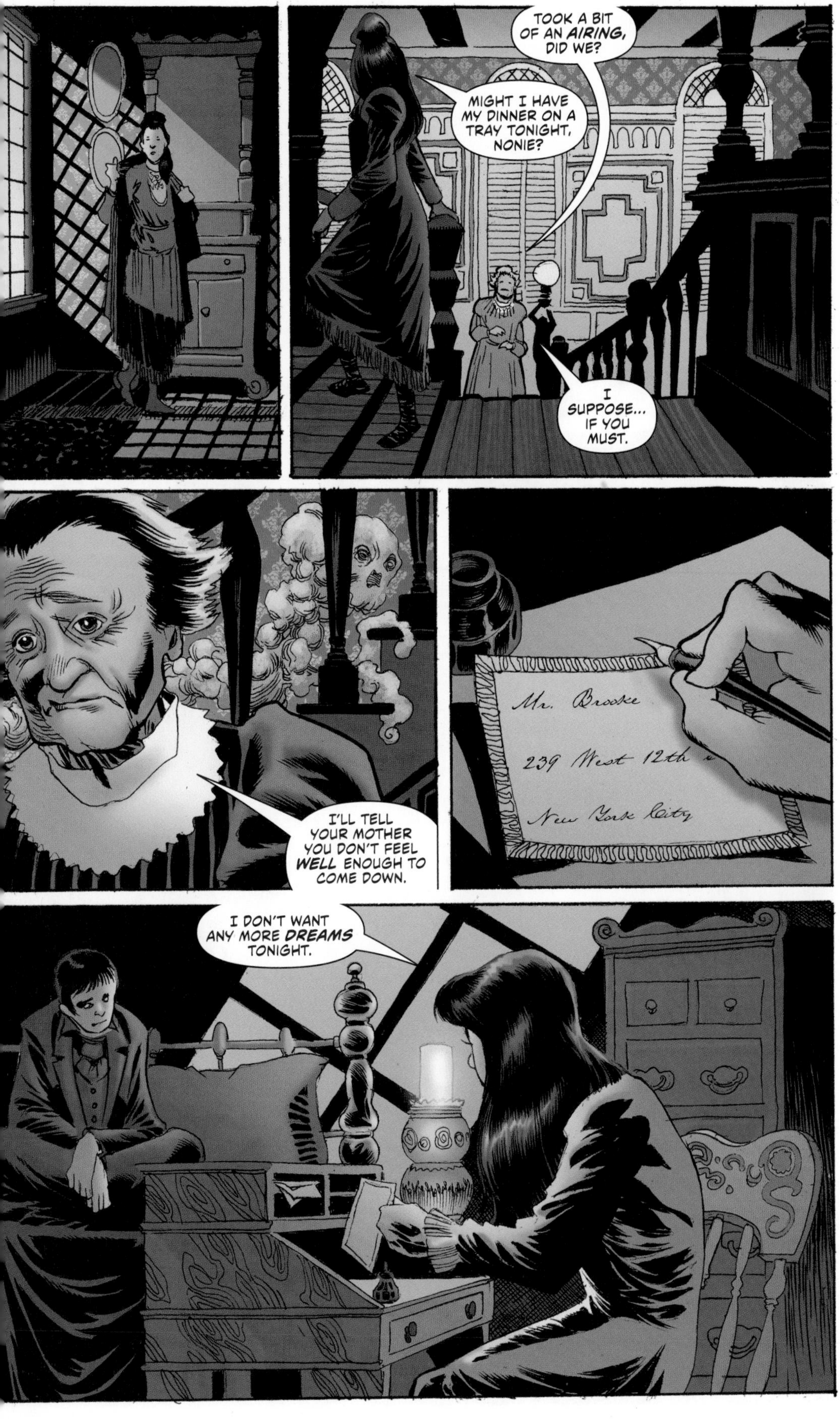
MIGHT I HAVE MY DINNER ON A TRAY TONIGHT, NONIE?
TOOK A BIT OF AN AIRING, DID WE?
I SUPPOSE... IF YOU MUST.
I'LL TELL YOUR MOTHER YOU DON'T FEEL WELL ENOUGH TO COME DOWN.
Mr. Brooke
239 West 12th
New York City
I DON'T WANT ANY MORE DREAMS TONIGHT.

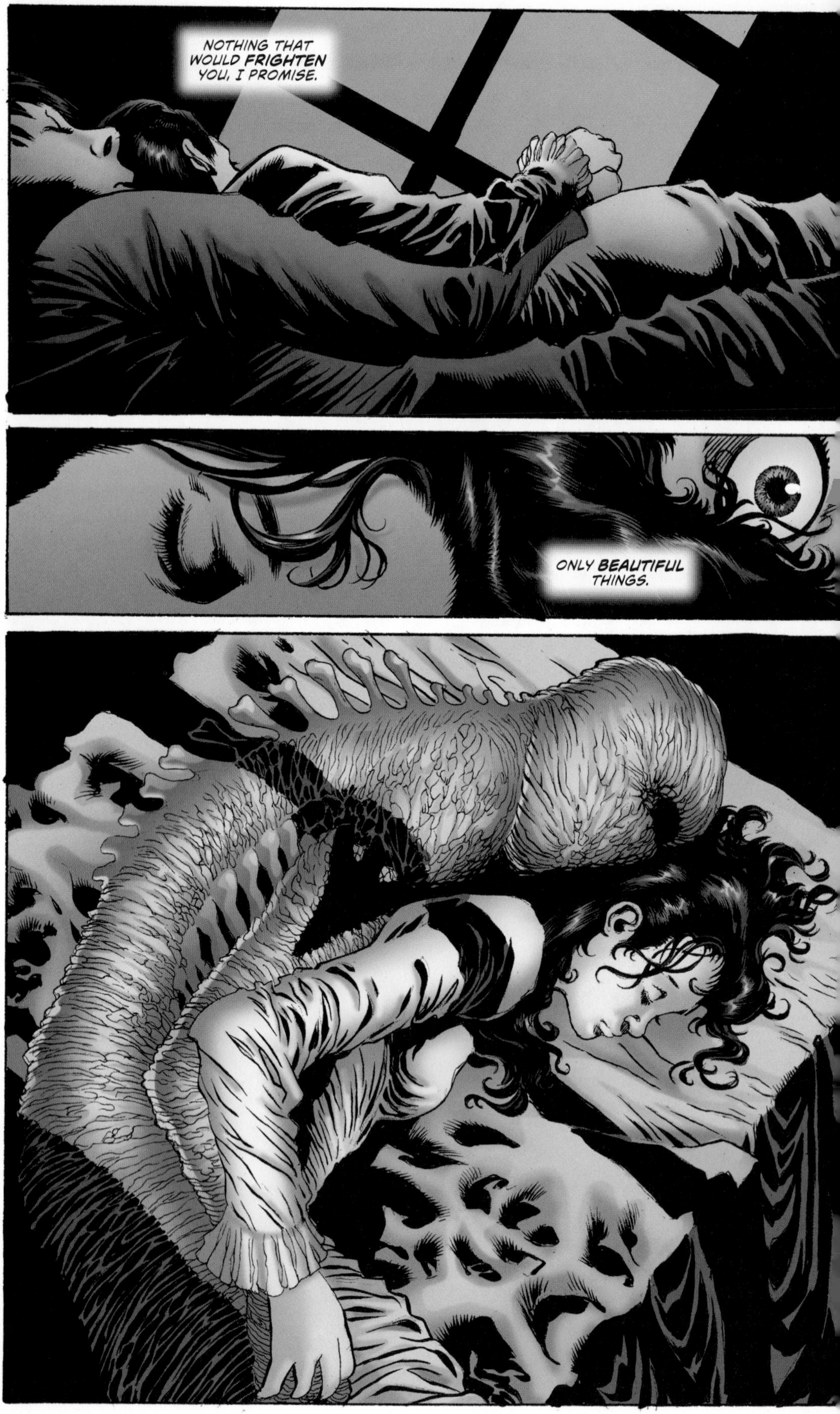
NOTHING THAT WOULD FRIGHTEN YOU, I PROMISE.
ONLY BEAUTIFUL THINGS.

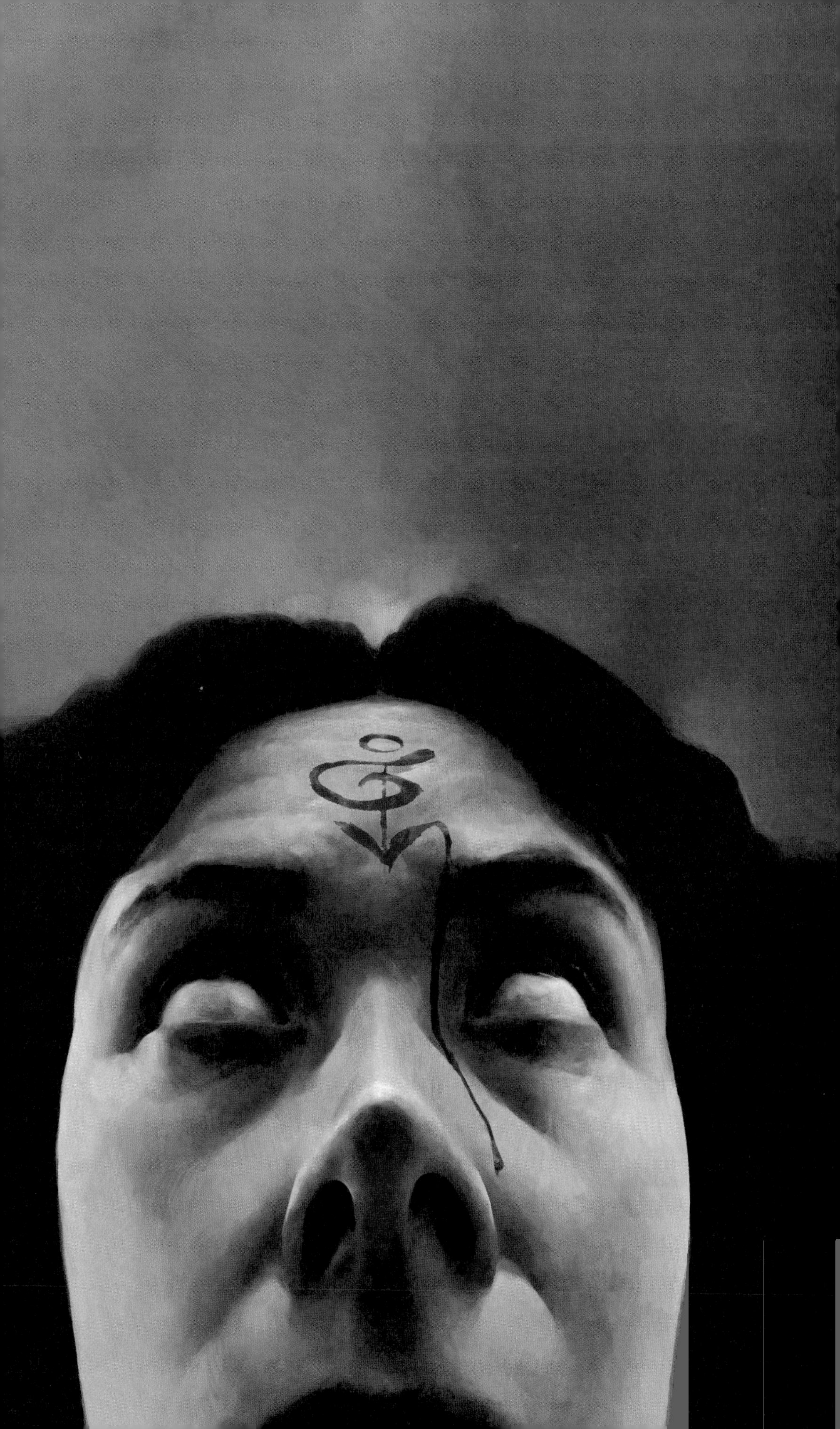

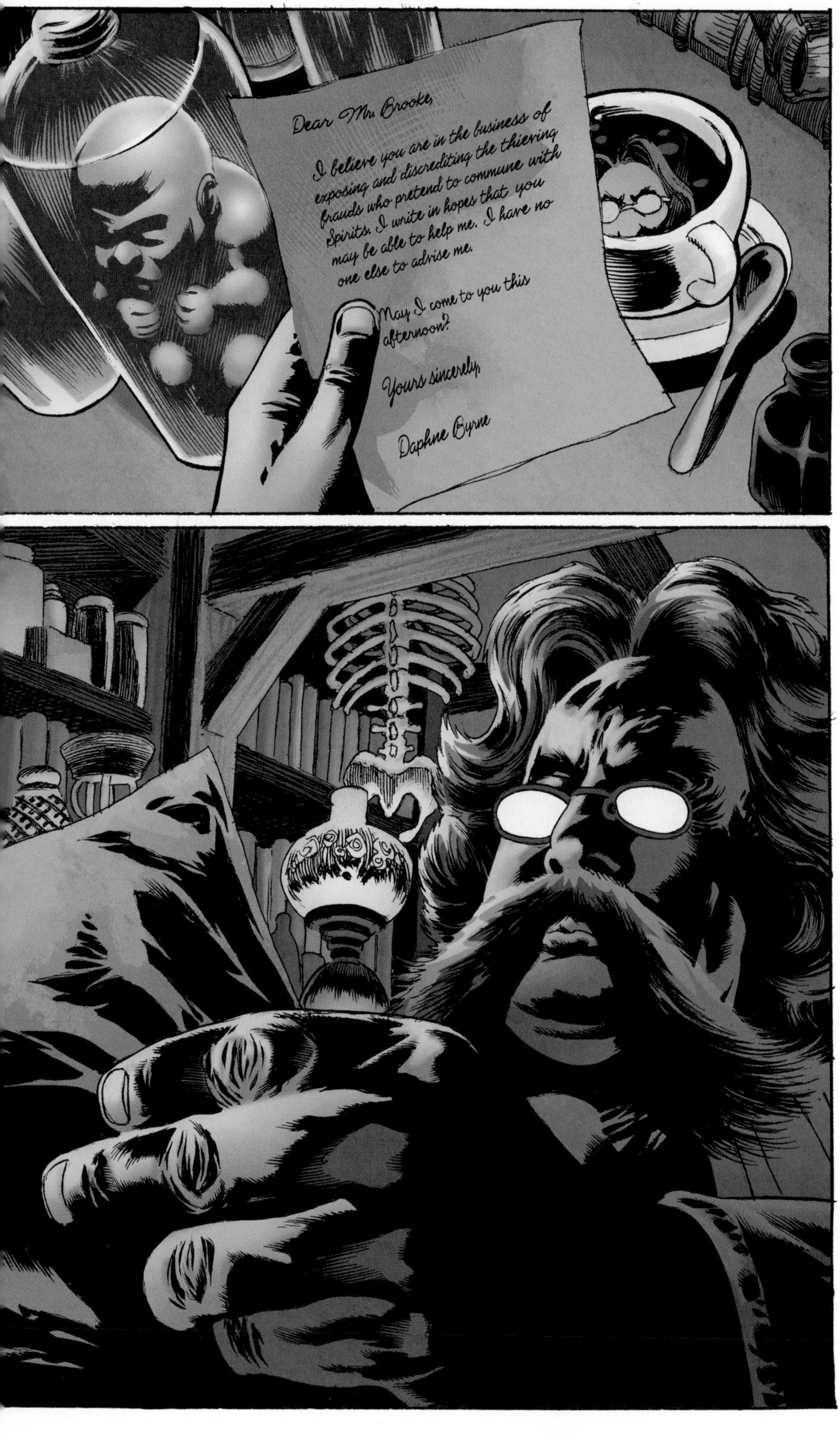
Dear Mr. Brooke,
I believe you are in the business of exposing and discrediting the thieving frauds who pretend to commune with Spirits. I write in hopes that you may be able to help me. I have no one else to advise me.
May I come to you this afternoon?
Yours sincerely,
Daphne Byrne

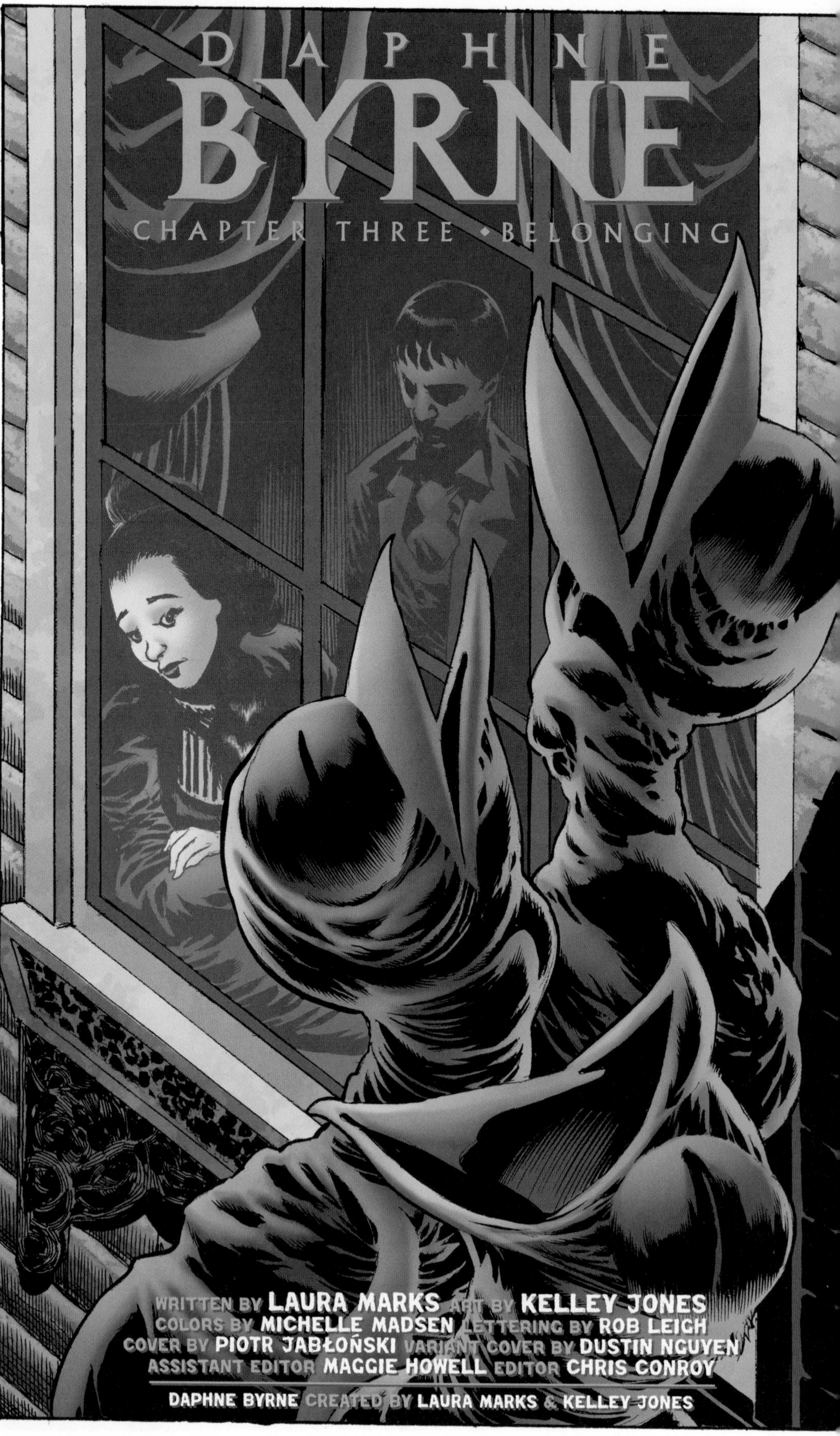
DAPHNE
BYRNE
CHAPTER THREE • BELONGING
WRITTEN BY LAURA MARKS ART BY KELLEY JONES
COLORS BY MICHELLE MADSEN LETTERING BY ROB LEIGH
COVER BY PIOTR JABŁOŃSKI VARIANT COVER BY DUSTIN NGUYEN
ASSISTANT EDITOR MAGGIE HOWELL EDITOR CHRIS CONROY
DAPHNE BYRNE CREATED BY LAURA MARKS & KELLEY JONES

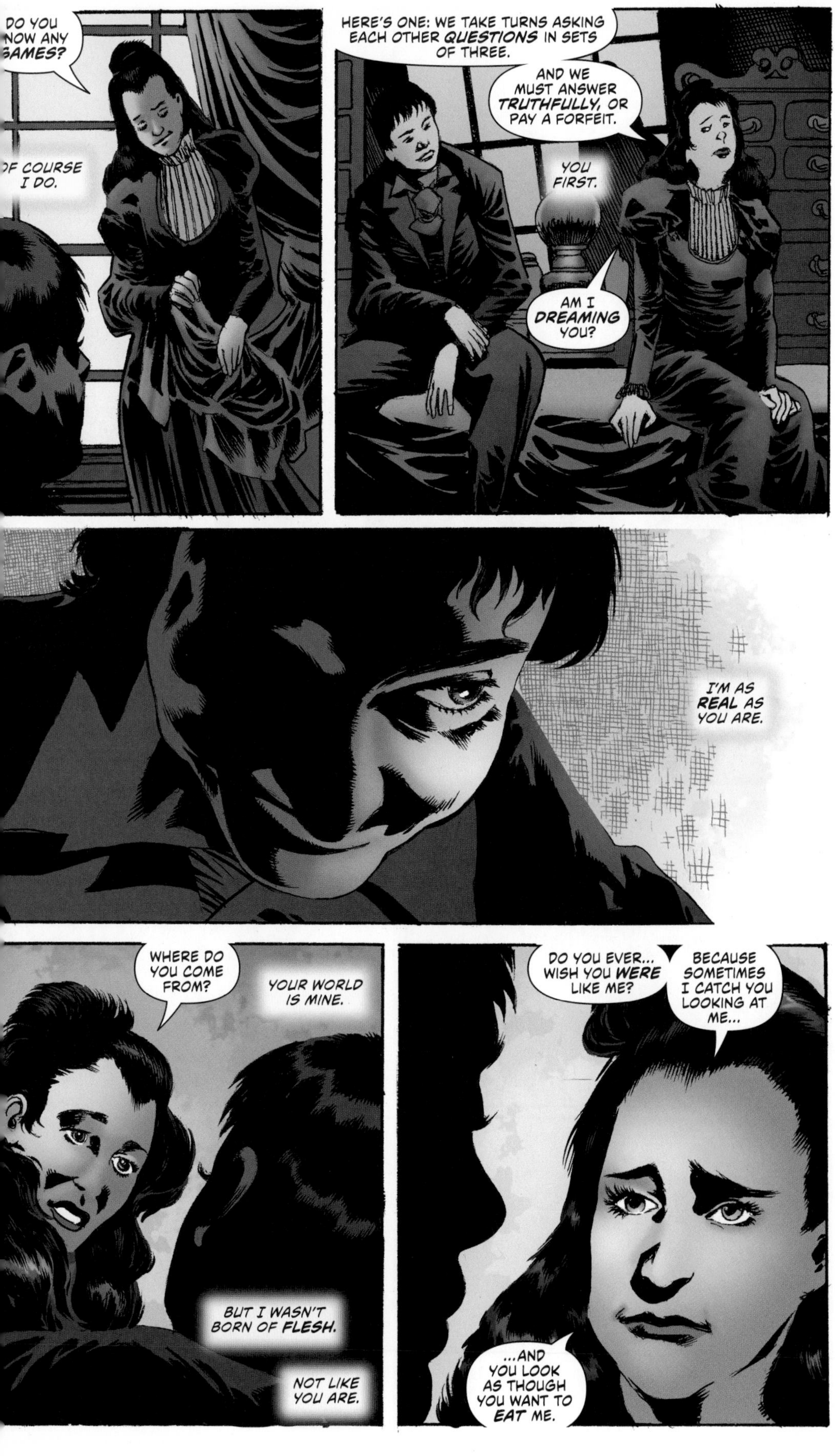
DO YOU
NOW ANY
GAMES?
OF COURSE
I DO.
HERE'S ONE: WE TAKE TURNS ASKING EACH OTHER QUESTIONS IN SETS OF THREE.
AND WE MUST ANSWER TRUTHFULLY, OR PAY A FORFEIT.
YOU FIRST.
AM I DREAMING YOU?
I'M AS REAL AS YOU ARE.
WHERE DO YOU COME FROM?
YOUR WORLD IS MINE.
BUT I WASN'T BORN OF FLESH.
NOT LIKE YOU ARE.
DO YOU EVER... WISH YOU WERE LIKE ME?
BECAUSE SOMETIMES I CATCH YOU LOOKING AT ME...
...AND YOU LOOK AS THOUGH YOU WANT TO EAT ME.

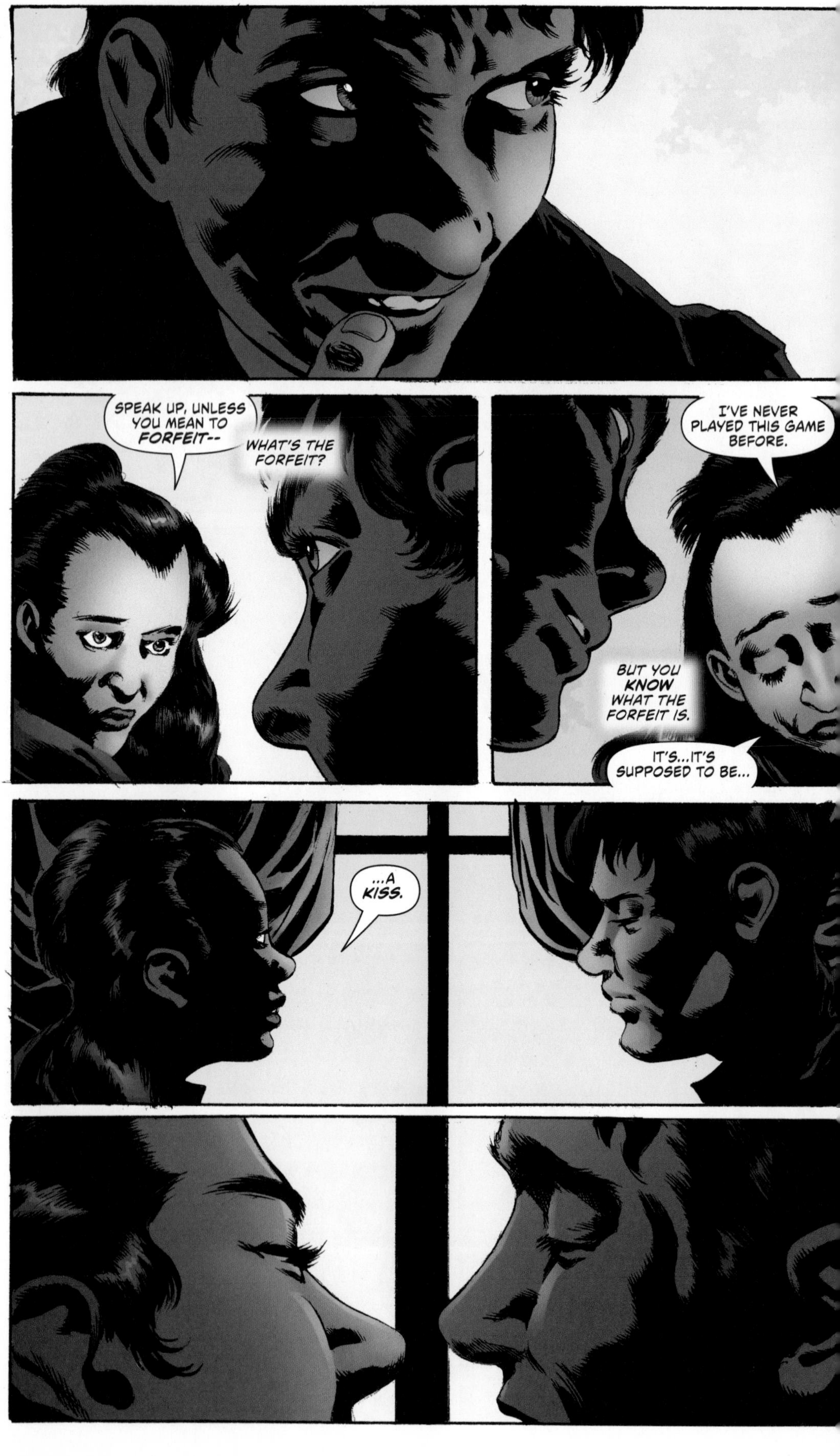
SPEAK UP, UNLESS YOU MEAN TO FORFEIT--
WHAT'S THE FORFEIT?
I'VE NEVER PLAYED THIS GAME BEFORE.
BUT YOU KNOW WHAT THE FORFEIT IS.
IT'S...IT'S SUPPOSED TO BE...
...A KISS.

DAPHNE!

I'VE JUST HAD A VISIT FROM MRS. JAMES. MINNIE'S MOTHER. SHE SAYS YOU *ATTACKED* HER DAUGHTER IN THE STREET.

MAMMA, I--I WOULD NEVER--

"THAT'S EXACTLY WHAT I SAID.

"YOU MUST BE MISTAKEN. DAPHNE WOULD NEVER DO SUCH A THING--AND BESIDES, SHE WAS HOME ALL DAY."

BUT SHE SAID THAT TWO *OTHER* GIRLS SAW YOU.

THEY'RE LYING, I *SWEAR* IT! I WENT OUT FOR A BIT--FOR A CHANGE OF AIR--AND I *SAW* THEM, BUT...THAT'S ALL.

THEY'RE ONLY MAKING UP A *STORY*.

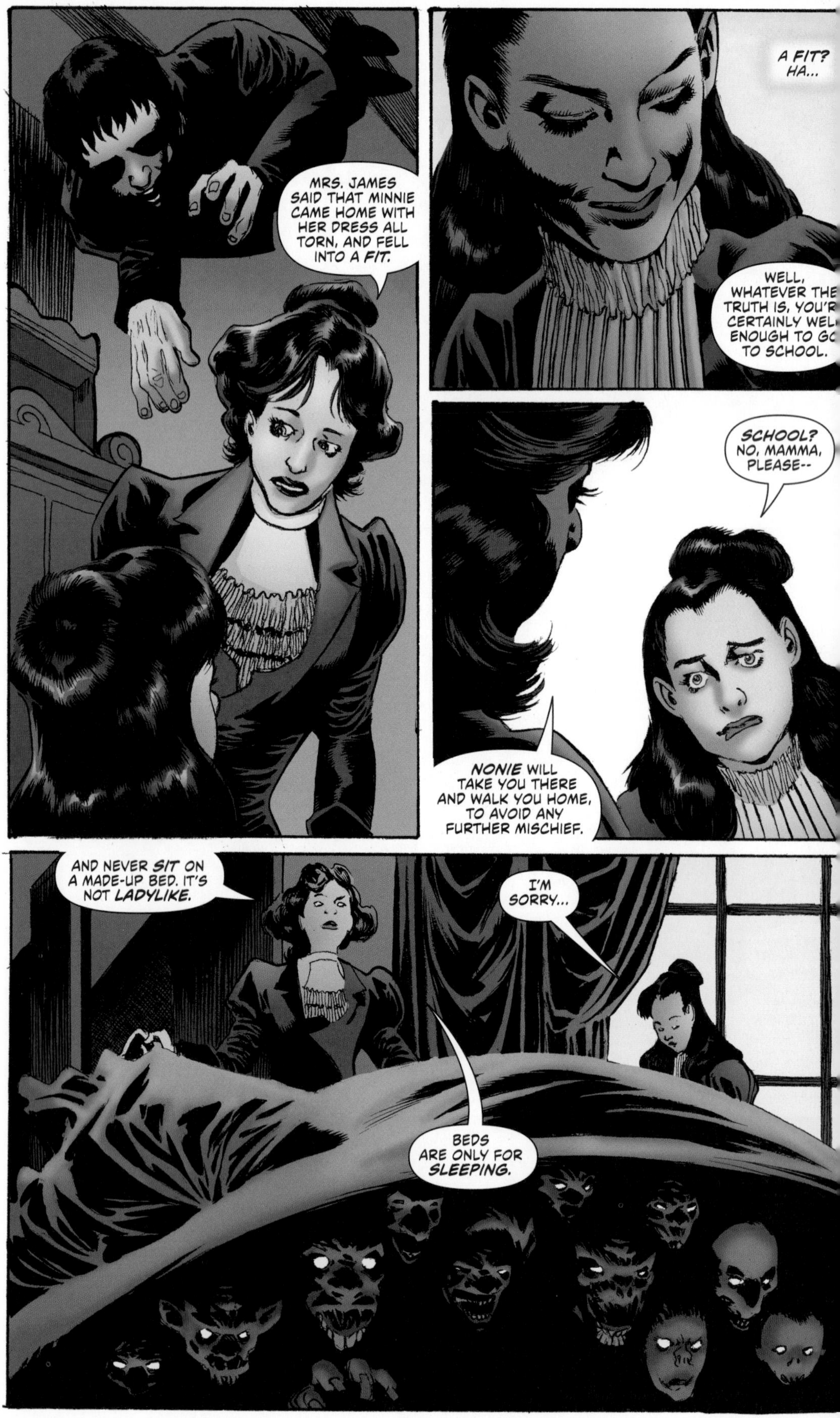
MRS. JAMES SAID THAT MINNIE CAME HOME WITH HER DRESS ALL TORN, AND FELL INTO A *FIT*.
A *FIT?* HA...
WELL, WHATEVER THE TRUTH IS, YOU'R CERTAINLY WEL ENOUGH TO GO TO SCHOOL.
SCHOOL? NO, MAMMA, PLEASE--
NONIE WILL TAKE YOU THERE AND WALK YOU HOME, TO AVOID ANY FURTHER MISCHIEF.
AND NEVER *SIT* ON A MADE-UP BED. IT'S NOT *LADYLIKE*.
I'M SORRY...
BEDS ARE ONLY FOR *SLEEPING*.

CHEER UP, LITTLE DAPHNE. YOUR MOTHER WAS QUITE RIGHT TO SEND ME ALONG.

FINE LADIES LIKE MRS. ASTOR *ALWAYS* HAVE THEIR MAIDS WITH THEM WHEN THEY GO OUT WALKING.

AND IT'S ONLY *SCHOOL*. YOU ACT AS IF YOU'RE GOING TO THE *GUILLOTINE*.

OLD *SOW*. SHE DOESN'T KNOW THAT YOU WANTED TO GO AND VISIT *MR. BROOKE* TODAY.

BUT I DON'T KNOW WHY YOU THINK *HE* CAN HELP YOU.

YOU COULD HAVE ASKED *ME*.

WHAT DO *YOU* KNOW ABOUT IT?

THAT'S ROUGH CHEEK FROM YOU, MISS.

I-I DIDN'T MEAN *YOU*, NONIE...

YOU DON'T HAVE TO *SPEAK* TO ME OUT LOUD.

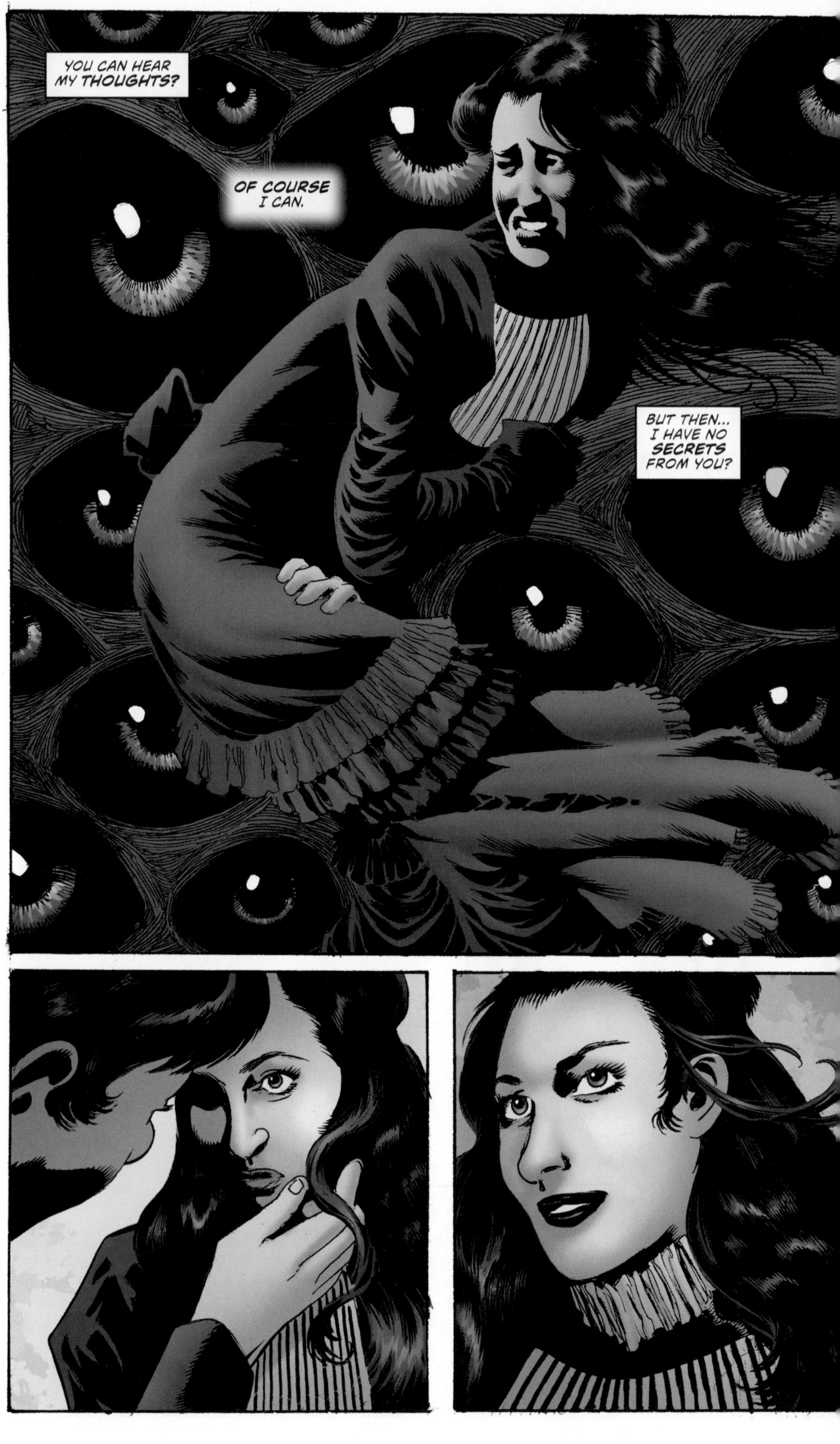
YOU CAN HEAR MY THOUGHTS?
OF COURSE I CAN.
BUT THEN... I HAVE NO SECRETS FROM YOU?

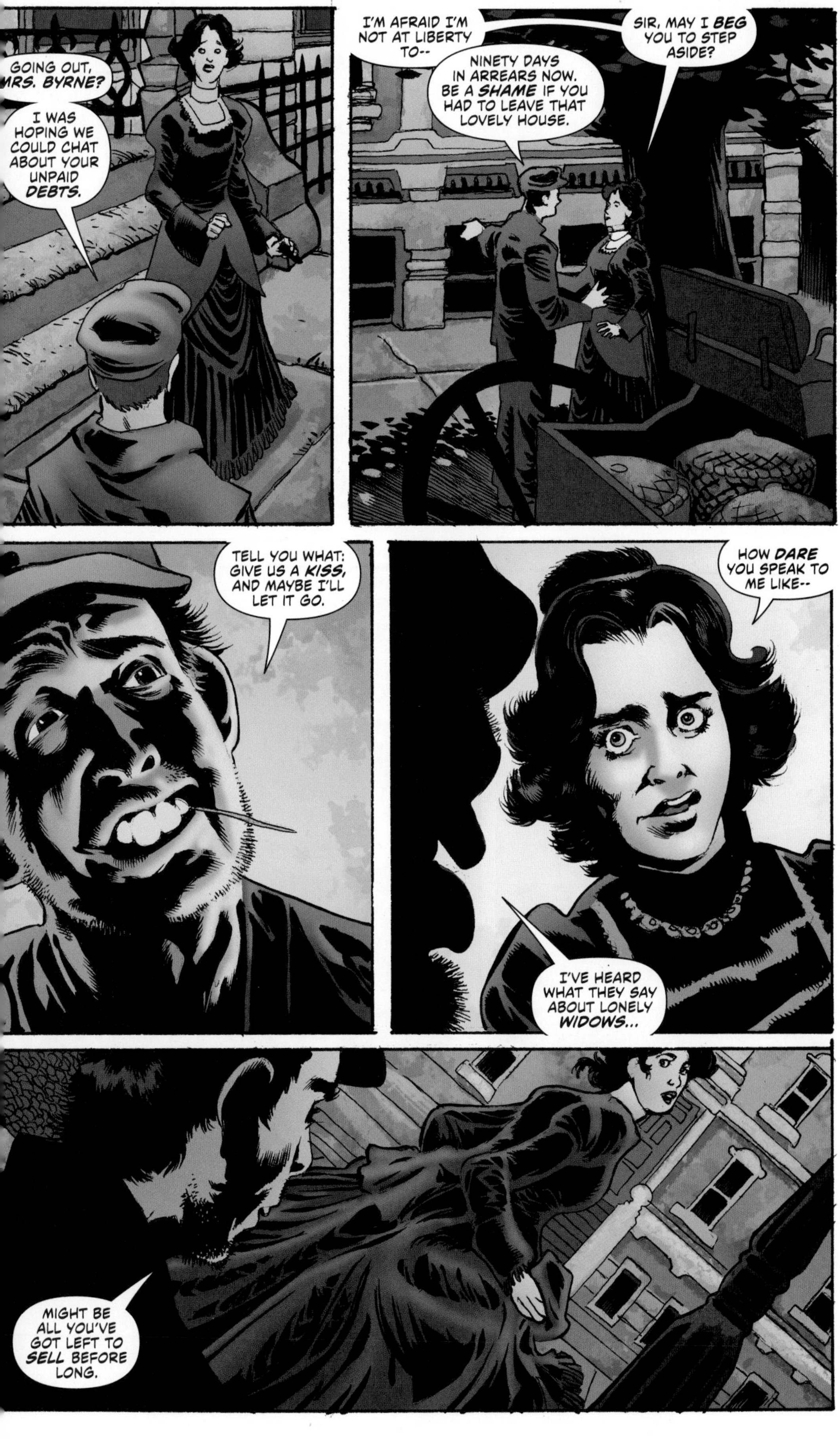
GOING OUT, MRS. BYRNE?
I WAS HOPING WE COULD CHAT ABOUT YOUR UNPAID DEBTS.
I'M AFRAID I'M NOT AT LIBERTY TO--
NINETY DAYS IN ARREARS NOW. BE A SHAME IF YOU HAD TO LEAVE THAT LOVELY HOUSE.
SIR, MAY I BEG YOU TO STEP ASIDE?
TELL YOU WHAT: GIVE US A KISS, AND MAYBE I'LL LET IT GO.
HOW DARE YOU SPEAK TO ME LIKE--
I'VE HEARD WHAT THEY SAY ABOUT LONELY WIDOWS...
MIGHT BE ALL YOU'VE GOT LEFT TO SELL BEFORE LONG.

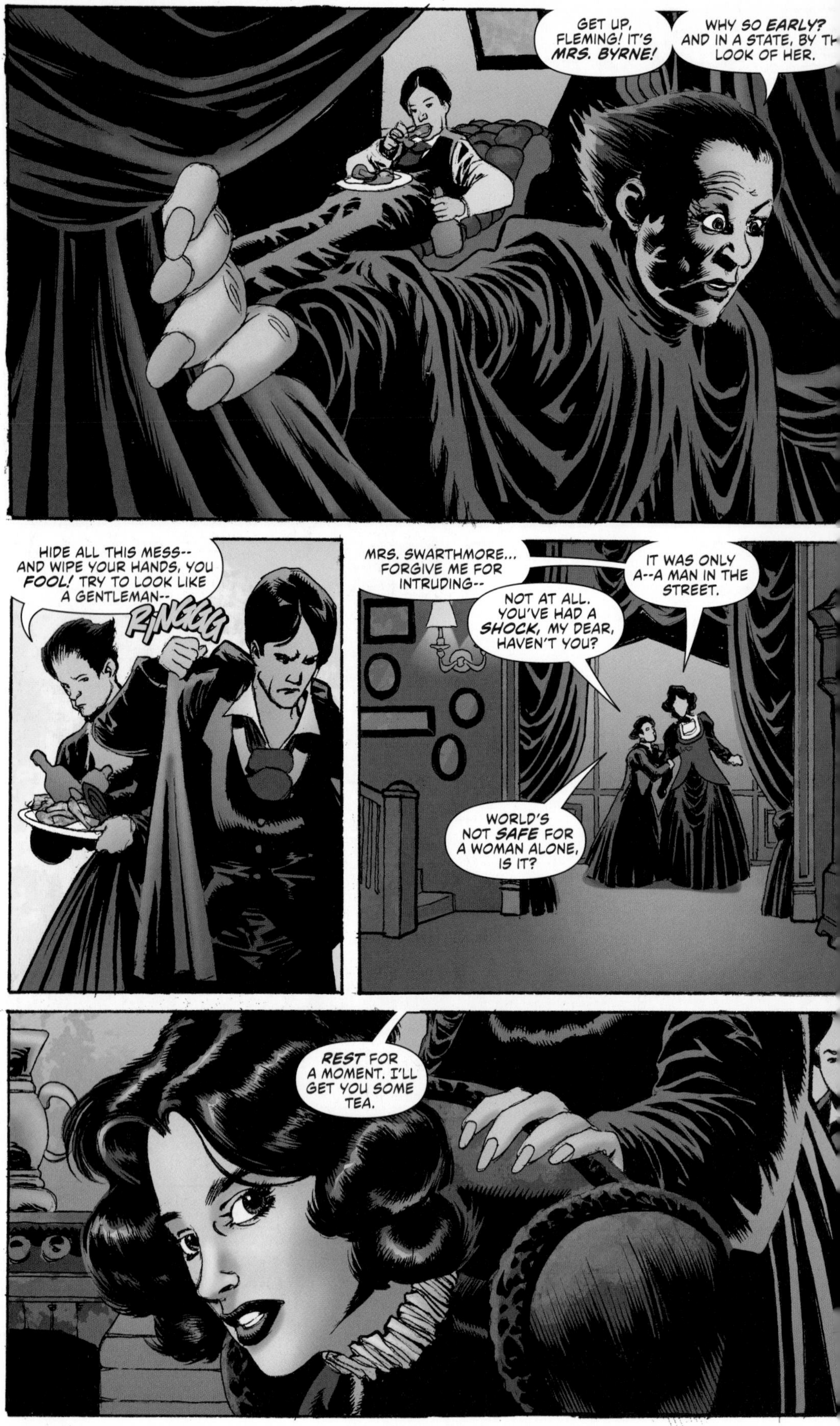
GET UP, FLEMING! IT'S MRS. BYRNE!
WHY SO EARLY? AND IN A STATE, BY TH LOOK OF HER.
HIDE ALL THIS MESS-- AND WIPE YOUR HANDS, YOU FOOL! TRY TO LOOK LIKE A GENTLEMAN--
RiNGGG
MRS. SWARTHMORE... FORGIVE ME FOR INTRUDING--
IT WAS ONLY A--A MAN IN THE STREET.
NOT AT ALL. YOU'VE HAD A SHOCK, MY DEAR, HAVEN'T YOU?
WORLD'S NOT SAFE FOR A WOMAN ALONE, IS IT?
REST FOR A MOMENT. I'LL GET YOU SOME TEA.

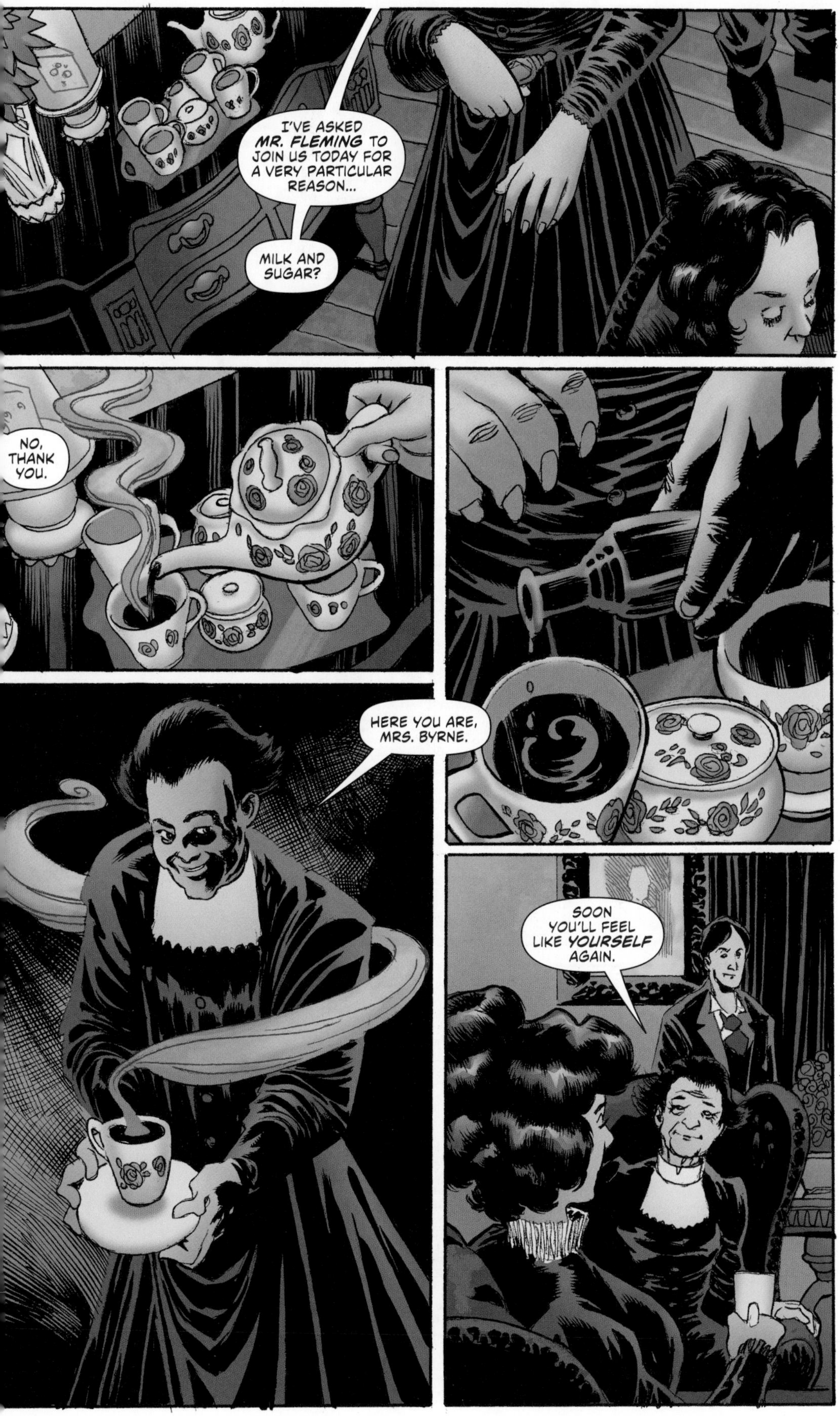

I'VE ASKED *MR. FLEMING* TO JOIN US TODAY FOR A VERY PARTICULAR REASON...
MILK AND SUGAR?
NO, THANK YOU.
HERE YOU ARE, MRS. BYRNE.
SOON YOU'LL FEEL LIKE *YOURSELF* AGAIN.

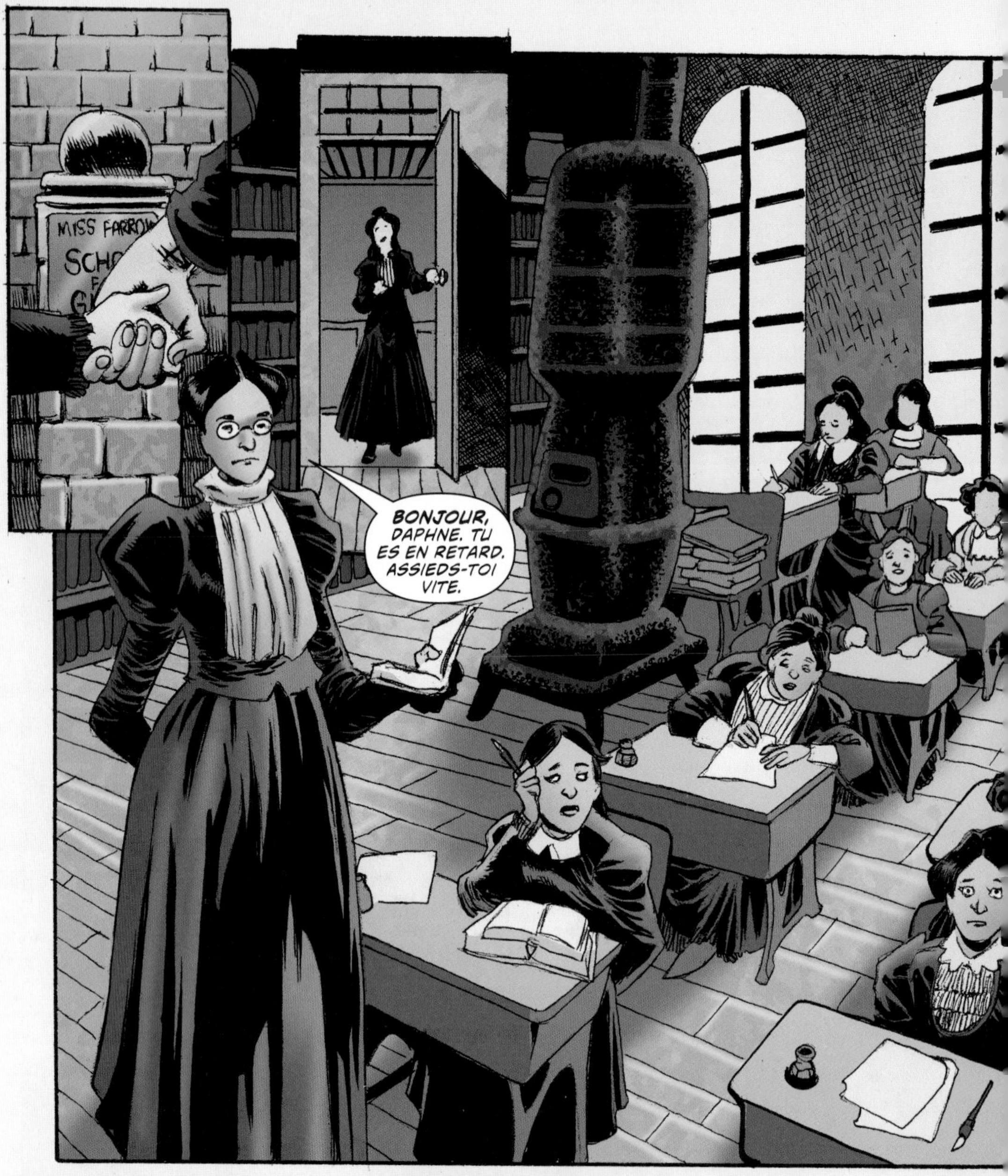
MISS FARROW
SCHO
BONJOUR, DAPHNE. TU ES EN RETARD. ASSIEDS-TOI VITE.

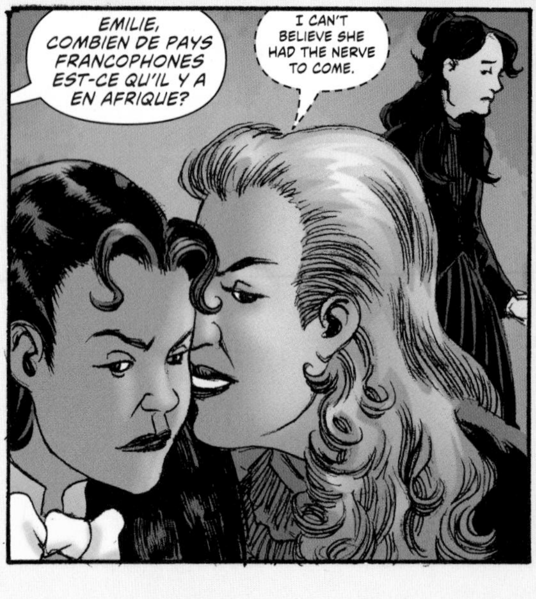
EMILIE, COMBIEN DE PAYS FRANCOPHONES EST-CE QU'IL Y A EN AFRIQUE?
I CAN'T BELIEVE SHE HAD THE NERVE TO COME.

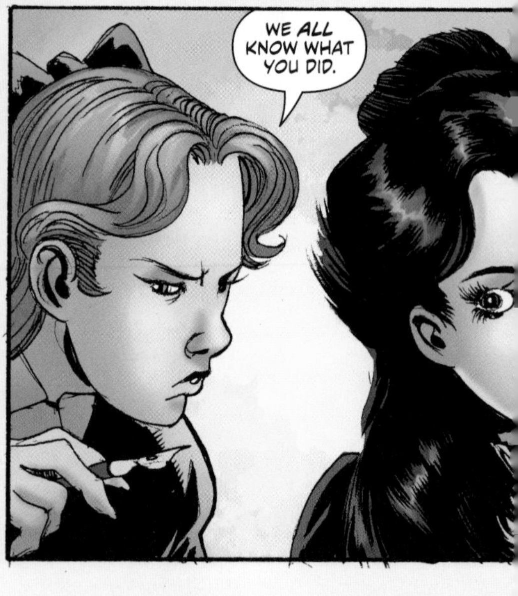
WE ALL KNOW WHAT YOU DID.

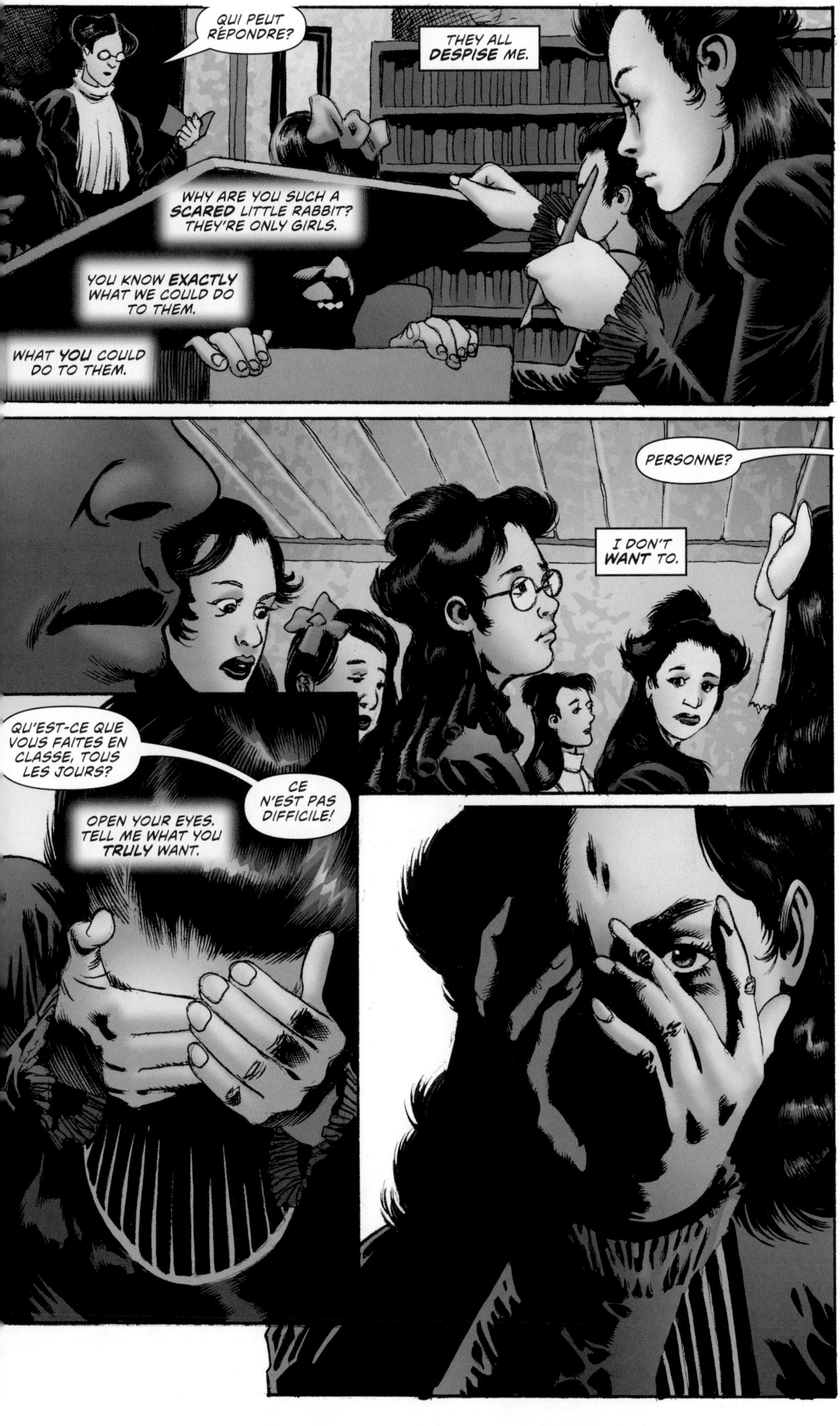
QUI PEUT RÉPONDRE?
THEY ALL DESPISE ME.
WHY ARE YOU SUCH A SCARED LITTLE RABBIT? THEY'RE ONLY GIRLS.
YOU KNOW EXACTLY WHAT WE COULD DO TO THEM.
WHAT YOU COULD DO TO THEM.
PERSONNE?
I DON'T WANT TO.
QU'EST-CE QUE VOUS FAITES EN CLASSE, TOUS LES JOURS?
CE N'EST PAS DIFFICILE!
OPEN YOUR EYES. TELL ME WHAT YOU TRULY WANT.

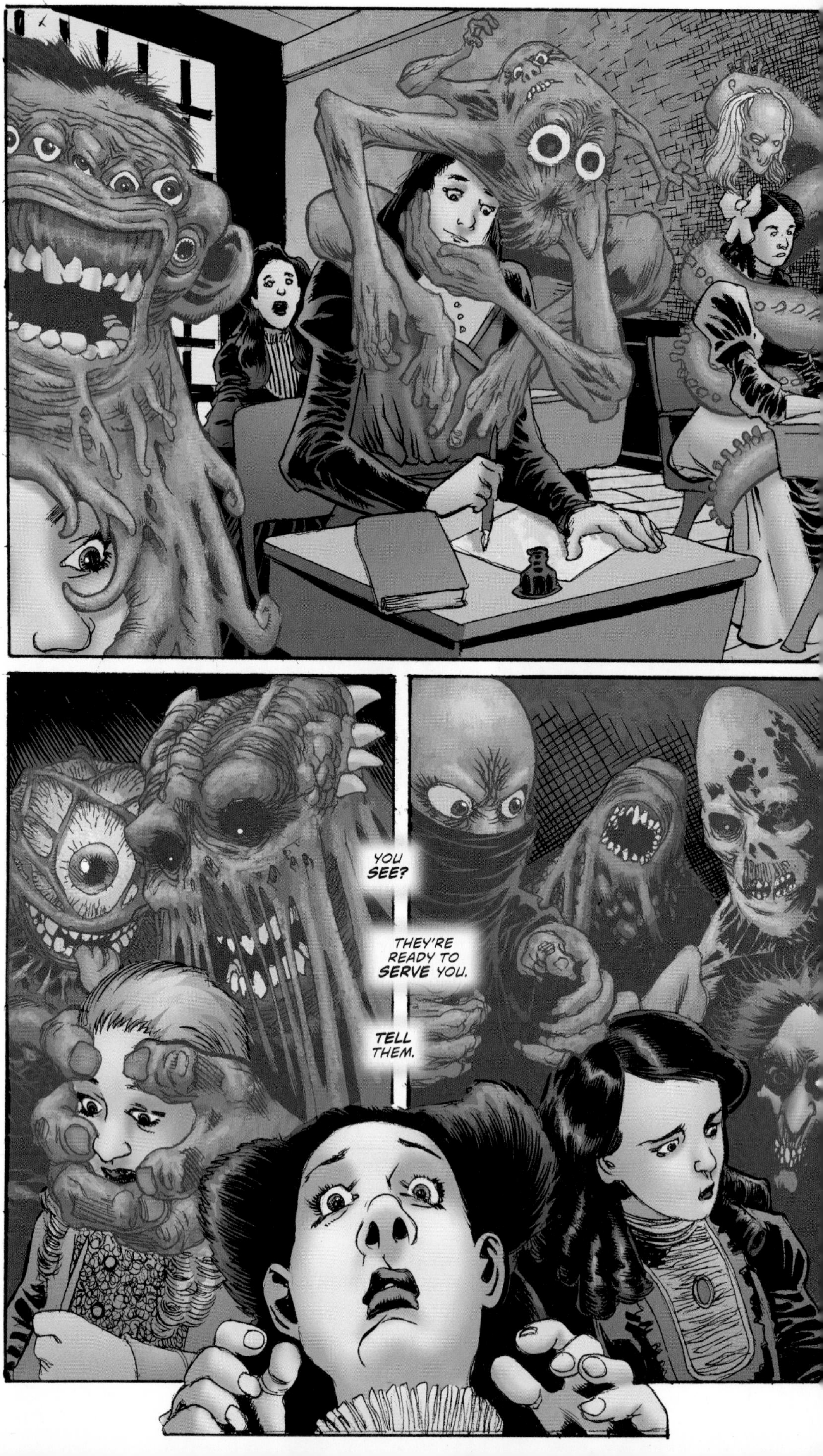
YOU SEE?
THEY'RE READY TO SERVE YOU.
TELL THEM.

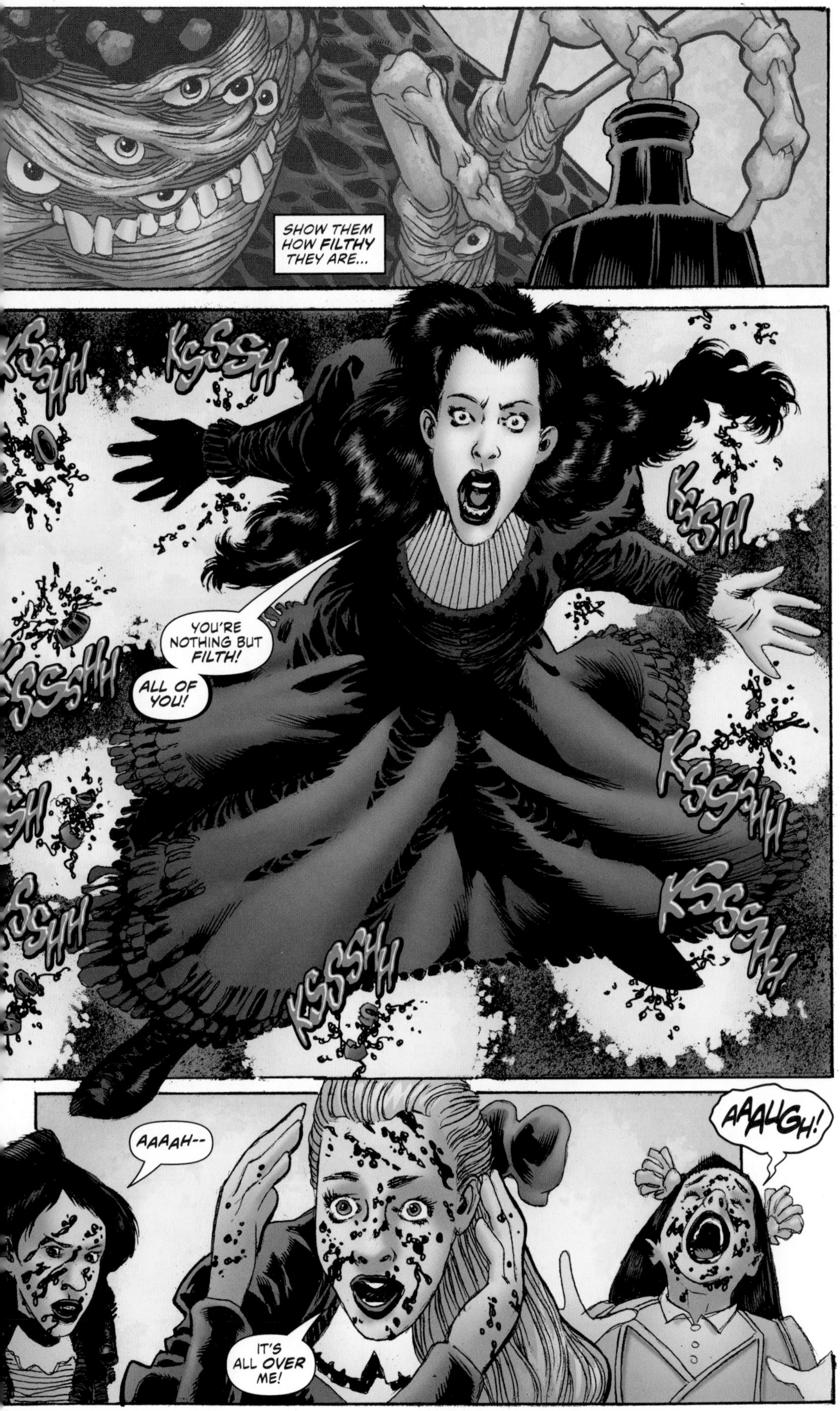
SHOW THEM HOW FILTHY THEY ARE...
KSSSH
KSSSH
KSSH
YOU'RE NOTHING BUT FILTH!
ALL OF YOU!
KSSSHH
KSSSHH
KSSSHH
KSSSH
AAAAH--
AAAAUGH!
IT'S ALL OVER ME!

Huh-- huh--

IT'S IN MY EYES!

I CAN'T SEE!

SHE DID IT! I SAW HER...

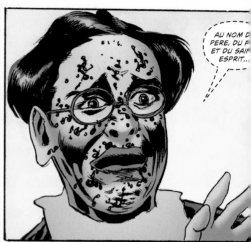

AU NOM D PERE, DU P ET DU SAI ESPRIT...

I CAN NEVER COME BACK HERE AGAIN.

BUT WHY WOULD YOU EVER WANT TO?

I'M AN ABOMINATION.

NO, YOU'RE NOT. YOU'RE MY PRINCESS.

WHERE SHALL WE GO? THE WHOLE CITY IS OURS NOW.

I WANT TO GO HOME.

WHY? NO ONE'S THERE. NONIE'S OUT SHOPPING...

...AND YOU CAN GUESS WHERE YOUR MOTHER IS.

YOU'RE RIGHT.

WE WON' GO HOME

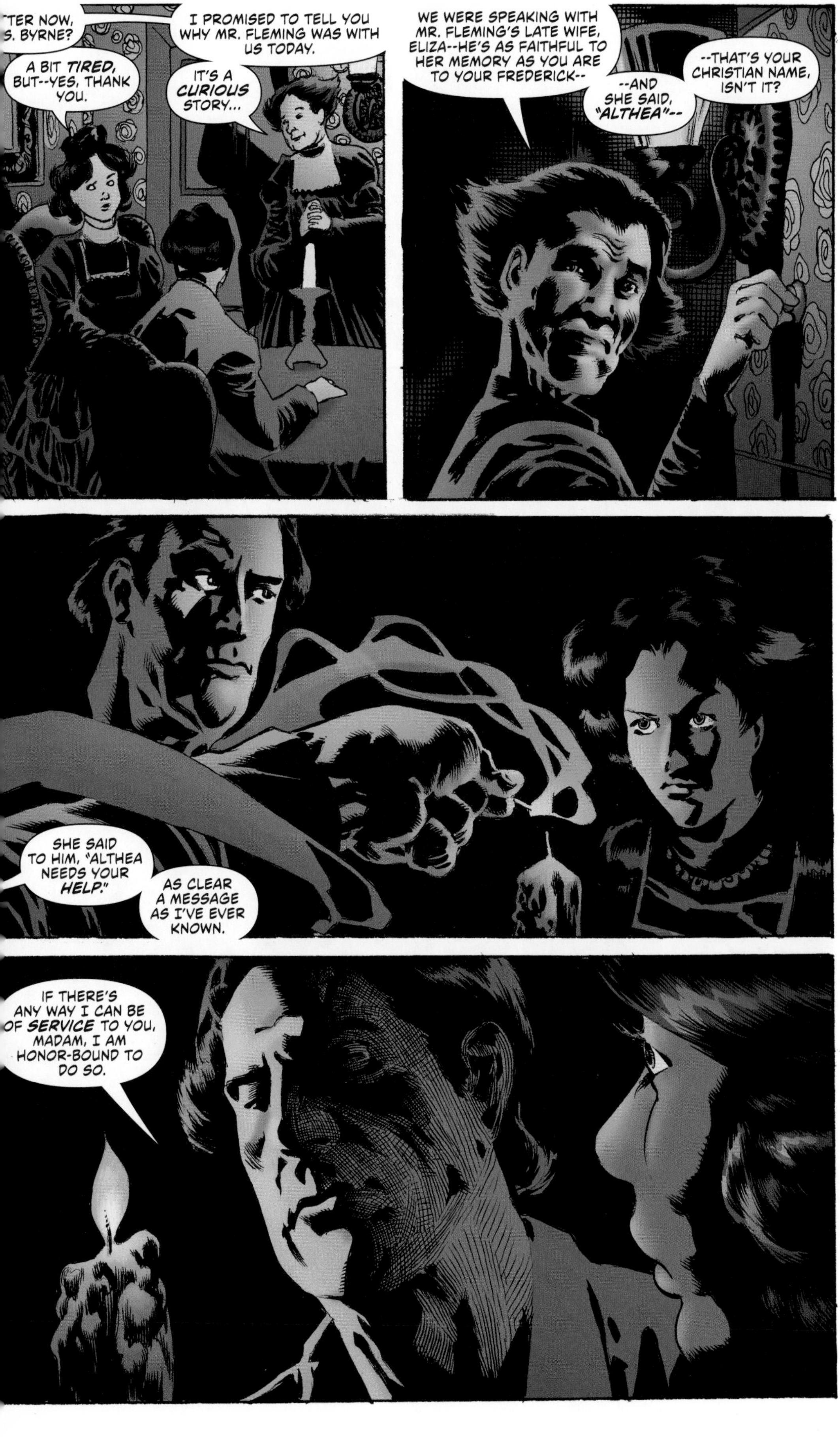

-TER NOW,
S. BYRNE?
A BIT TIRED, BUT--YES, THANK YOU.
I PROMISED TO TELL YOU WHY MR. FLEMING WAS WITH US TODAY.
IT'S A CURIOUS STORY...
WE WERE SPEAKING WITH MR. FLEMING'S LATE WIFE, ELIZA--HE'S AS FAITHFUL TO HER MEMORY AS YOU ARE TO YOUR FREDERICK--
--AND SHE SAID, "ALTHEA"--
--THAT'S YOUR CHRISTIAN NAME, ISN'T IT?
SHE SAID TO HIM, "ALTHEA NEEDS YOUR HELP."
AS CLEAR A MESSAGE AS I'VE EVER KNOWN.
IF THERE'S ANY WAY I CAN BE OF SERVICE TO YOU, MADAM, I AM HONOR-BOUND TO DO SO.

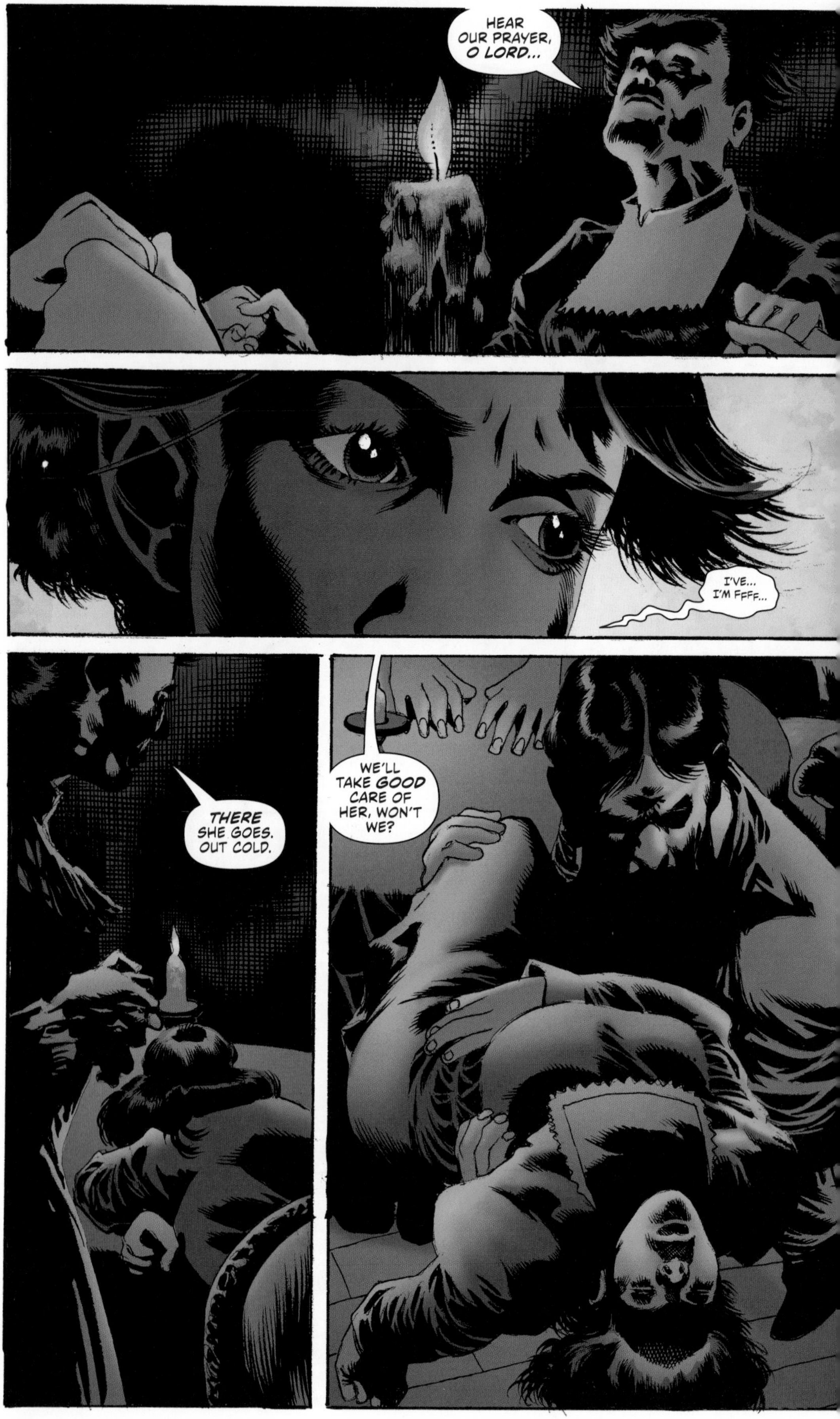
HEAR OUR PRAYER, O LORD...
I'VE... I'M FFFF...
THERE SHE GOES. OUT COLD.
WE'LL TAKE GOOD CARE OF HER, WON'T WE?

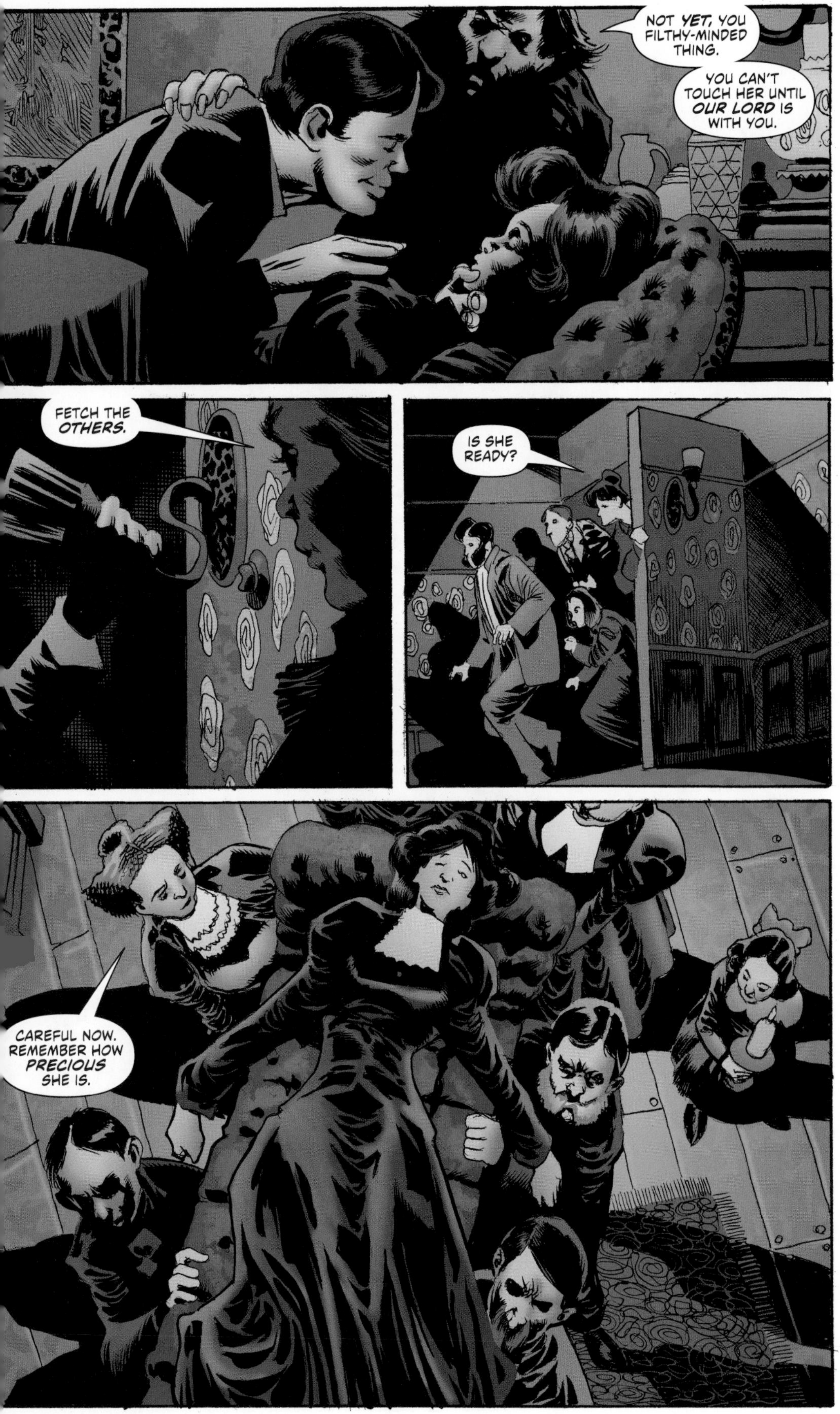

NOT *YET*, YOU FILTHY-MINDED THING.
YOU CAN'T TOUCH HER UNTIL *OUR LORD* IS WITH YOU.
FETCH THE *OTHERS*.
IS SHE READY?
CAREFUL NOW. REMEMBER HOW *PRECIOUS* SHE IS.

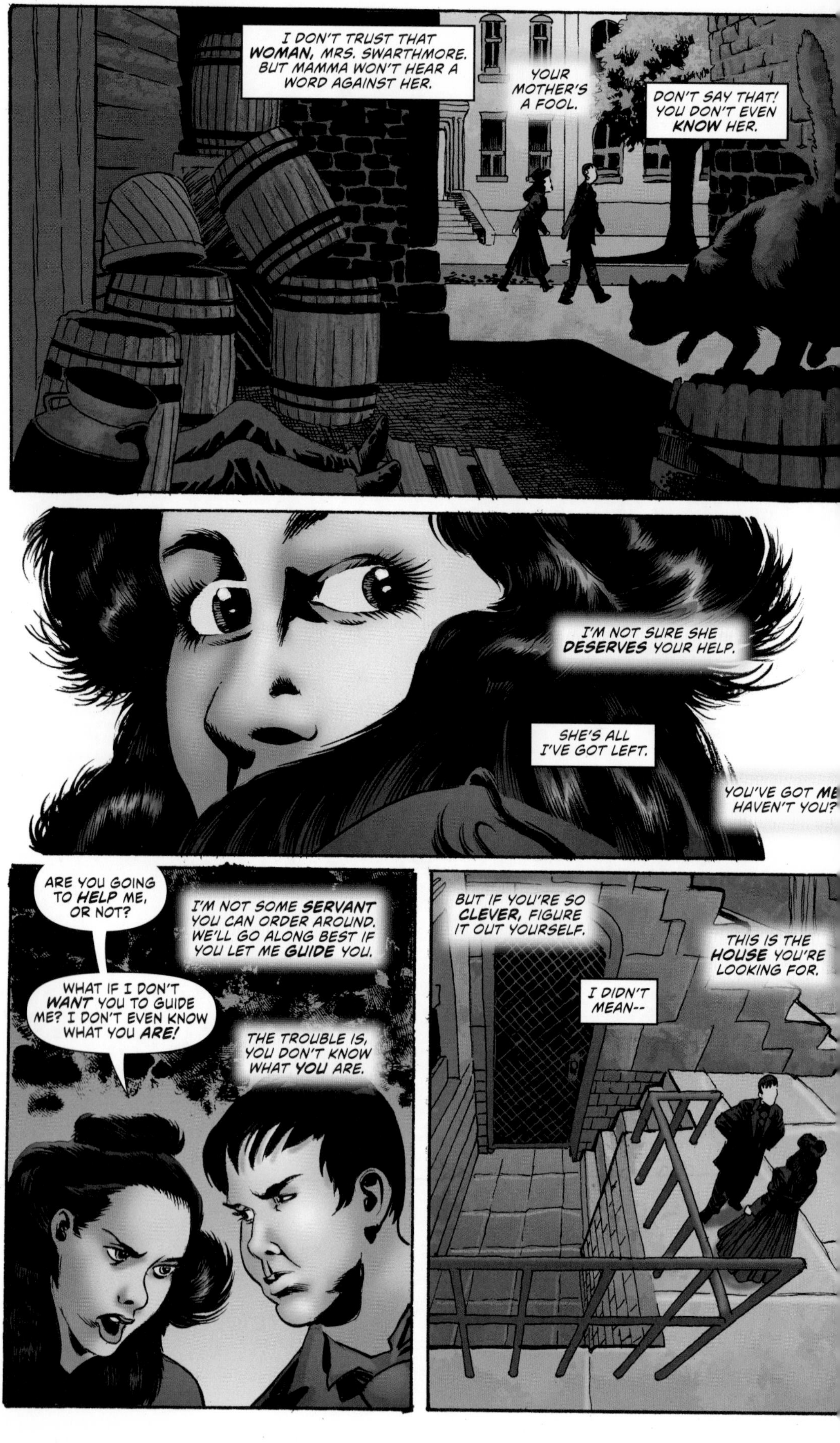
I DON'T TRUST THAT WOMAN, MRS. SWARTHMORE. BUT MAMMA WON'T HEAR A WORD AGAINST HER.
YOUR MOTHER'S A FOOL.
DON'T SAY THAT! YOU DON'T EVEN KNOW HER.
I'M NOT SURE SHE DESERVES YOUR HELP.
SHE'S ALL I'VE GOT LEFT.
YOU'VE GOT ME HAVEN'T YOU?
ARE YOU GOING TO HELP ME, OR NOT?
I'M NOT SOME SERVANT YOU CAN ORDER AROUND. WE'LL GO ALONG BEST IF YOU LET ME GUIDE YOU.
WHAT IF I DON'T WANT YOU TO GUIDE ME? I DON'T EVEN KNOW WHAT YOU ARE!
THE TROUBLE IS, YOU DON'T KNOW WHAT YOU ARE.
BUT IF YOU'RE SO CLEVER, FIGURE IT OUT YOURSELF.
I DIDN'T MEAN--
THIS IS THE HOUSE YOU'RE LOOKING FOR.

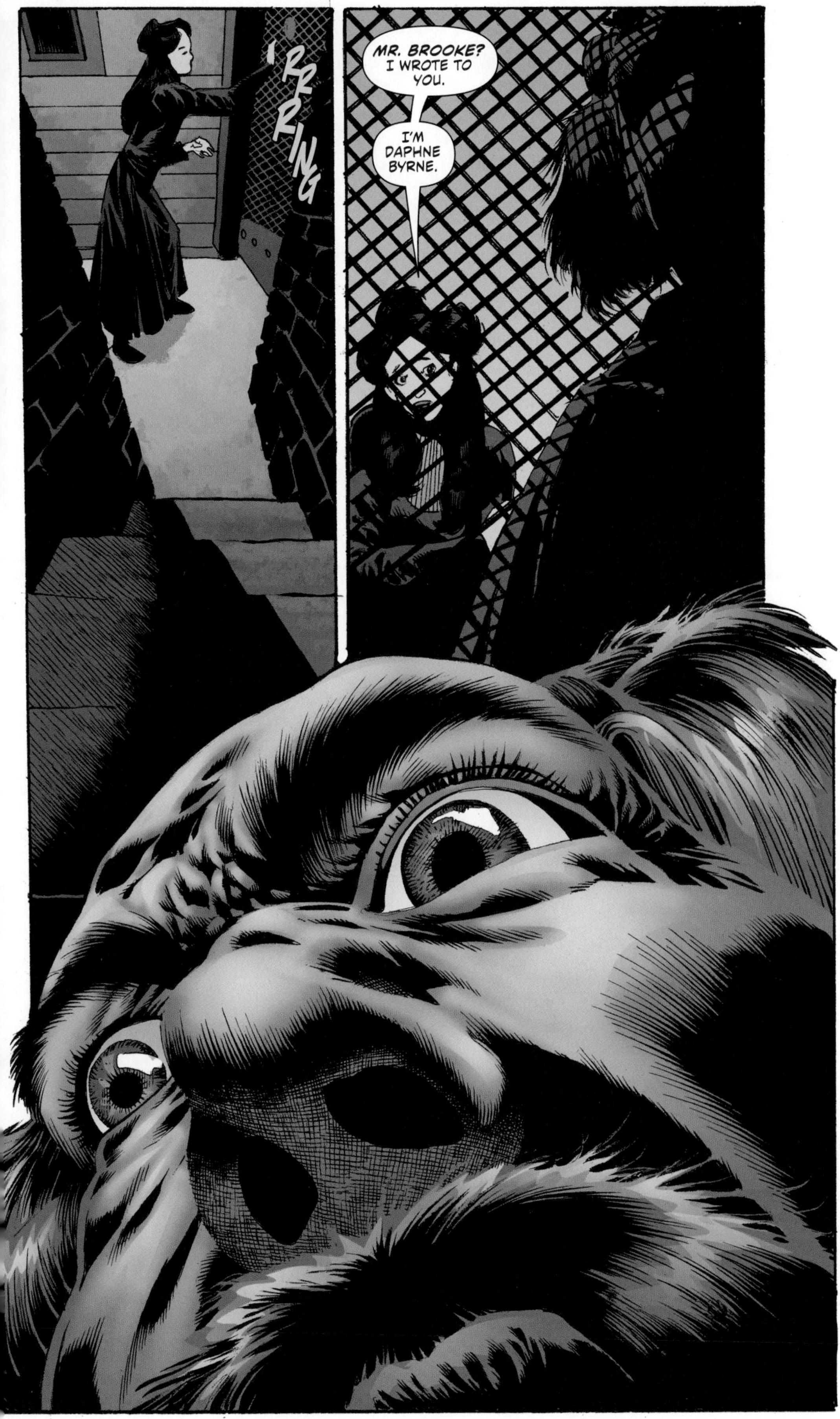
RRRING
MR. BROOKE? I WROTE TO YOU.
I'M DAPHNE BYRNE.

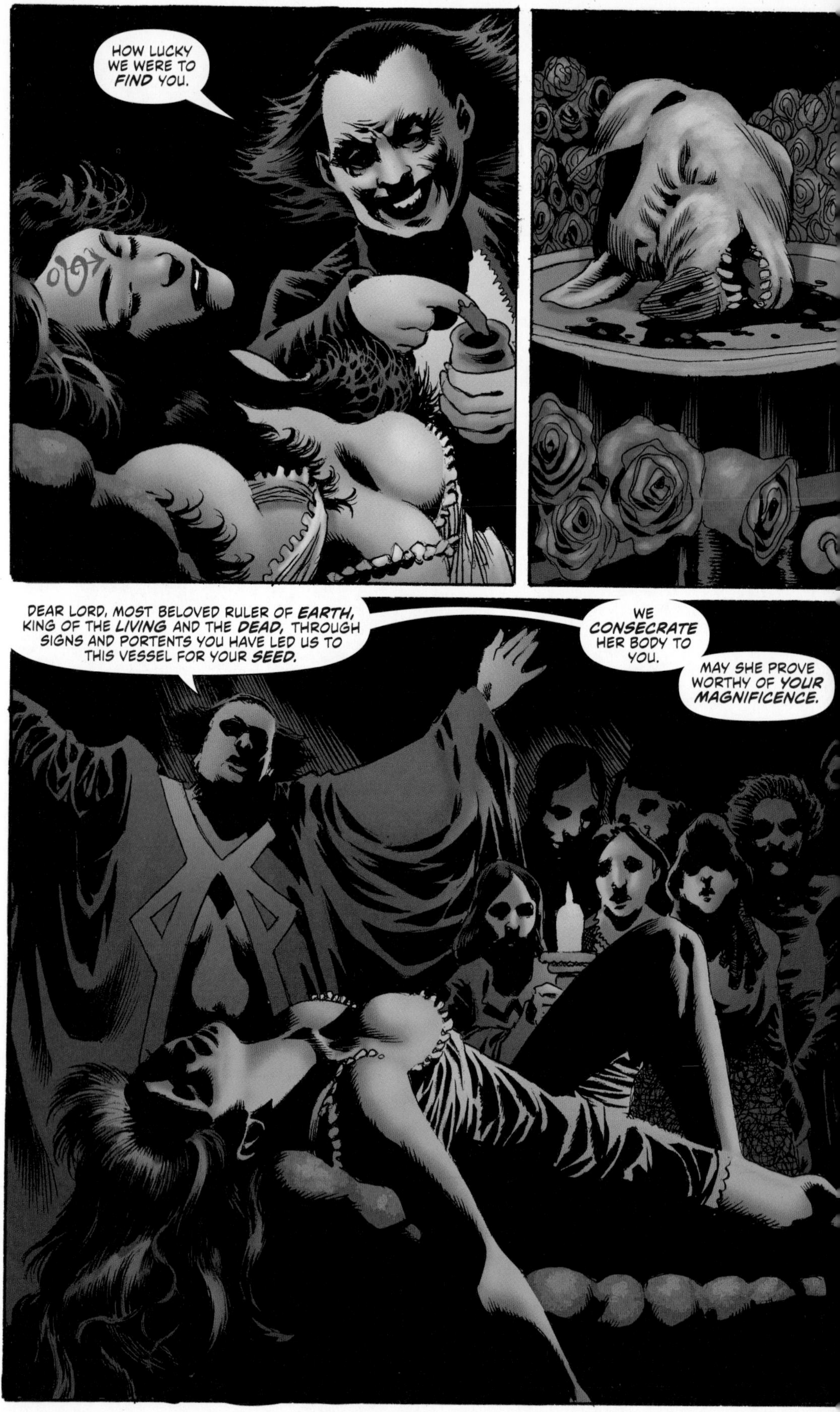
HOW LUCKY WE WERE TO FIND YOU.
DEAR LORD, MOST BELOVED RULER OF EARTH, KING OF THE LIVING AND THE DEAD, THROUGH SIGNS AND PORTENTS YOU HAVE LED US TO THIS VESSEL FOR YOUR SEED.
WE CONSECRATE HER BODY TO YOU.
MAY SHE PROVE WORTHY OF YOUR MAGNIFICENCE.

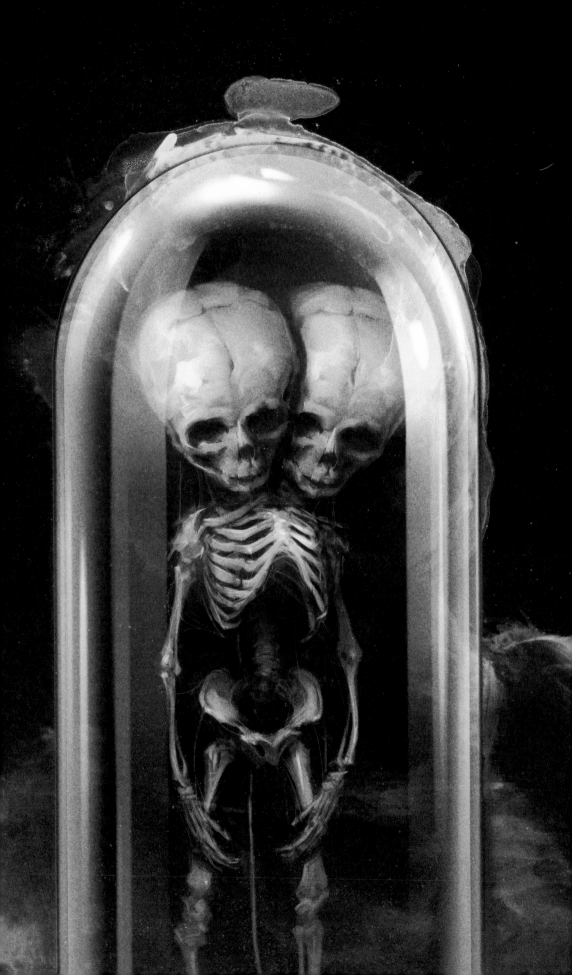

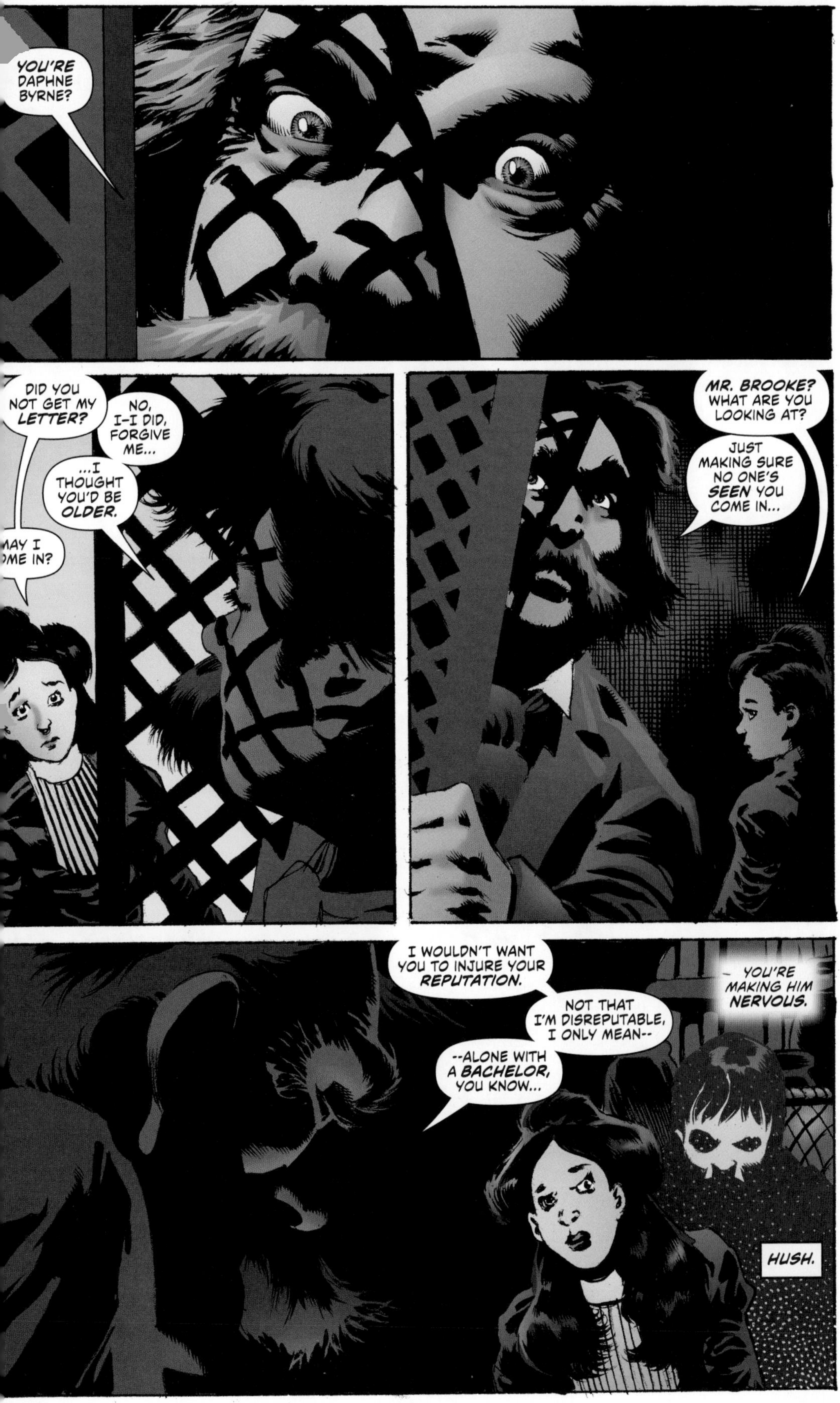
YOU'RE DAPHNE BYRNE?
DID YOU NOT GET MY LETTER?
NO, I--I DID, FORGIVE ME...
...I THOUGHT YOU'D BE OLDER.
MAY I COME IN?
MR. BROOKE? WHAT ARE YOU LOOKING AT?
JUST MAKING SURE NO ONE'S SEEN YOU COME IN...
I WOULDN'T WANT YOU TO INJURE YOUR REPUTATION.
NOT THAT I'M DISREPUTABLE, I ONLY MEAN--
--ALONE WITH A BACHELOR, YOU KNOW...
YOU'RE MAKING HIM NERVOUS.
HUSH.

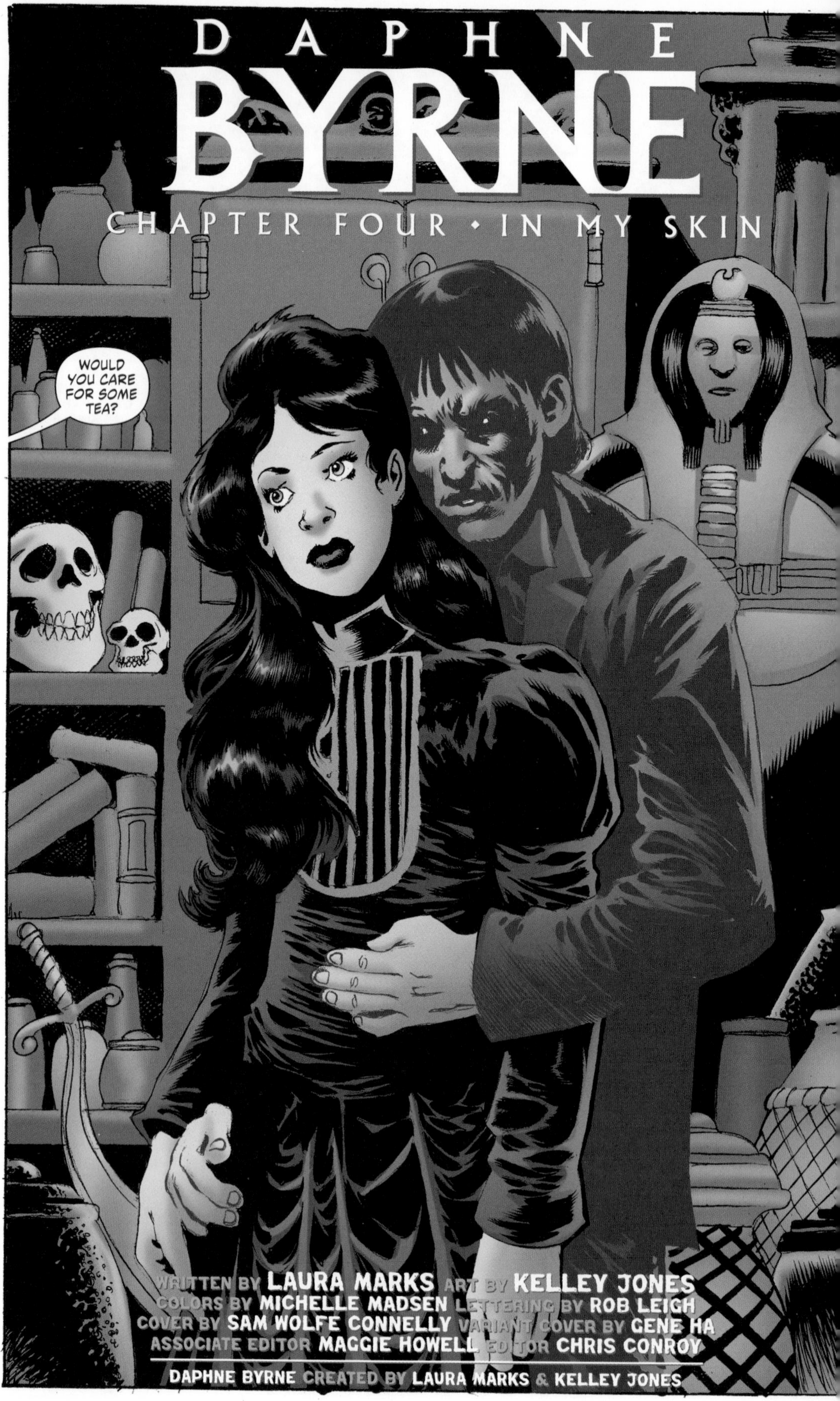
DAPHNE
BYRNE
CHAPTER FOUR • IN MY SKIN
WOULD YOU CARE FOR SOME TEA?
WRITTEN BY LAURA MARKS ART BY KELLEY JONES
COLORS BY MICHELLE MADSEN LETTERING BY ROB LEIGH
COVER BY SAM WOLFE CONNELLY VARIANT COVER BY GENE HA
ASSOCIATE EDITOR MAGGIE HOWELL EDITOR CHRIS CONROY
DAPHNE BYRNE CREATED BY LAURA MARKS & KELLEY JONES

AT IS AT? IT'S NOT **REAL**. SEE THE SEAM IN THE MIDDLE, WHERE SOMEONE'S **GLUED** IT TOGETHER?

I KEEP IT TO REMIND MYSELF THAT MOST PEOPLE WILL **BELIEVE** ANYTHING.

HOW MUCH DID IT **COST** YOU?

RATHER A **LOT**, FOR AN IRONIC GESTURE!

YOU'RE RIGHT. I SUPPOSE **I'M** THE FOOL.

THAT'S CALLED A--

TRILOBITE. I KNOW.

I SEE U'RE NOT RAID OF VES AND HINGS.

THAT'S BECAUSE...

...I'M **AFRAID** THERE'S SOMETHING **WRONG** WITH ME.

NO, MISS BYRNE. I'M SURE THAT'S NOT TRUE.

WHY DON'T YOU SIT DOWN AND TELL ME WHY YOU'VE COME.

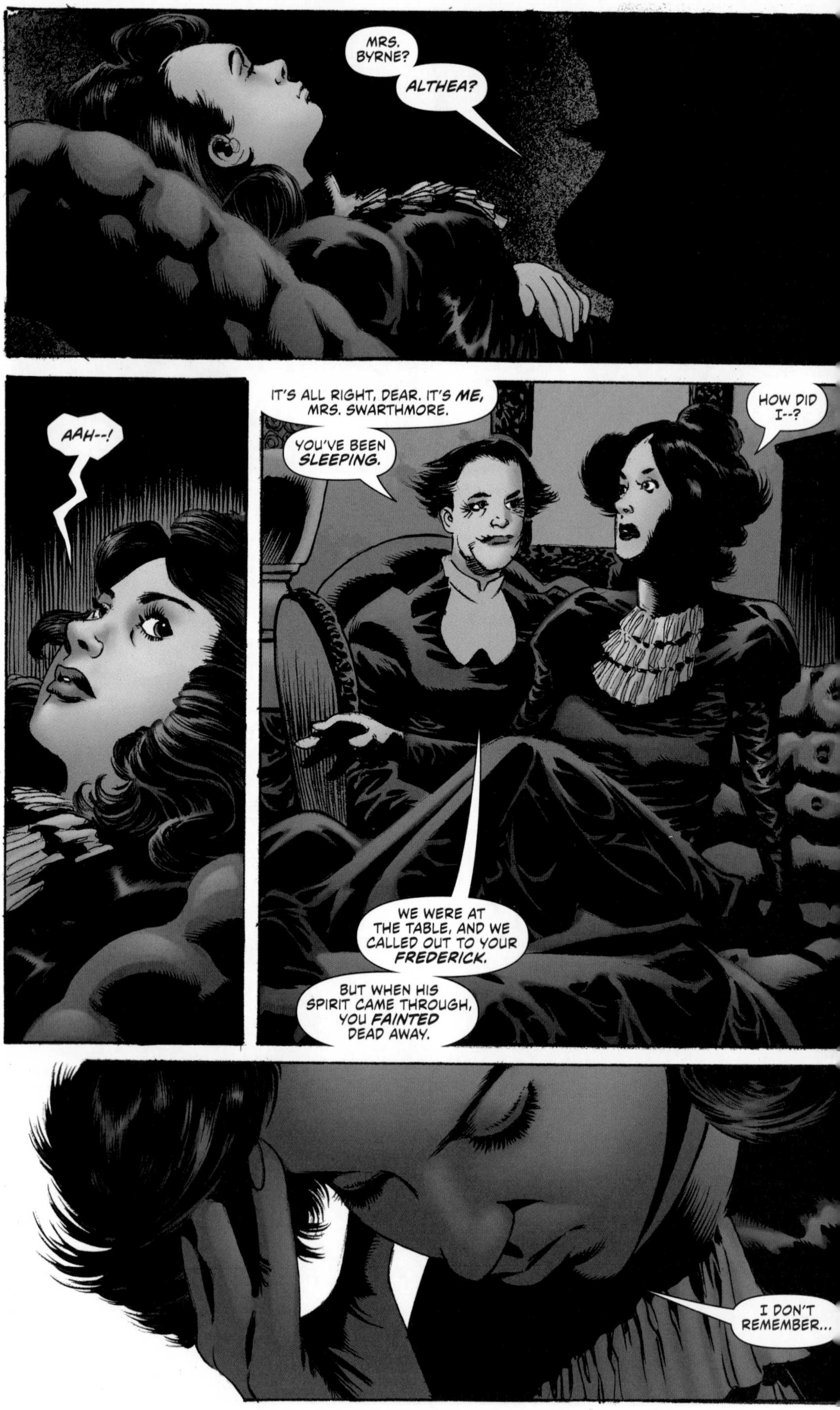
MRS. BYRNE?
ALTHEA?
AAH--!
IT'S ALL RIGHT, DEAR. IT'S ME, MRS. SWARTHMORE.
YOU'VE BEEN SLEEPING.
HOW DID I--?
WE WERE AT THE TABLE, AND WE CALLED OUT TO YOUR FREDERICK.
BUT WHEN HIS SPIRIT CAME THROUGH, YOU FAINTED DEAD AWAY.
I DON'T REMEMBER...

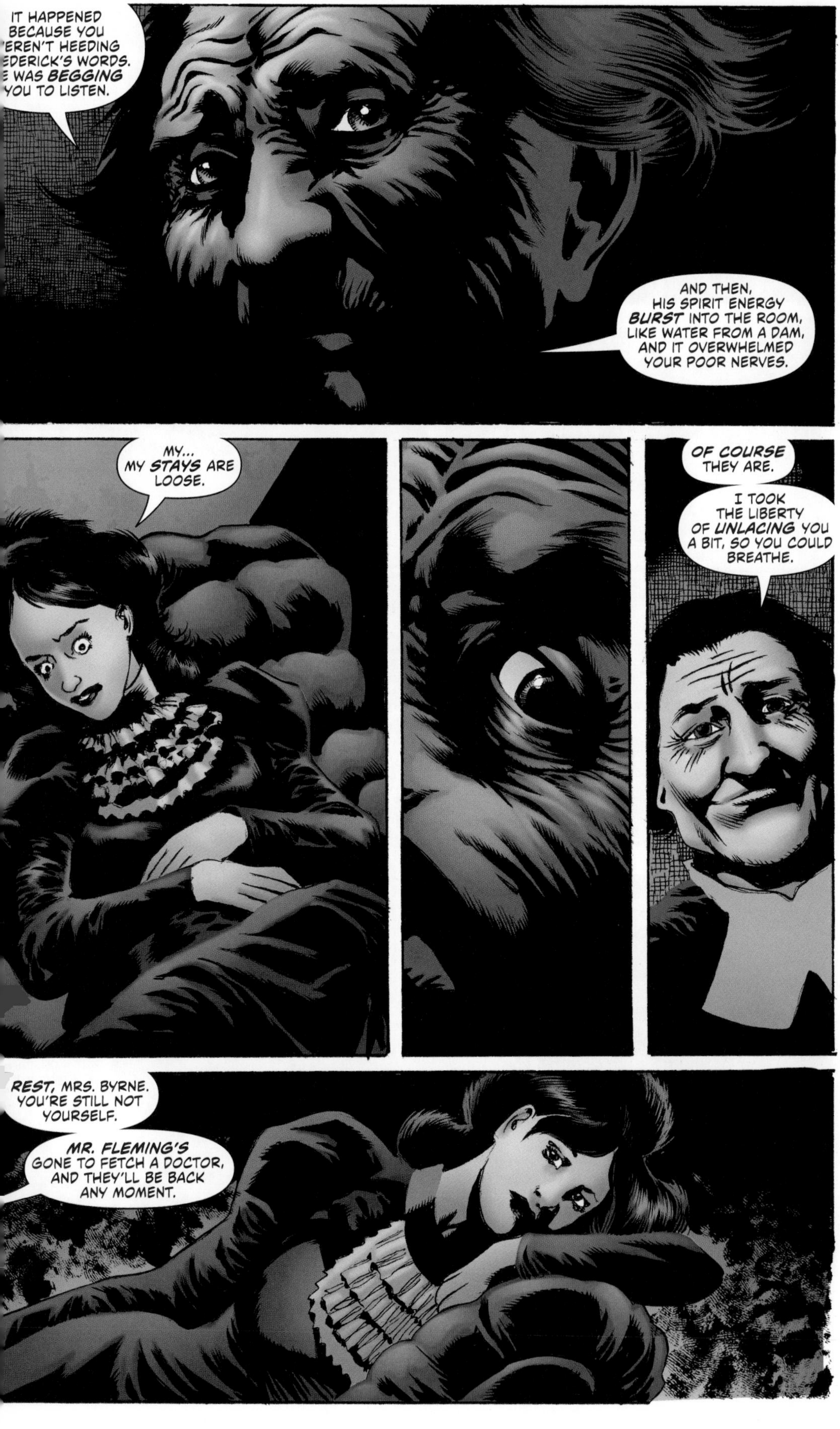
IT HAPPENED BECAUSE YOU 'EREN'T HEEDING EDERICK'S WORDS. E WAS BEGGING YOU TO LISTEN.
AND THEN, HIS SPIRIT ENERGY BURST INTO THE ROOM, LIKE WATER FROM A DAM, AND IT OVERWHELMED YOUR POOR NERVES.
MY... MY STAYS ARE LOOSE.
OF COURSE THEY ARE.
I TOOK THE LIBERTY OF UNLACING YOU A BIT, SO YOU COULD BREATHE.
REST, MRS. BYRNE. YOU'RE STILL NOT YOURSELF.
MR. FLEMING'S GONE TO FETCH A DOCTOR, AND THEY'LL BE BACK ANY MOMENT.

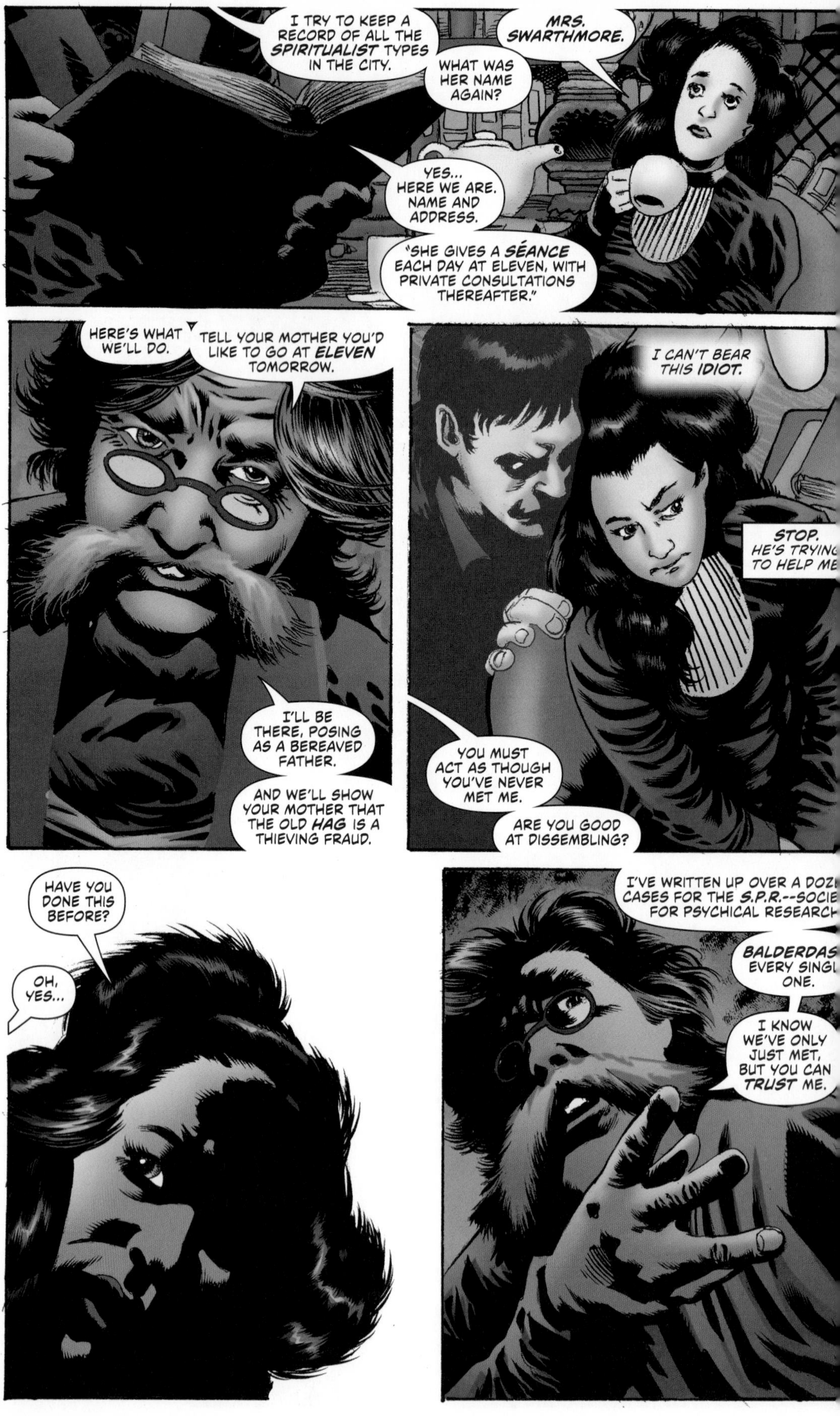
I TRY TO KEEP A RECORD OF ALL THE SPIRITUALIST TYPES IN THE CITY.
WHAT WAS HER NAME AGAIN?
MRS. SWARTHMORE.
YES... HERE WE ARE. NAME AND ADDRESS.
"SHE GIVES A SÉANCE EACH DAY AT ELEVEN, WITH PRIVATE CONSULTATIONS THEREAFTER."
HERE'S WHAT WE'LL DO.
TELL YOUR MOTHER YOU'D LIKE TO GO AT ELEVEN TOMORROW.
I'LL BE THERE, POSING AS A BEREAVED FATHER.
AND WE'LL SHOW YOUR MOTHER THAT THE OLD HAG IS A THIEVING FRAUD.
I CAN'T BEAR THIS IDIOT.
STOP. HE'S TRYIN TO HELP ME
YOU MUST ACT AS THOUGH YOU'VE NEVER MET ME.
ARE YOU GOOD AT DISSEMBLING?
HAVE YOU DONE THIS BEFORE?
OH, YES...
I'VE WRITTEN UP OVER A DOZ CASES FOR THE S.P.R.--SOCIE FOR PSYCHICAL RESEARCH
BALDERDAS EVERY SING ONE.
I KNOW WE'VE ONLY JUST MET, BUT YOU CAN TRUST ME.

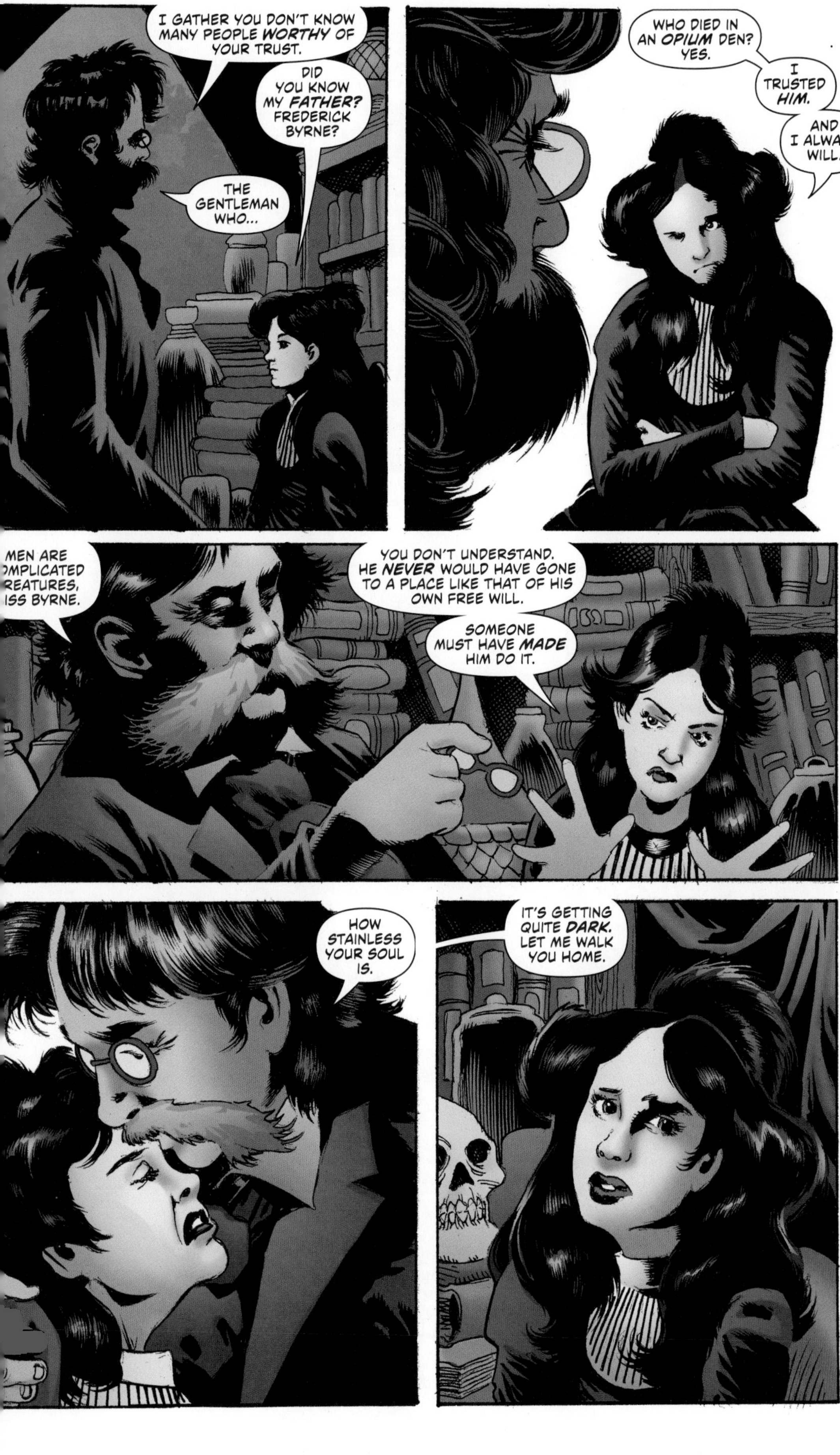
I GATHER YOU DON'T KNOW MANY PEOPLE *WORTHY* OF YOUR TRUST.
DID YOU KNOW MY *FATHER?* FREDERICK BYRNE?
THE GENTLEMAN WHO...
WHO DIED IN AN *OPIUM* DEN? YES.
I TRUSTED *HIM.*
AND I ALWAYS WILL.
MEN ARE OMPLICATED REATURES, ISS BYRNE.
YOU DON'T UNDERSTAND. HE *NEVER* WOULD HAVE GONE TO A PLACE LIKE THAT OF HIS OWN FREE WILL.
SOMEONE MUST HAVE *MADE* HIM DO IT.
HOW STAINLESS YOUR SOUL IS.
IT'S GETTING QUITE *DARK.* LET ME WALK YOU HOME.

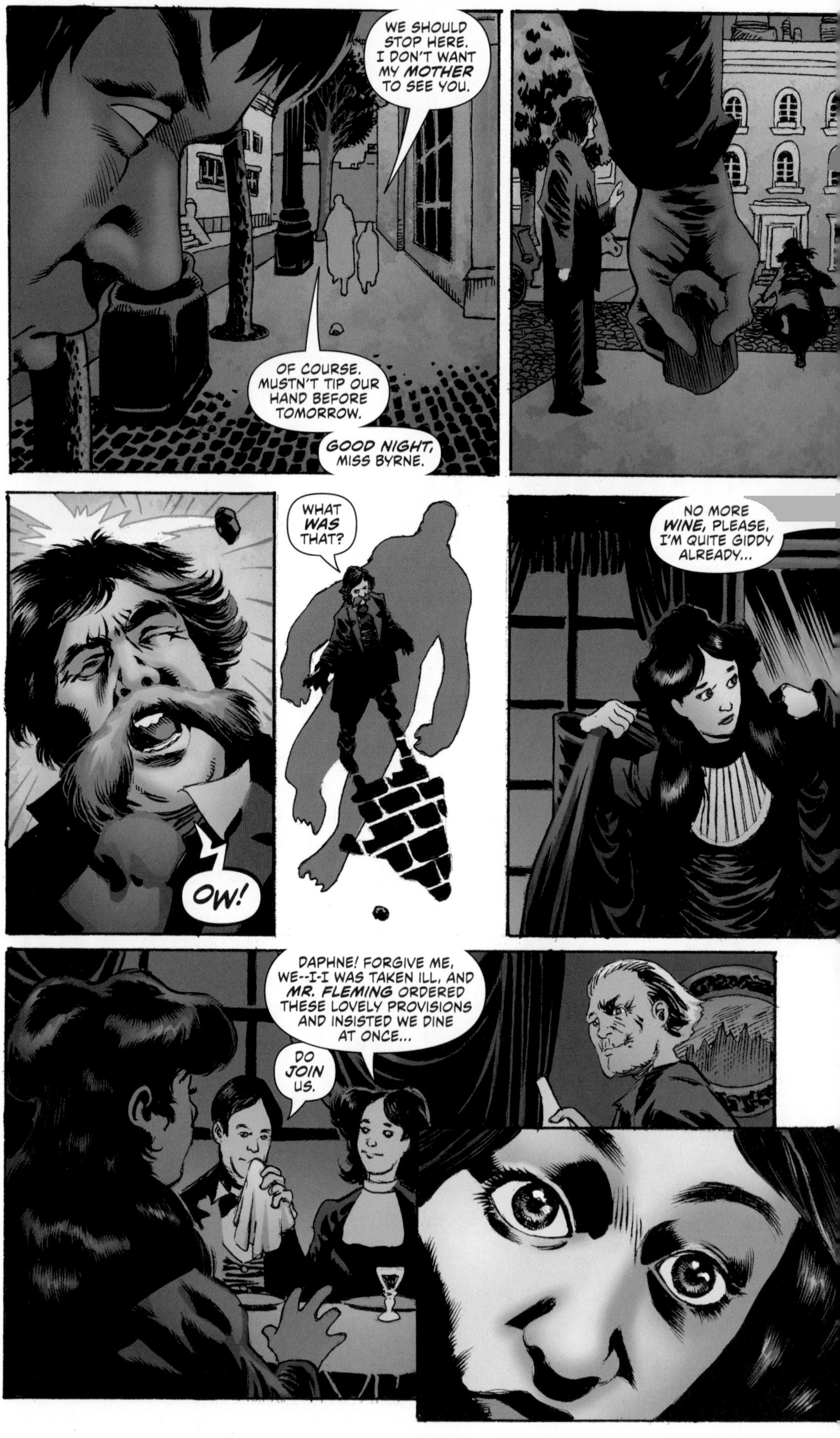
WE SHOULD STOP HERE. I DON'T WANT MY MOTHER TO SEE YOU.
OF COURSE. MUSTN'T TIP OUR HAND BEFORE TOMORROW.
GOOD NIGHT, MISS BYRNE.
OW!
WHAT WAS THAT?
NO MORE WINE, PLEASE, I'M QUITE GIDDY ALREADY...
DAPHNE! FORGIVE ME, WE--I-I WAS TAKEN ILL, AND MR. FLEMING ORDERED THESE LOVELY PROVISIONS AND INSISTED WE DINE AT ONCE...
DO JOIN US.

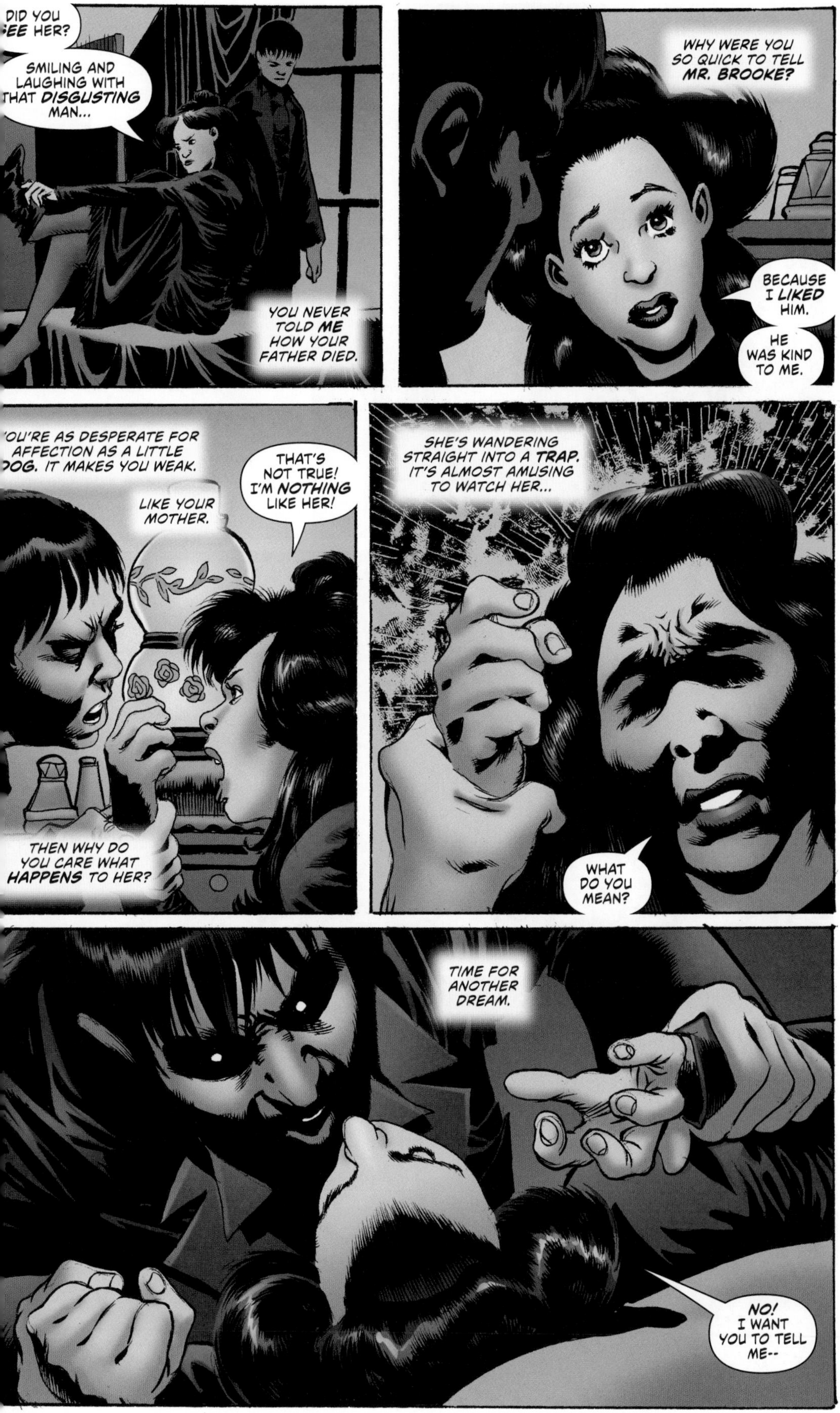

DID YOU SEE HER?
SMILING AND LAUGHING WITH THAT DISGUSTING MAN...
YOU NEVER TOLD ME HOW YOUR FATHER DIED.
WHY WERE YOU SO QUICK TO TELL MR. BROOKE?
BECAUSE I LIKED HIM.
HE WAS KIND TO ME.
YOU'RE AS DESPERATE FOR AFFECTION AS A LITTLE DOG. IT MAKES YOU WEAK.
LIKE YOUR MOTHER.
THAT'S NOT TRUE! I'M NOTHING LIKE HER!
THEN WHY DO YOU CARE WHAT HAPPENS TO HER?
SHE'S WANDERING STRAIGHT INTO A TRAP. IT'S ALMOST AMUSING TO WATCH HER...
WHAT DO YOU MEAN?
TIME FOR ANOTHER DREAM.
NO! I WANT YOU TO TELL ME--

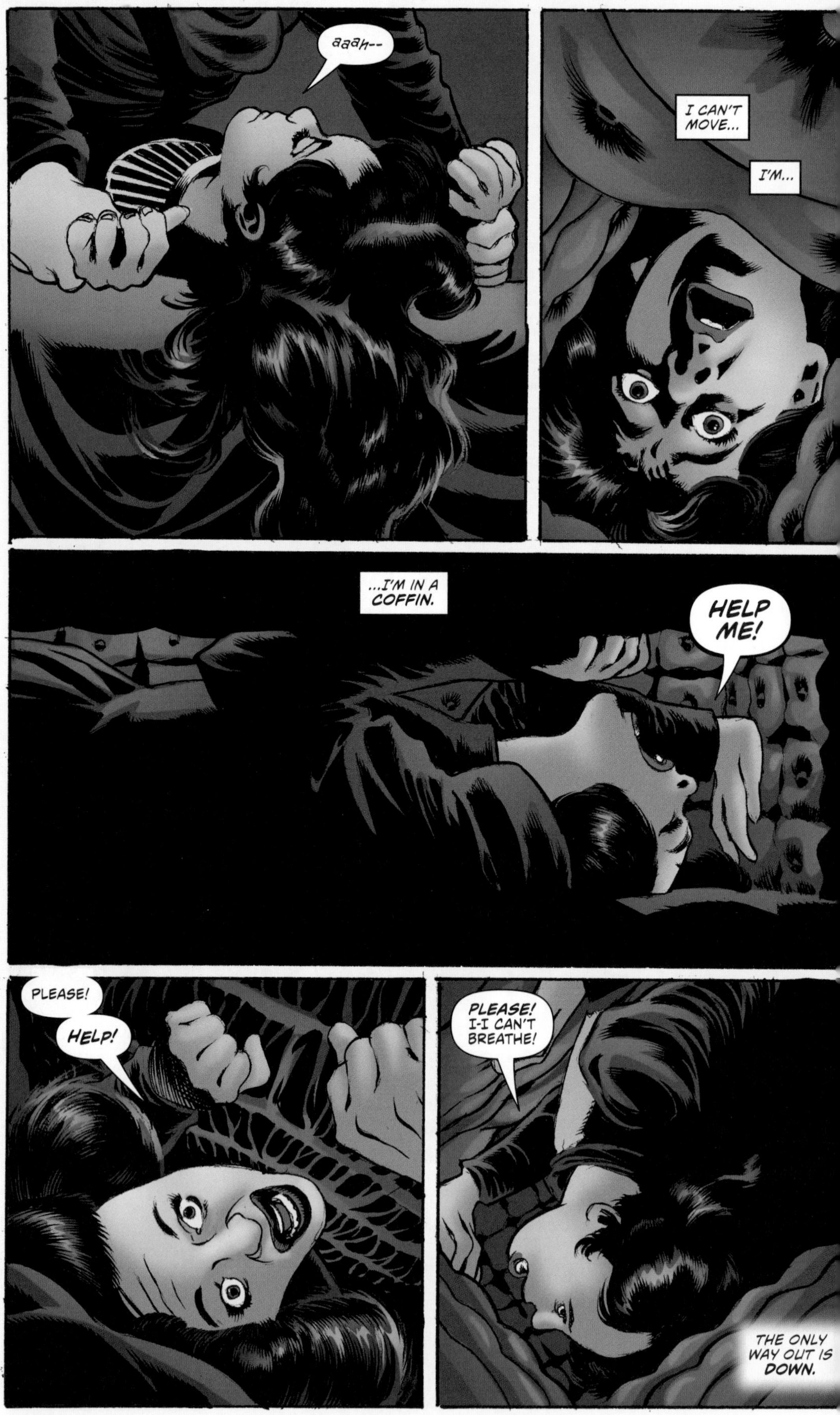
aaah--
I CAN'T MOVE...
I'M...
...I'M IN A COFFIN.
HELP ME!
PLEASE!
HELP!
PLEASE! I-I CAN'T BREATHE!
THE ONLY WAY OUT IS DOWN.

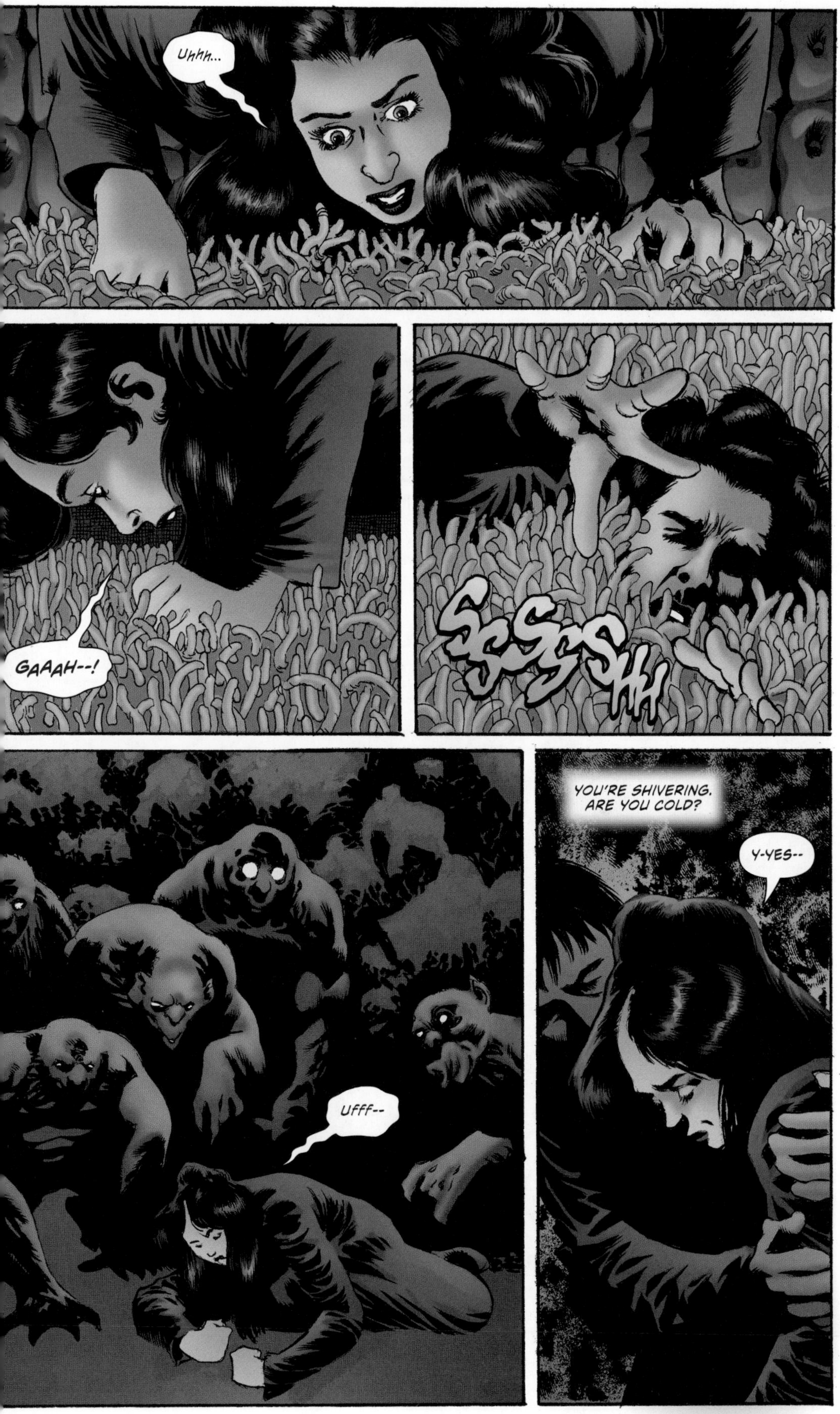

Uhhh...
GAAAH--!
SSSSSHH
UFFF--
YOU'RE SHIVERING. ARE YOU COLD?
Y-YES--

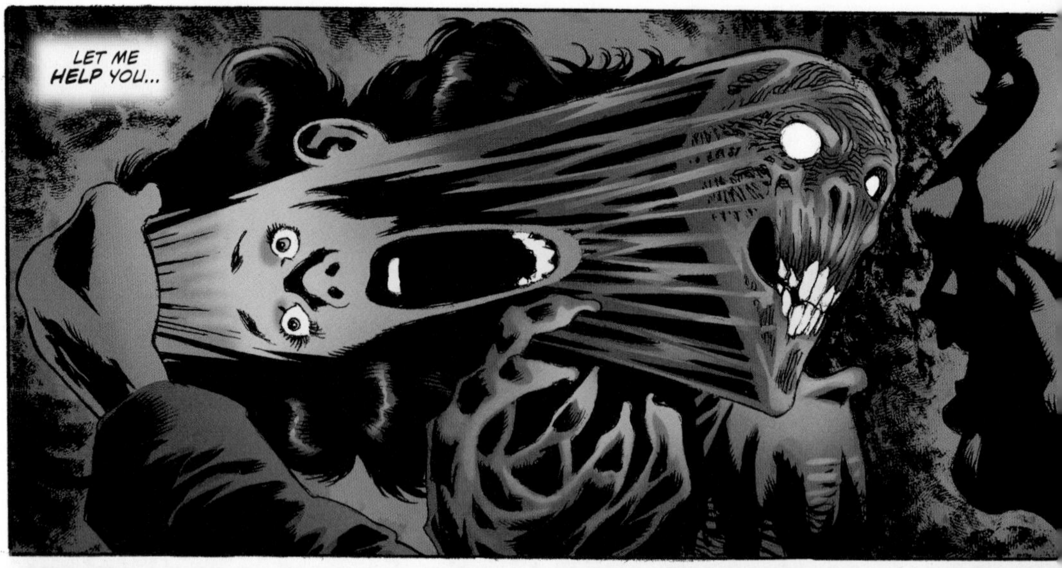
LET ME HELP YOU...

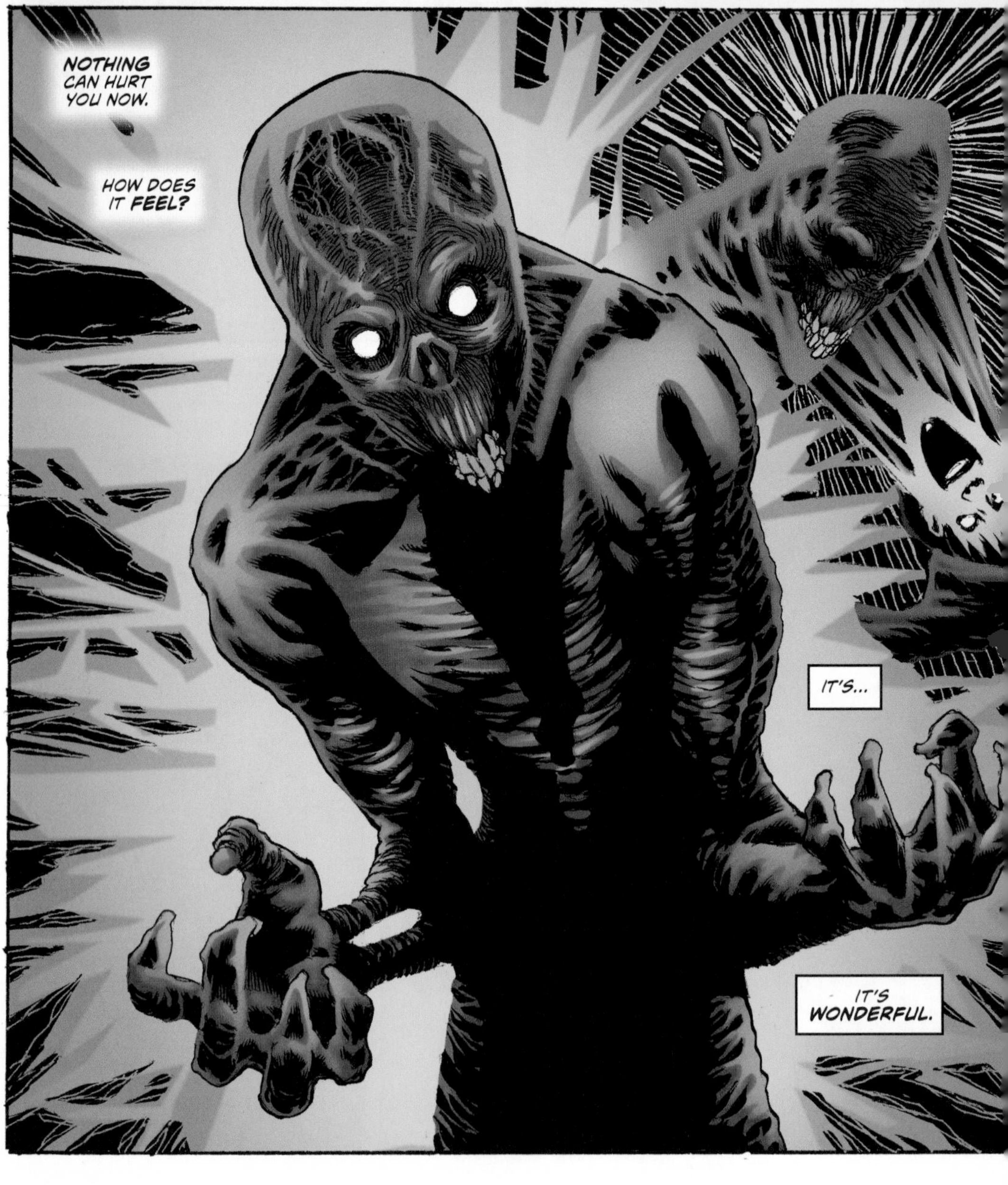
NOTHING CAN HURT YOU NOW.
HOW DOES IT FEEL?
IT'S...
IT'S WONDERFUL.

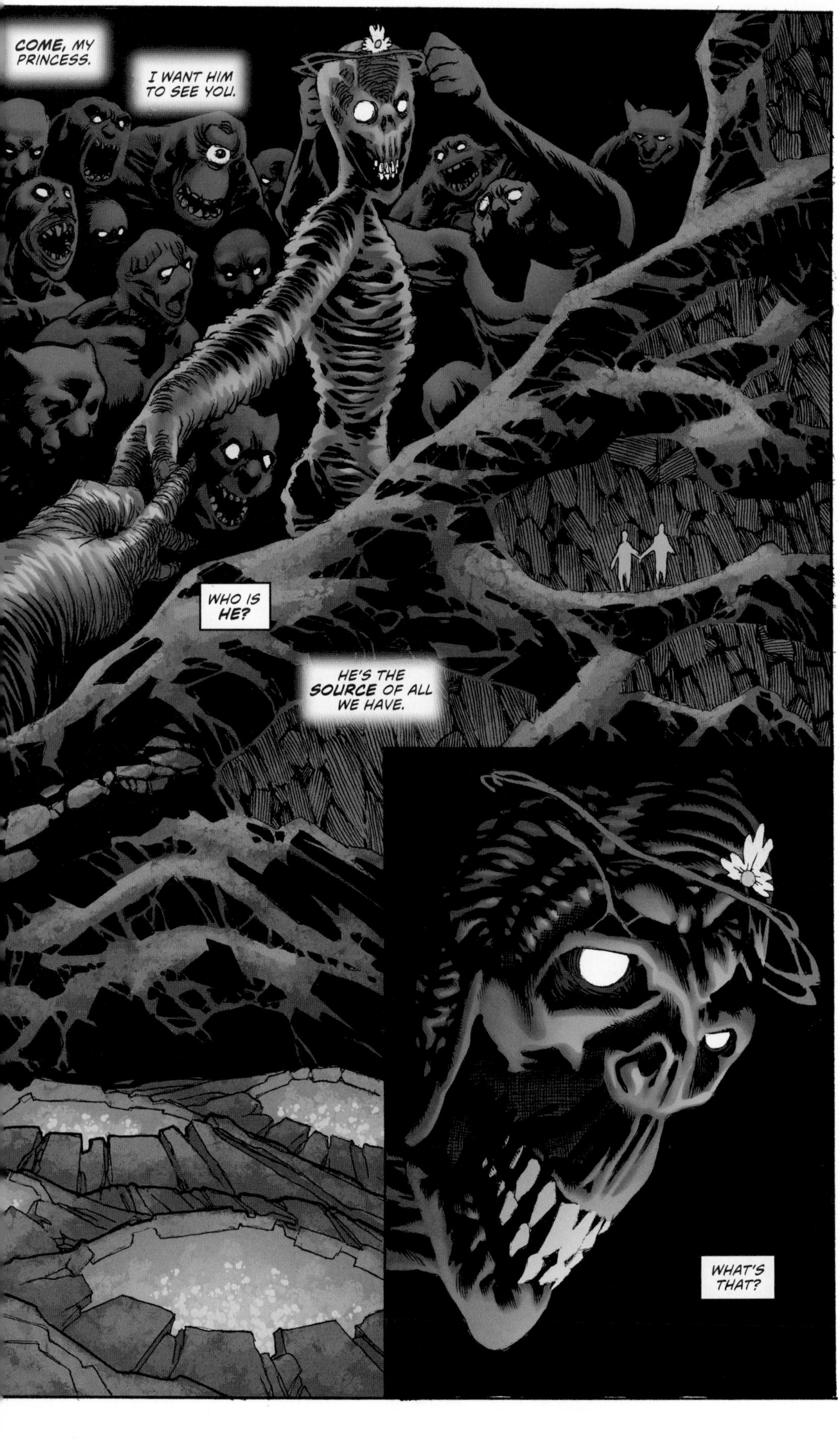
COME, MY PRINCESS.
I WANT HIM TO SEE YOU.
WHO IS HE?
HE'S THE SOURCE OF ALL WE HAVE.
WHAT'S THAT?

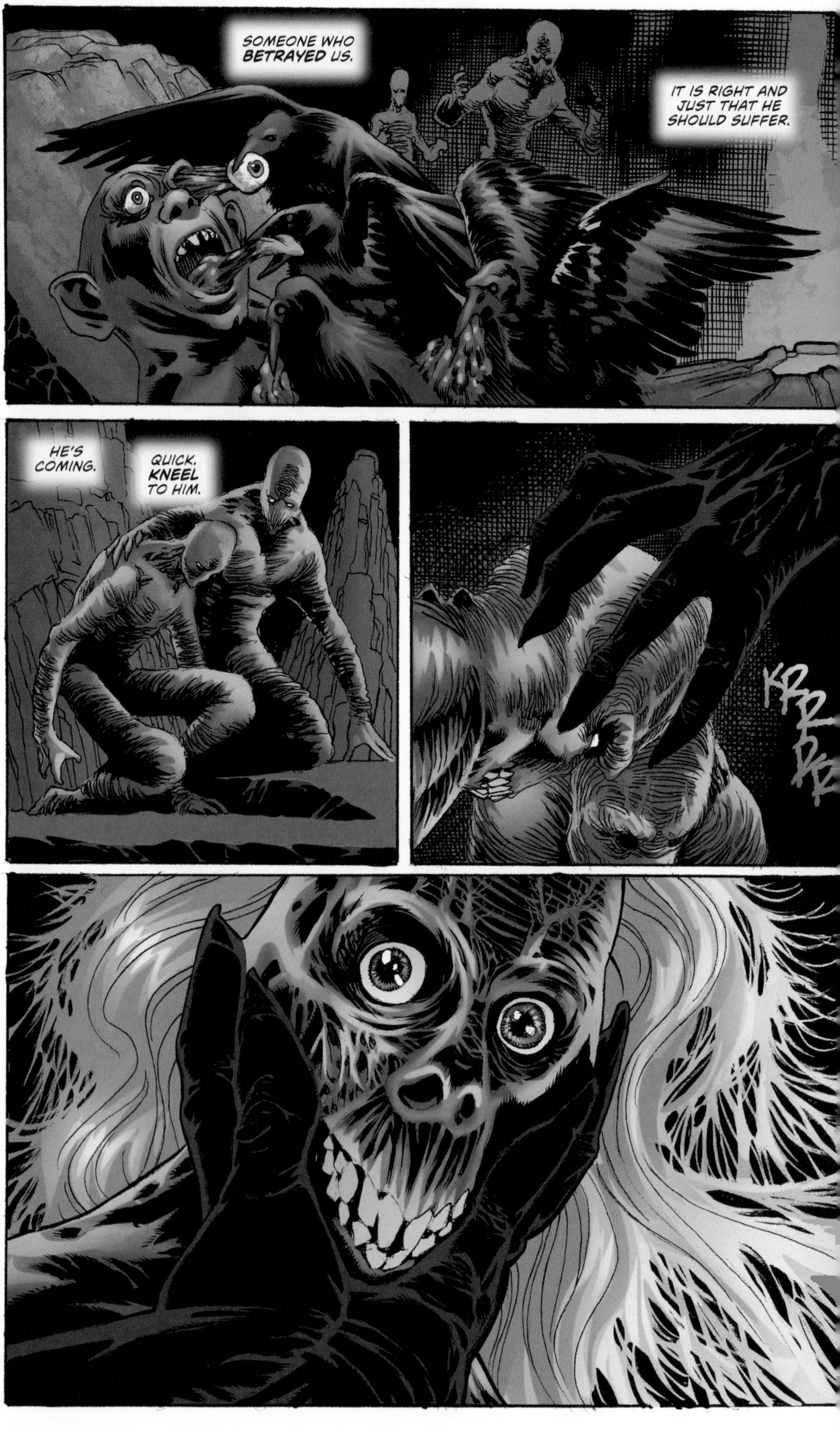
SOMEONE WHO BETRAYED US.
IT IS RIGHT AND JUST THAT HE SHOULD SUFFER.
HE'S COMING.
QUICK. KNEEL TO HIM.
KRRRRR

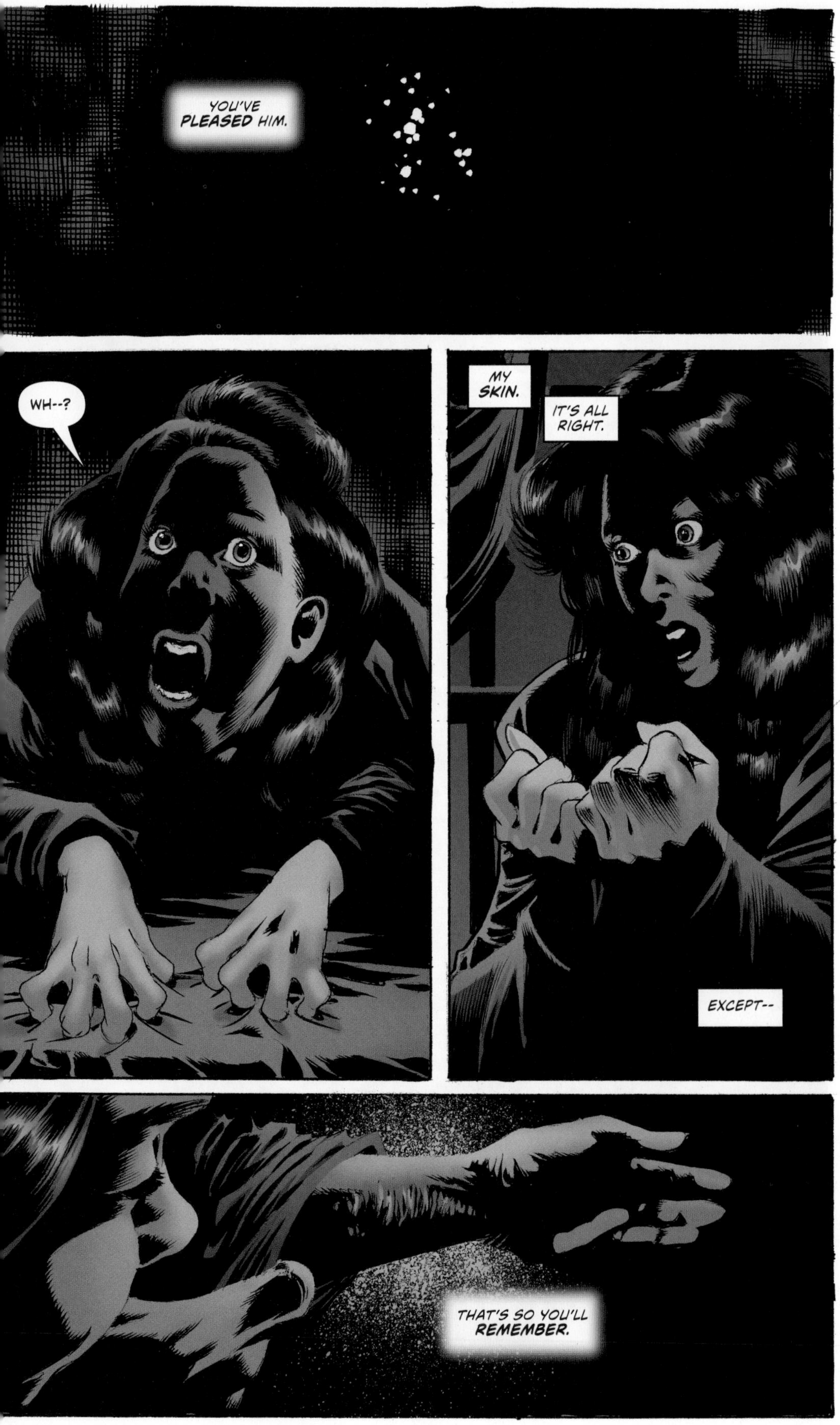
YOU'VE PLEASED HIM.
WH--?
MY SKIN.
IT'S ALL RIGHT.
EXCEPT--
THAT'S SO YOU'LL REMEMBER.

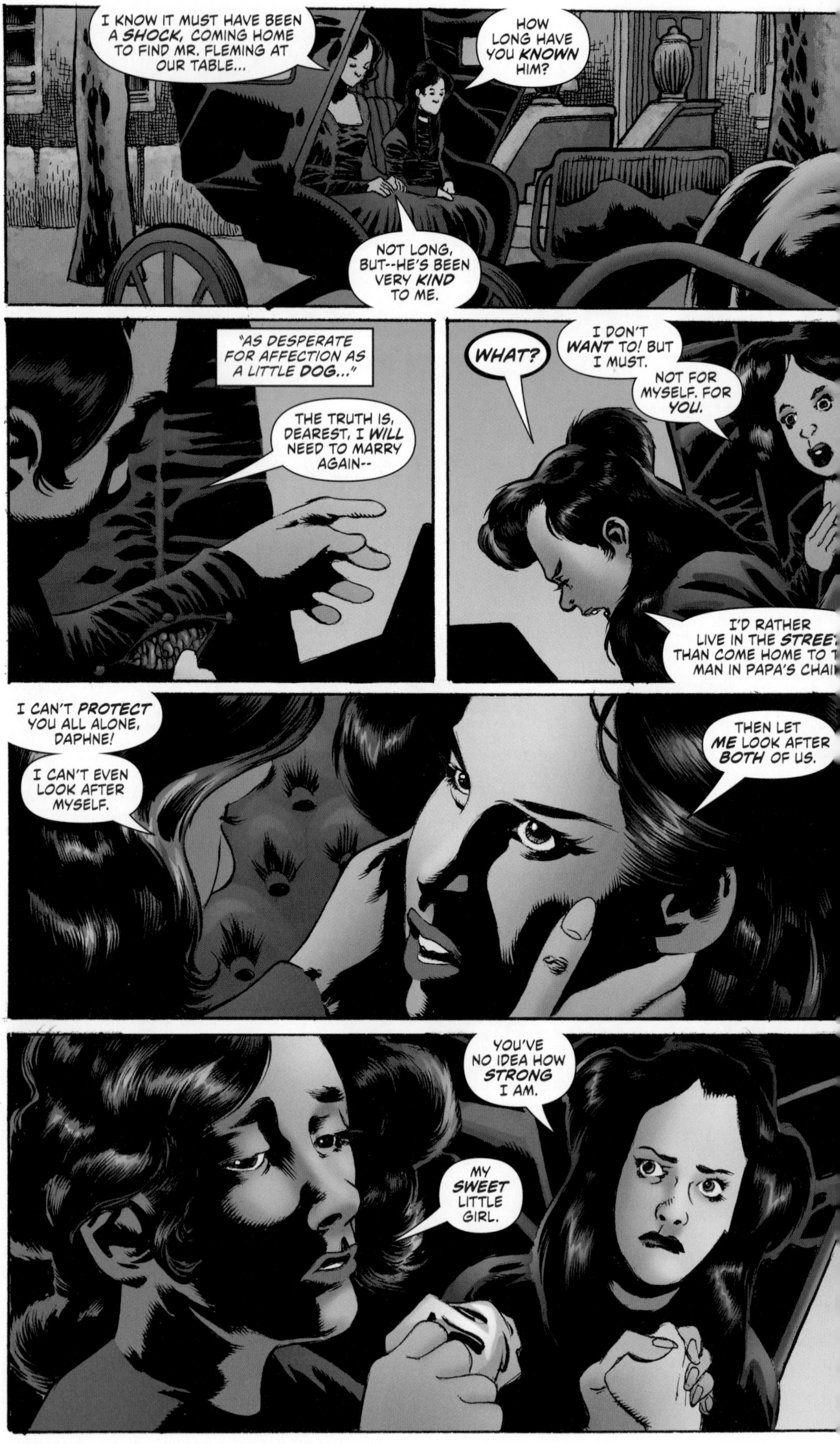
I KNOW IT MUST HAVE BEEN A SHOCK, COMING HOME TO FIND MR. FLEMING AT OUR TABLE...
HOW LONG HAVE YOU KNOWN HIM?
NOT LONG, BUT--HE'S BEEN VERY KIND TO ME.
"AS DESPERATE FOR AFFECTION AS A LITTLE DOG..."
THE TRUTH IS, DEAREST, I WILL NEED TO MARRY AGAIN--
WHAT?
I DON'T WANT TO! BUT I MUST.
NOT FOR MYSELF. FOR YOU.
I'D RATHER LIVE IN THE STREE THAN COME HOME TO T MAN IN PAPA'S CHAI
I CAN'T PROTECT YOU ALL ALONE, DAPHNE!
I CAN'T EVEN LOOK AFTER MYSELF.
THEN LET ME LOOK AFTER BOTH OF US.
YOU'VE NO IDEA HOW STRONG I AM.
MY SWEET LITTLE GIRL.

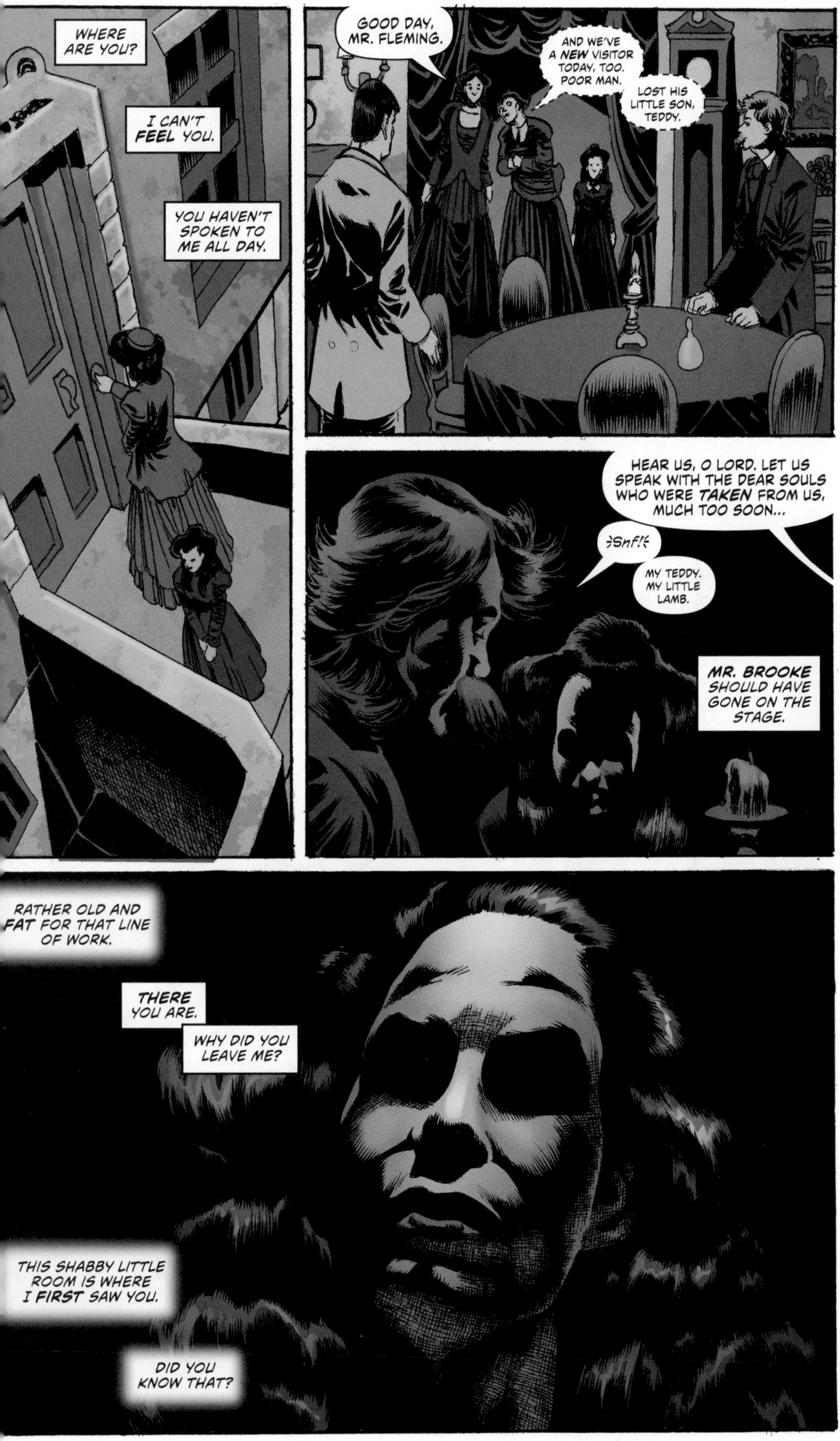
WHERE ARE YOU?
I CAN'T FEEL YOU.
YOU HAVEN'T SPOKEN TO ME ALL DAY.
GOOD DAY, MR. FLEMING.
AND WE'VE A NEW VISITOR TODAY, TOO. POOR MAN.
LOST HIS LITTLE SON, TEDDY.
HEAR US, O LORD. LET US SPEAK WITH THE DEAR SOULS WHO WERE TAKEN FROM US, MUCH TOO SOON...
SNF!
MY TEDDY. MY LITTLE LAMB.
MR. BROOKE SHOULD HAVE GONE ON THE STAGE.
RATHER OLD AND FAT FOR THAT LINE OF WORK.
THERE YOU ARE.
WHY DID YOU LEAVE ME?
THIS SHABBY LITTLE ROOM IS WHERE I FIRST SAW YOU.
DID YOU KNOW THAT?

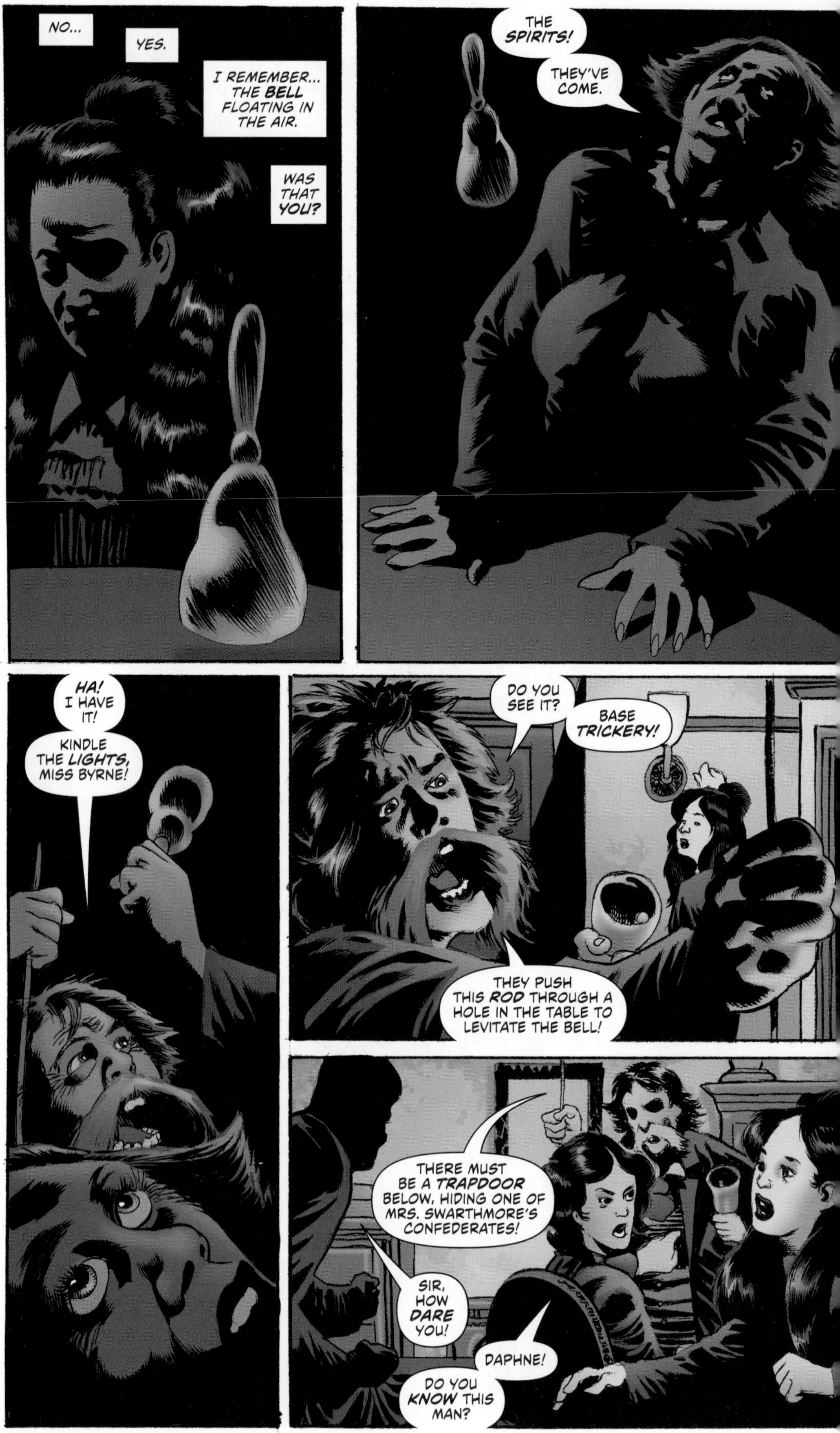
NO...
YES.
I REMEMBER... THE BELL FLOATING IN THE AIR.
WAS THAT YOU?
THE SPIRITS!
THEY'VE COME.
HA! I HAVE IT!
KINDLE THE LIGHTS, MISS BYRNE!
DO YOU SEE IT?
BASE TRICKERY!
THEY PUSH THIS ROD THROUGH A HOLE IN THE TABLE TO LEVITATE THE BELL!
THERE MUST BE A TRAPDOOR BELOW, HIDING ONE OF MRS. SWARTHMORE'S CONFEDERATES!
SIR, HOW DARE YOU!
DAPHNE!
DO YOU KNOW THIS MAN?

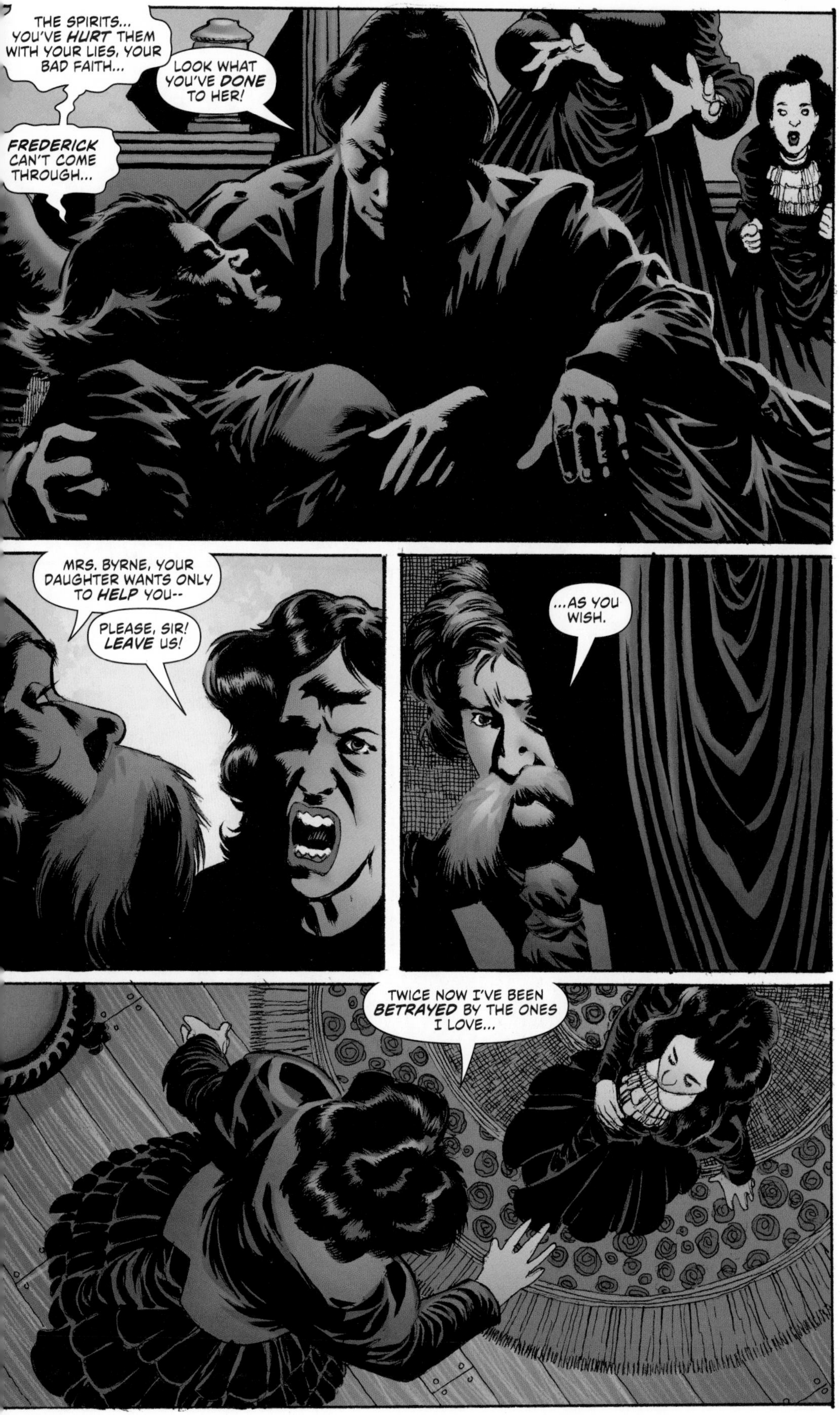

THE SPIRITS... YOU'VE HURT THEM WITH YOUR LIES, YOUR BAD FAITH...
FREDERICK CAN'T COME THROUGH...
LOOK WHAT YOU'VE DONE TO HER!
MRS. BYRNE, YOUR DAUGHTER WANTS ONLY TO HELP YOU--
PLEASE, SIR! LEAVE US!
...AS YOU WISH.
TWICE NOW I'VE BEEN BETRAYED BY THE ONES I LOVE...

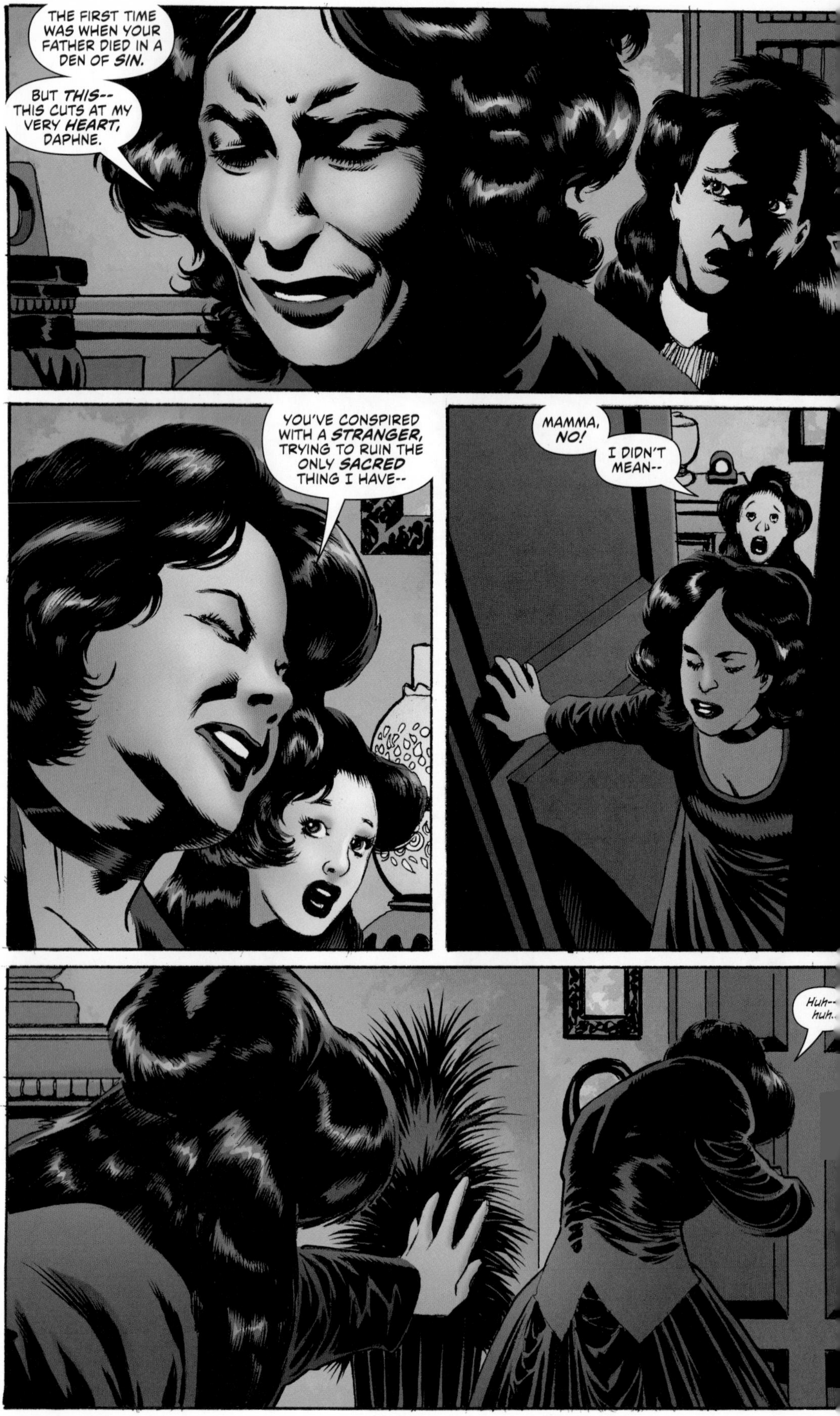
THE FIRST TIME WAS WHEN YOUR FATHER DIED IN A DEN OF *SIN.*
BUT *THIS--* THIS CUTS AT MY VERY *HEART,* DAPHNE.
YOU'VE CONSPIRED WITH A *STRANGER,* TRYING TO RUIN THE ONLY *SACRED* THING I HAVE--
MAMMA, *NO!*
I DIDN'T MEAN--

Mmmh--

I'M SO SORRY, BUT...YOU WOULDN'T *LISTEN* TO ME.

I DIDN'T KNOW HOW ELSE TO *SHOW* YOU.

IF YOU THINK I'M PERSUADED BY YOUR FRIEND'S *PREPOSTEROUS* TRICKS, YOU'RE MISTAKEN.

HEY'RE THE ES TRICKING OU, MAMMA!

YOUR NEW BEAU IS *HELPING* THAT VILE WOMAN, I'M SURE OF IT!

SLAP

Ah--!

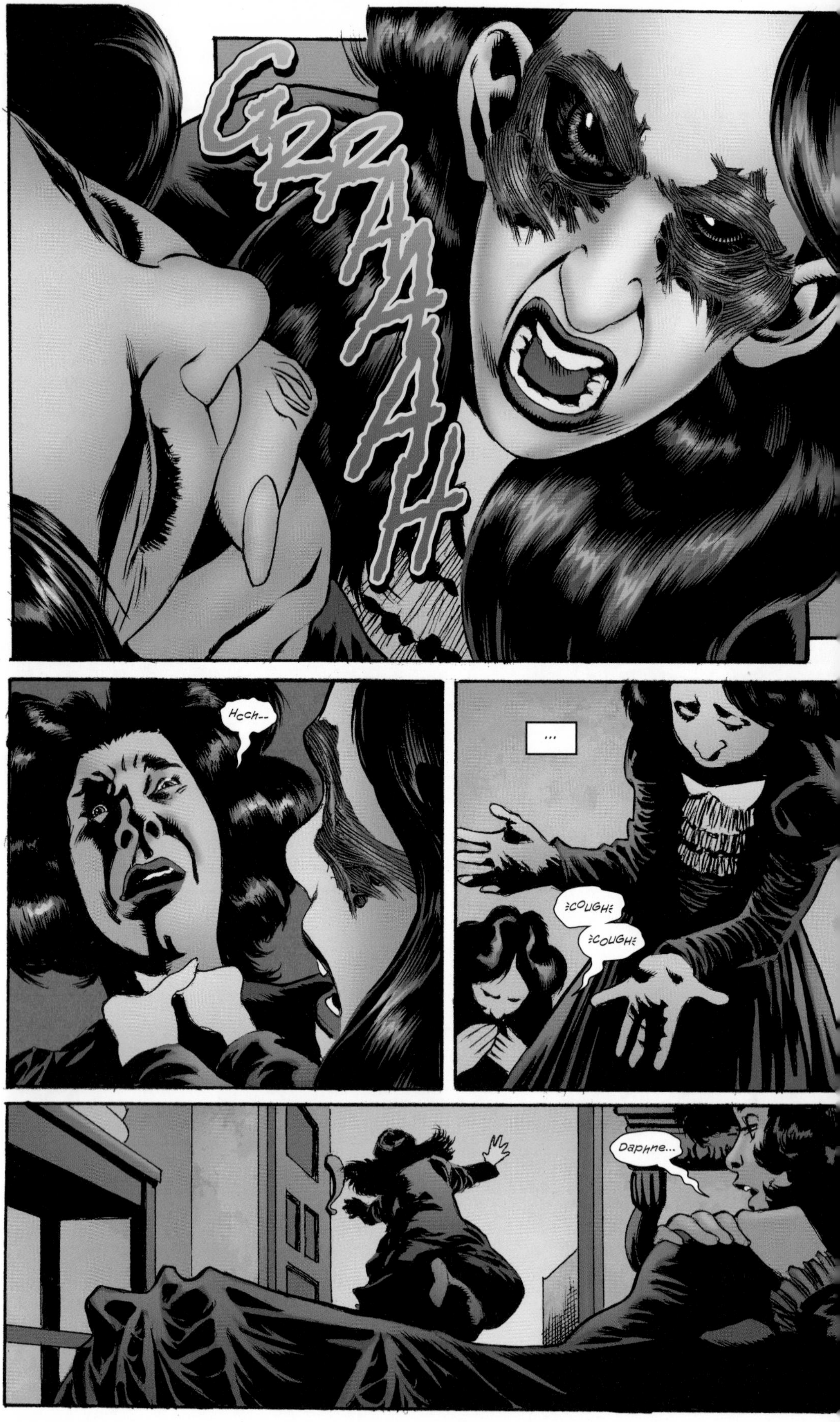
GRAAAH
Hcch--
...
COUGH
COUGH
Daphne...

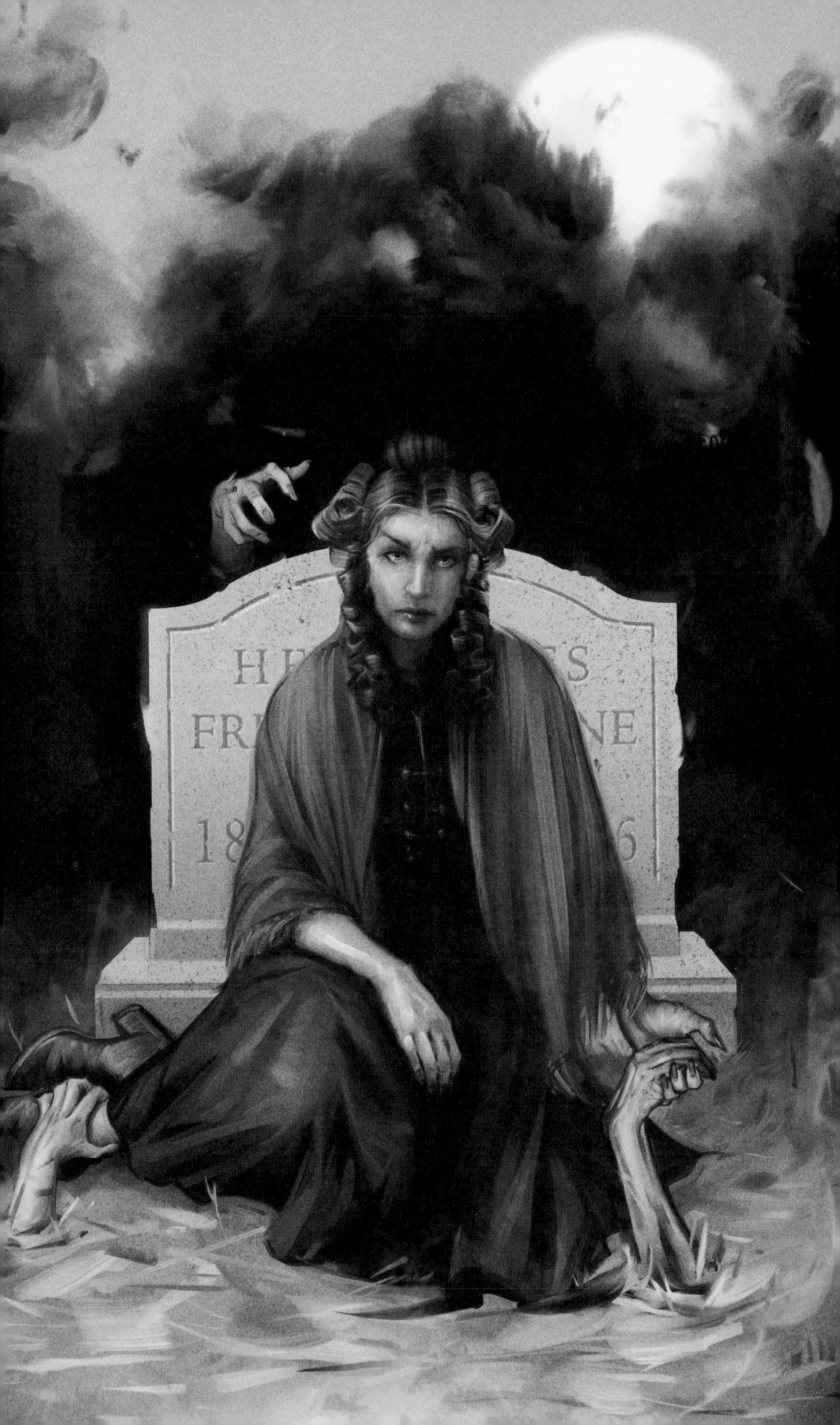

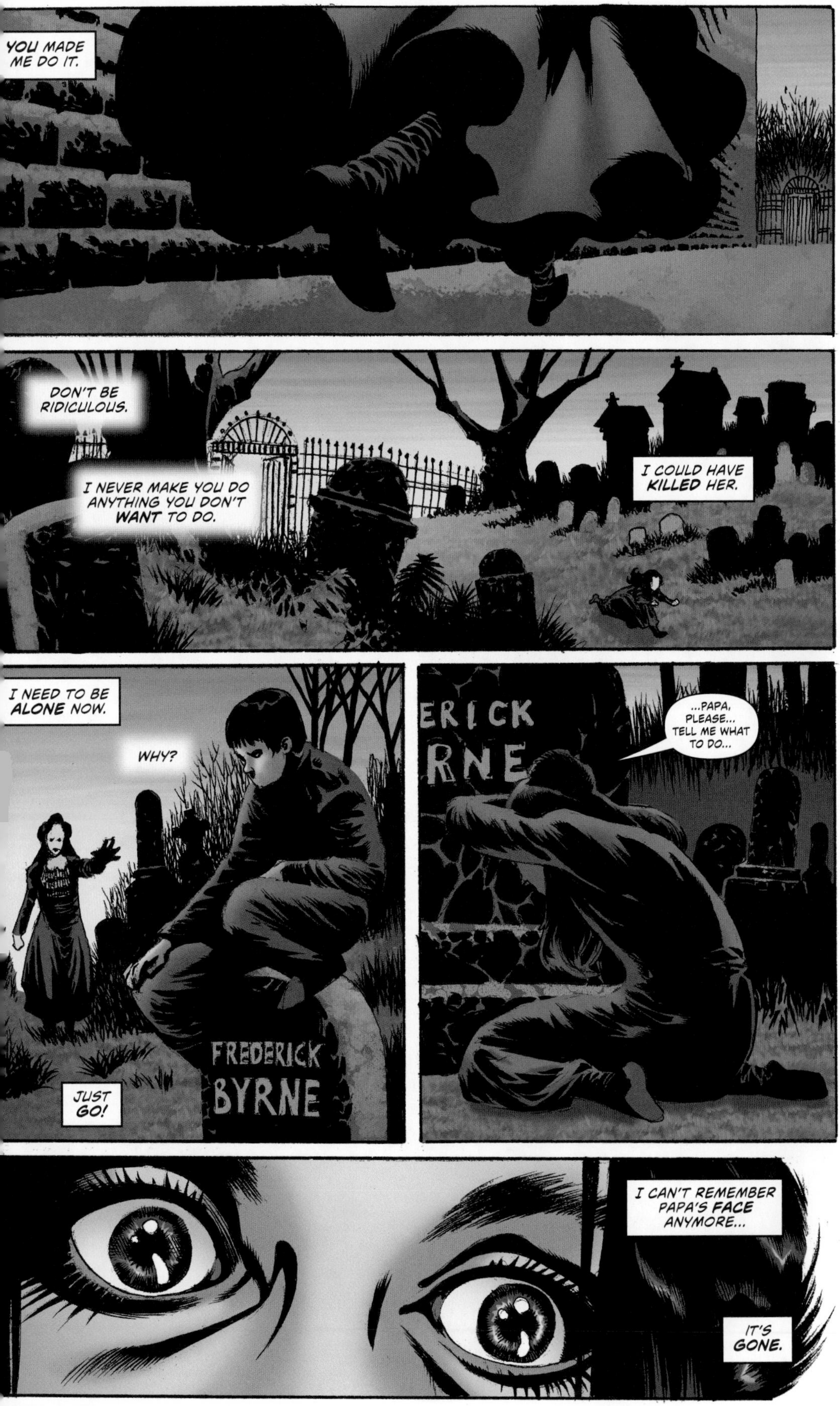

YOU MADE ME DO IT.
DON'T BE RIDICULOUS.
I NEVER MAKE YOU DO ANYTHING YOU DON'T WANT TO DO.
I COULD HAVE KILLED HER.
I NEED TO BE ALONE NOW.
WHY?
FREDERICK BYRNE
JUST GO!
ERICK
RNE
...PAPA, PLEASE... TELL ME WHAT TO DO...
I CAN'T REMEMBER PAPA'S FACE ANYMORE...
IT'S GONE.

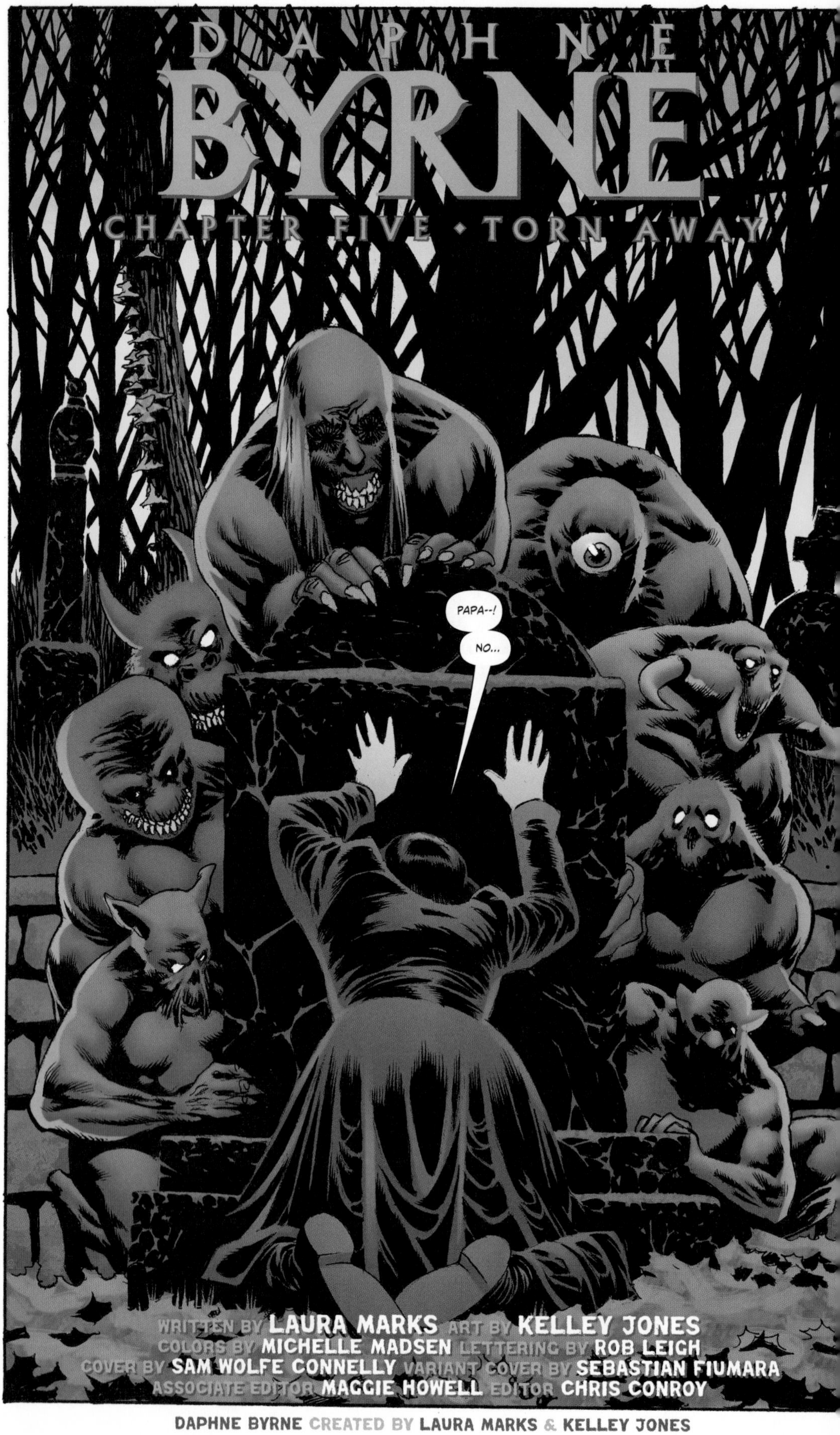
DAPHNE
BYRNE
CHAPTER FIVE • TORN AWAY
PAPA--!
NO...
WRITTEN BY LAURA MARKS ART BY KELLEY JONES
COLORS BY MICHELLE MADSEN LETTERING BY ROB LEIGH
COVER BY SAM WOLFE CONNELLY VARIANT COVER BY SEBASTIAN FIUMARA
ASSOCIATE EDITOR MAGGIE HOWELL EDITOR CHRIS CONROY

DAPHNE BYRNE CREATED BY LAURA MARKS & KELLEY JONES

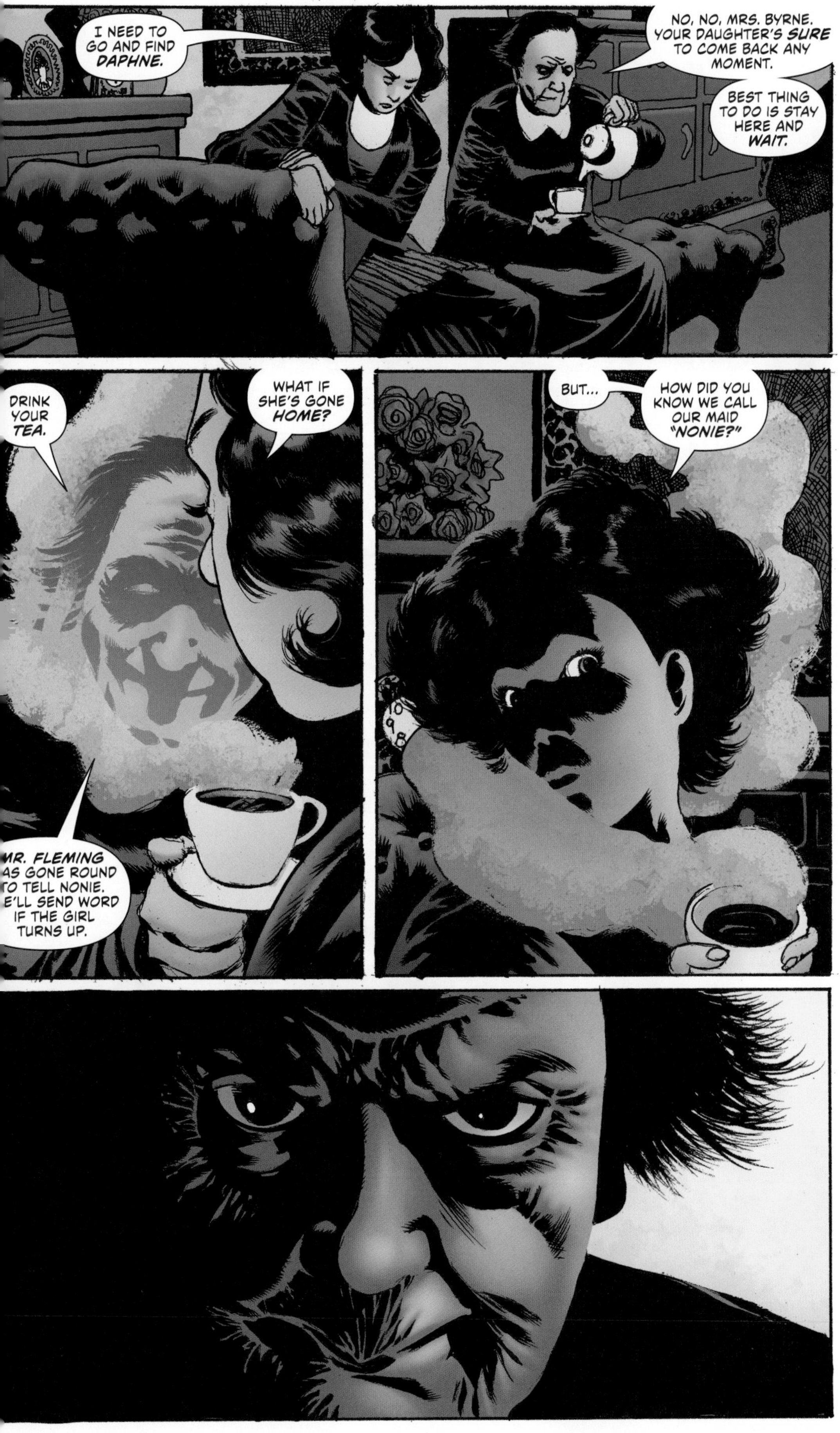
I NEED TO GO AND FIND *DAPHNE.*
NO, NO, MRS. BYRNE. YOUR DAUGHTER'S *SURE* TO COME BACK ANY MOMENT.
BEST THING TO DO IS STAY HERE AND *WAIT.*
WHAT IF SHE'S GONE *HOME?*
DRINK YOUR *TEA.*
MR. FLEMING HAS GONE ROUND TO TELL NONIE. HE'LL SEND WORD IF THE GIRL TURNS UP.
BUT...
HOW DID YOU KNOW WE CALL OUR MAID *"NONIE?"*

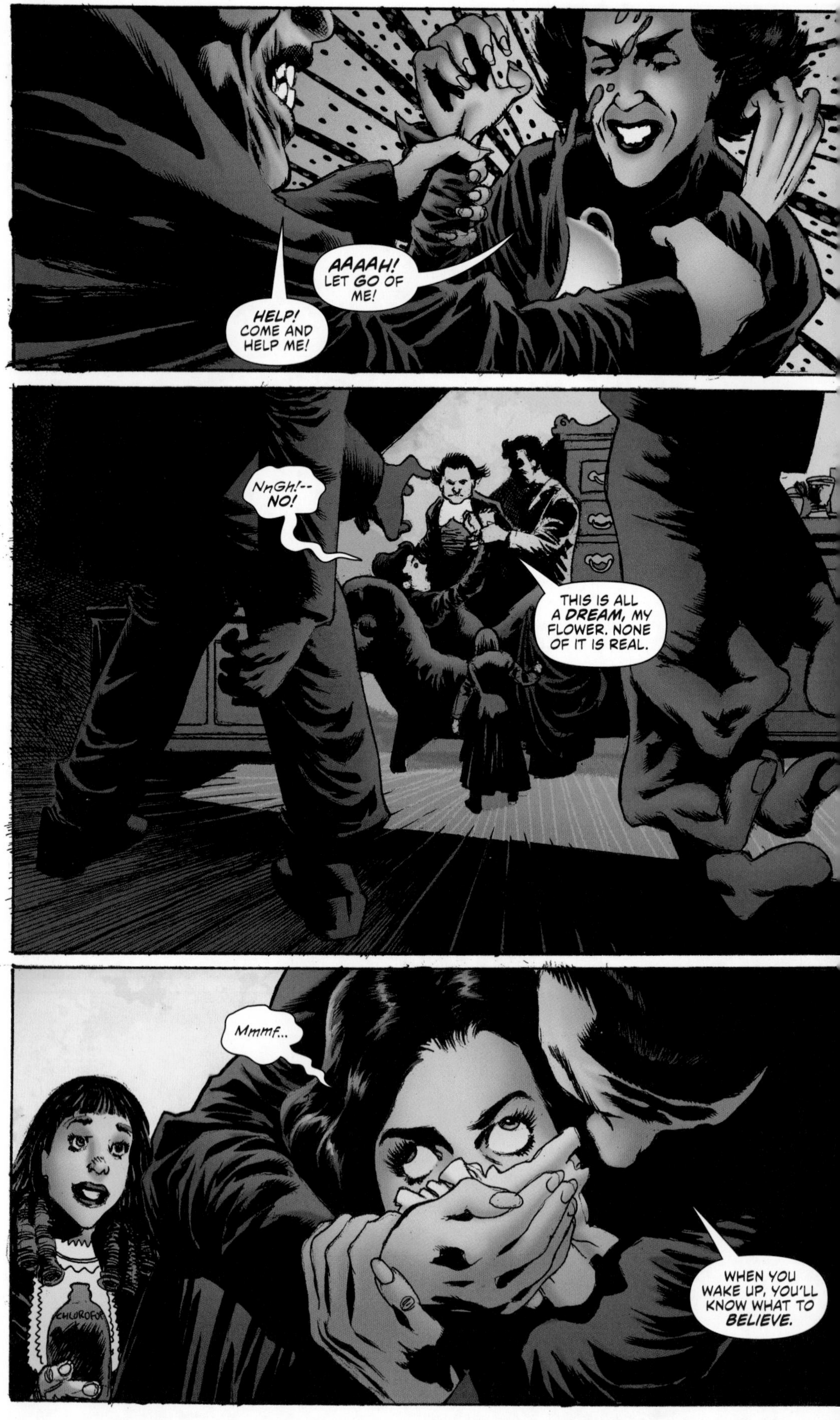
HELP! COME AND HELP ME!
AAAAH! LET GO OF ME!
NnGh!-- NO!
THIS IS ALL A DREAM, MY FLOWER. NONE OF IT IS REAL.
Mmmf...
WHEN YOU WAKE UP, YOU'LL KNOW WHAT TO BELIEVE.

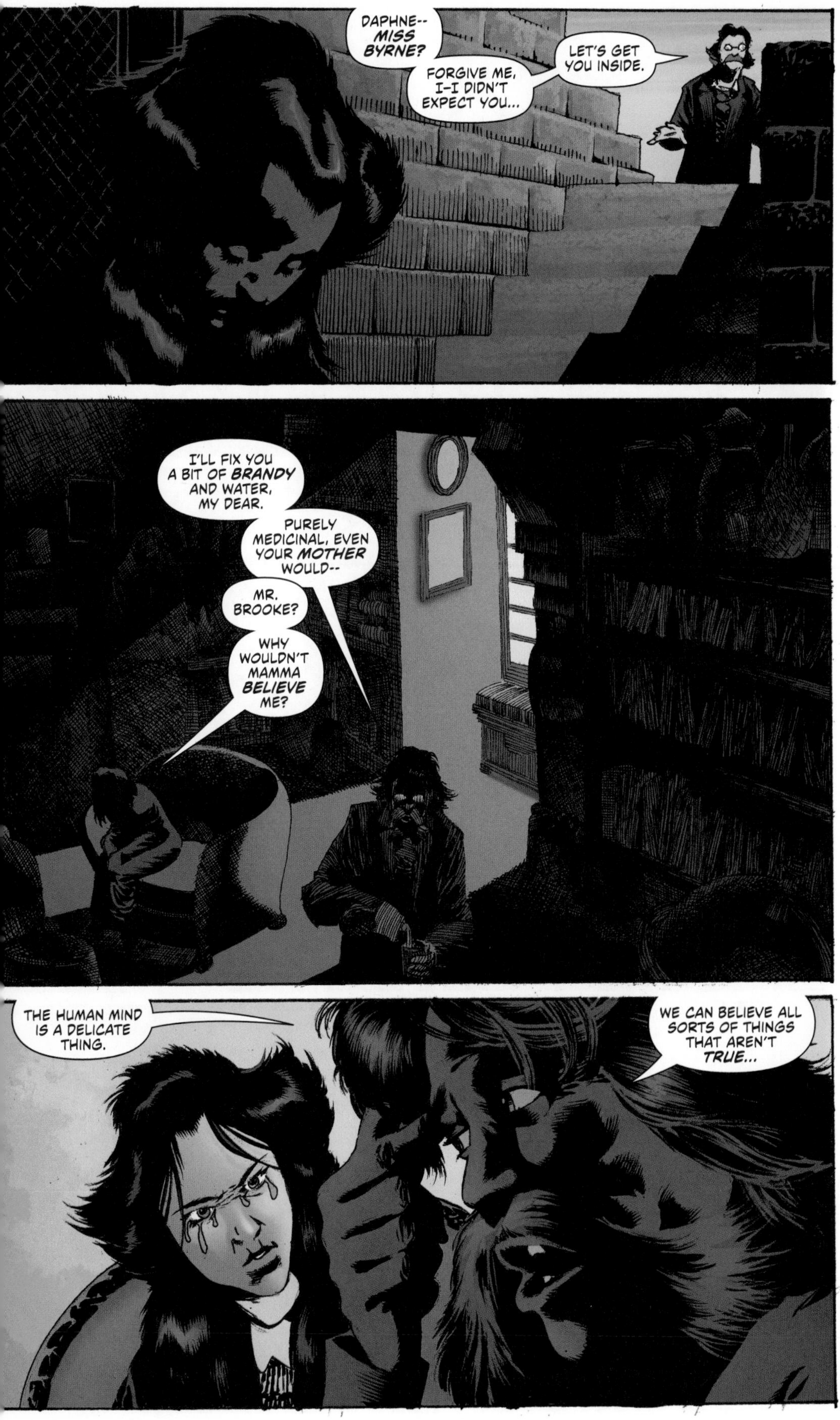
DAPHNE-- MISS BYRNE?
FORGIVE ME, I-I DIDN'T EXPECT YOU...
LET'S GET YOU INSIDE.
I'LL FIX YOU A BIT OF BRANDY AND WATER, MY DEAR.
PURELY MEDICINAL, EVEN YOUR MOTHER WOULD--
MR. BROOKE?
WHY WOULDN'T MAMMA BELIEVE ME?
THE HUMAN MIND IS A DELICATE THING.
WE CAN BELIEVE ALL SORTS OF THINGS THAT AREN'T TRUE...

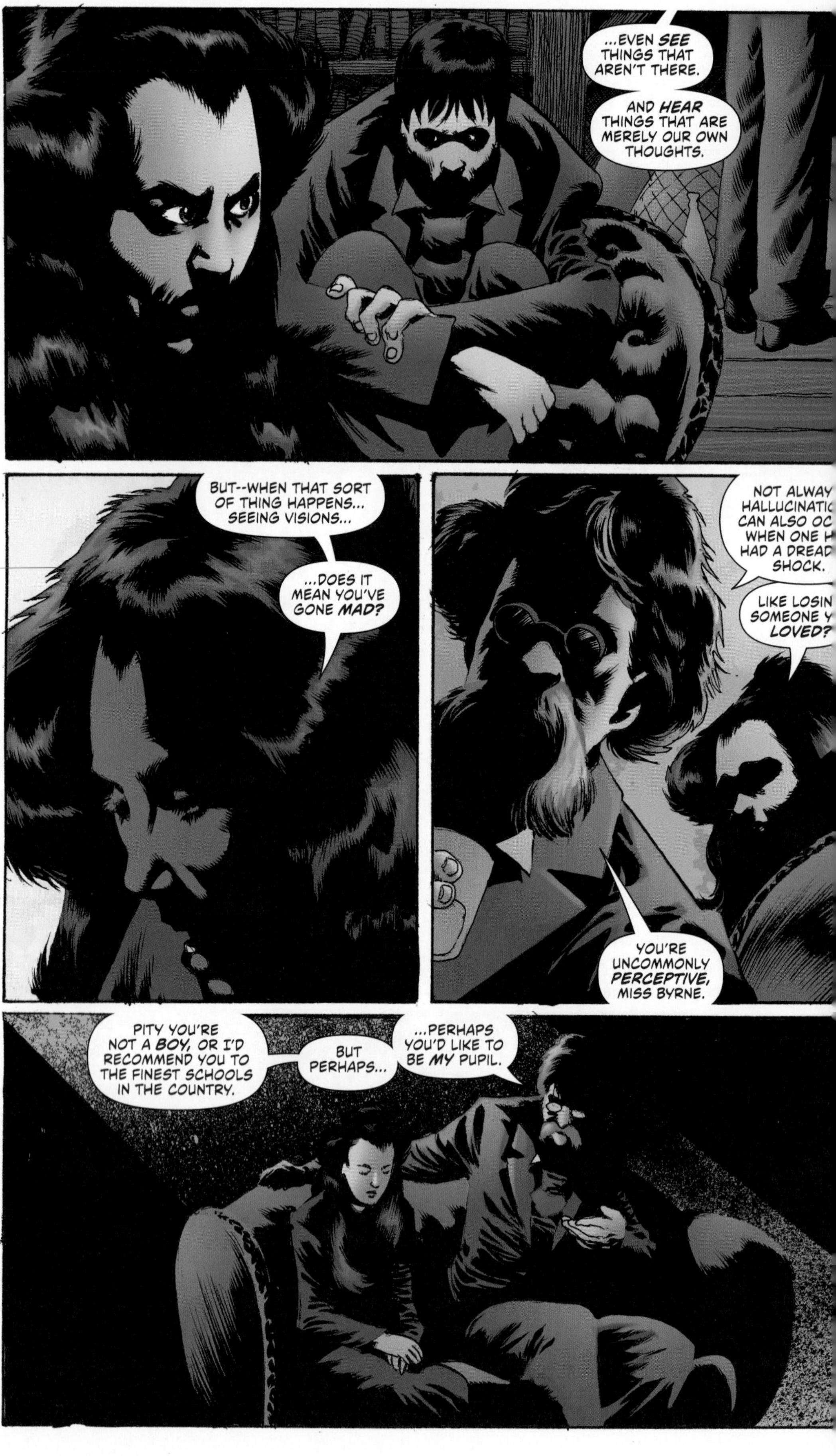
...EVEN SEE THINGS THAT AREN'T THERE.
AND HEAR THINGS THAT ARE MERELY OUR OWN THOUGHTS.
BUT--WHEN THAT SORT OF THING HAPPENS... SEEING VISIONS...
...DOES IT MEAN YOU'VE GONE MAD?
NOT ALWAY HALLUCINATIC CAN ALSO OC WHEN ONE H HAD A DREAD SHOCK.
LIKE LOSIN SOMEONE Y LOVED?
YOU'RE UNCOMMONLY PERCEPTIVE, MISS BYRNE.
PITY YOU'RE NOT A BOY, OR I'D RECOMMEND YOU TO THE FINEST SCHOOLS IN THE COUNTRY.
BUT PERHAPS...
...PERHAPS YOU'D LIKE TO BE MY PUPIL.

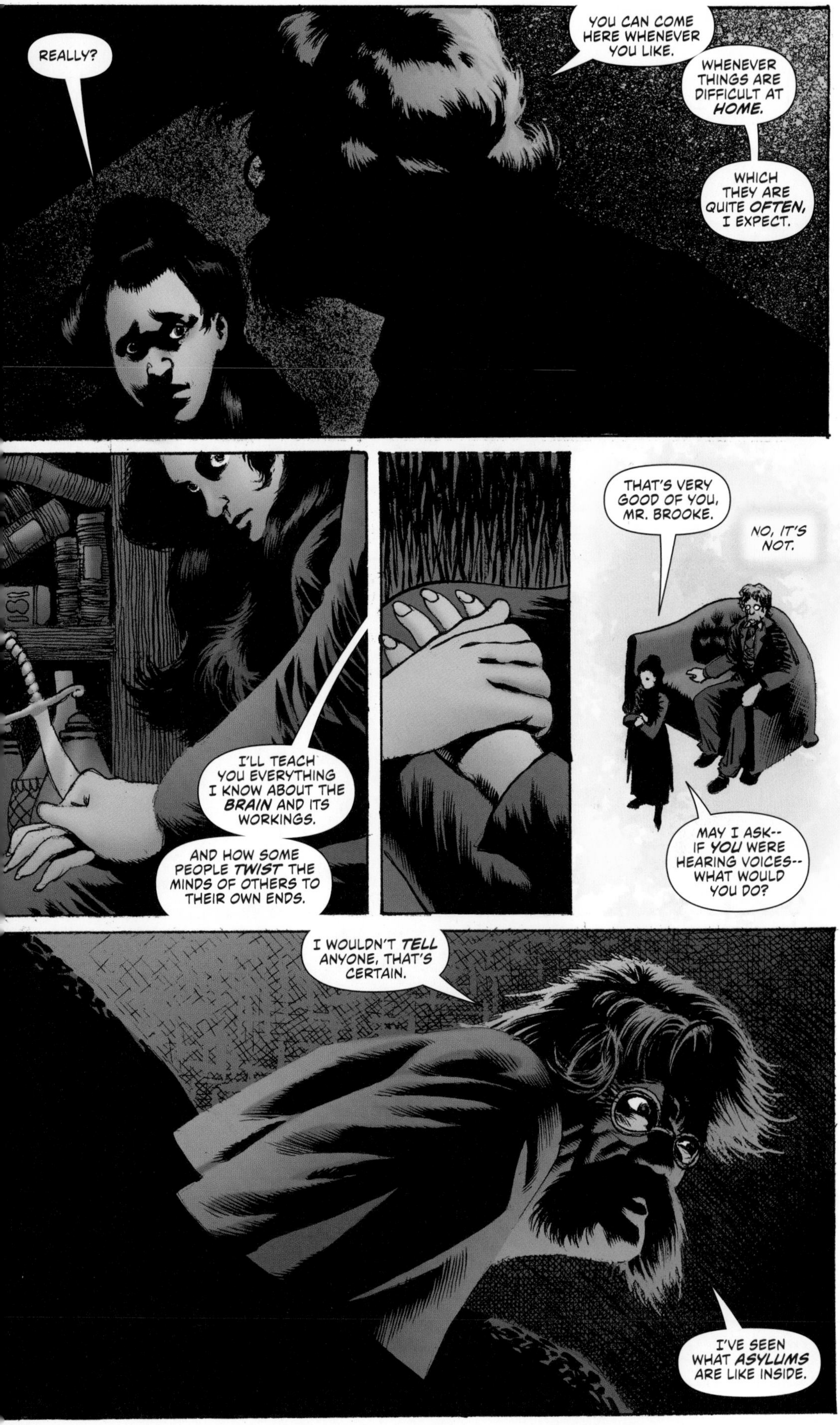
REALLY?
YOU CAN COME HERE WHENEVER YOU LIKE.
WHENEVER THINGS ARE DIFFICULT AT HOME.
WHICH THEY ARE QUITE OFTEN, I EXPECT.
I'LL TEACH YOU EVERYTHING I KNOW ABOUT THE BRAIN AND ITS WORKINGS.
AND HOW SOME PEOPLE TWIST THE MINDS OF OTHERS TO THEIR OWN ENDS.
THAT'S VERY GOOD OF YOU, MR. BROOKE.
NO, IT'S NOT.
MAY I ASK-- IF YOU WERE HEARING VOICES-- WHAT WOULD YOU DO?
I WOULDN'T TELL ANYONE, THAT'S CERTAIN.
I'VE SEEN WHAT ASYLUMS ARE LIKE INSIDE.

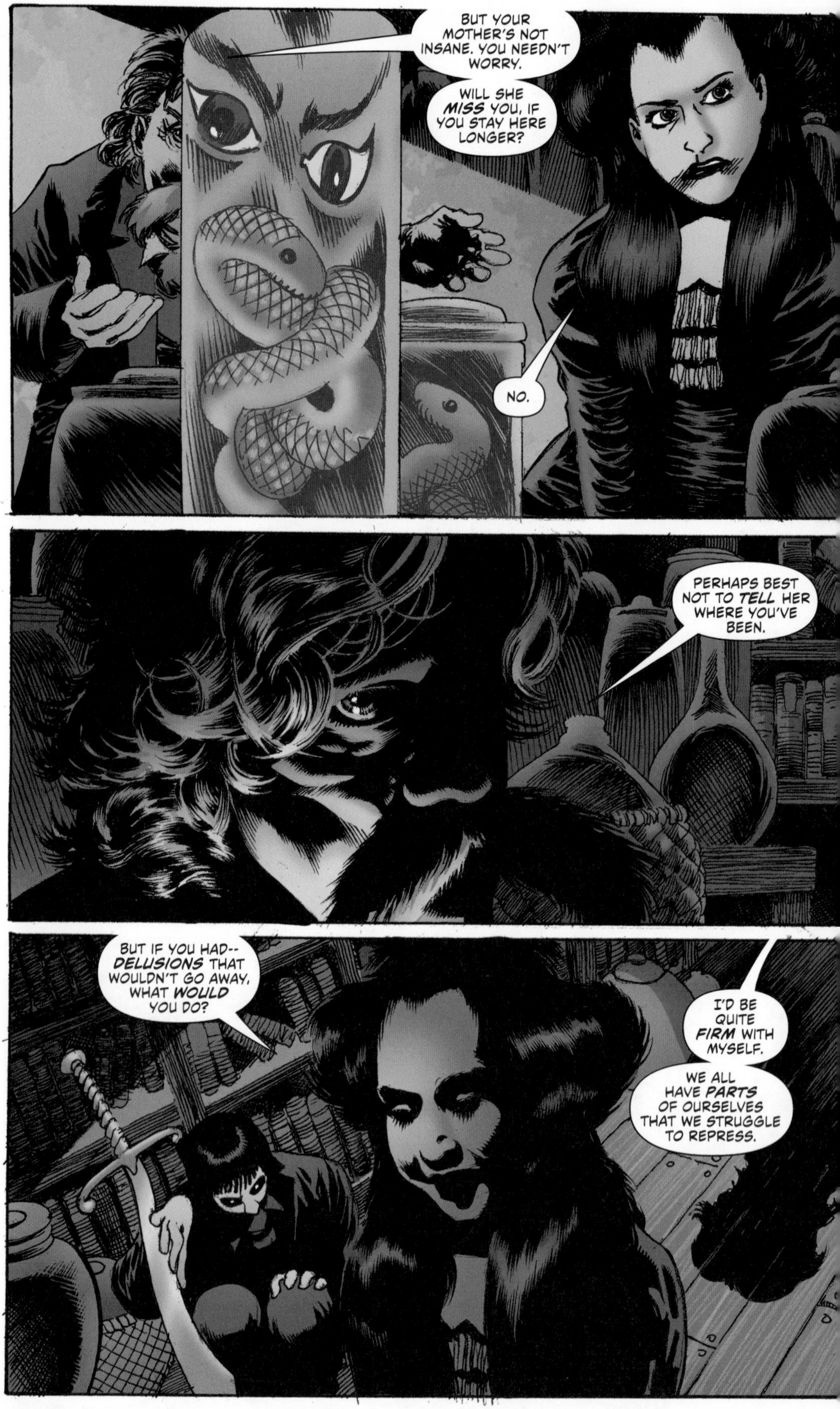
BUT YOUR MOTHER'S NOT INSANE. YOU NEEDN'T WORRY.
WILL SHE MISS YOU, IF YOU STAY HERE LONGER?
NO.
PERHAPS BEST NOT TO TELL HER WHERE YOU'VE BEEN.
BUT IF YOU HAD-- DELUSIONS THAT WOULDN'T GO AWAY, WHAT WOULD YOU DO?
I'D BE QUITE FIRM WITH MYSELF.
WE ALL HAVE PARTS OF OURSELVES THAT WE STRUGGLE TO REPRESS.

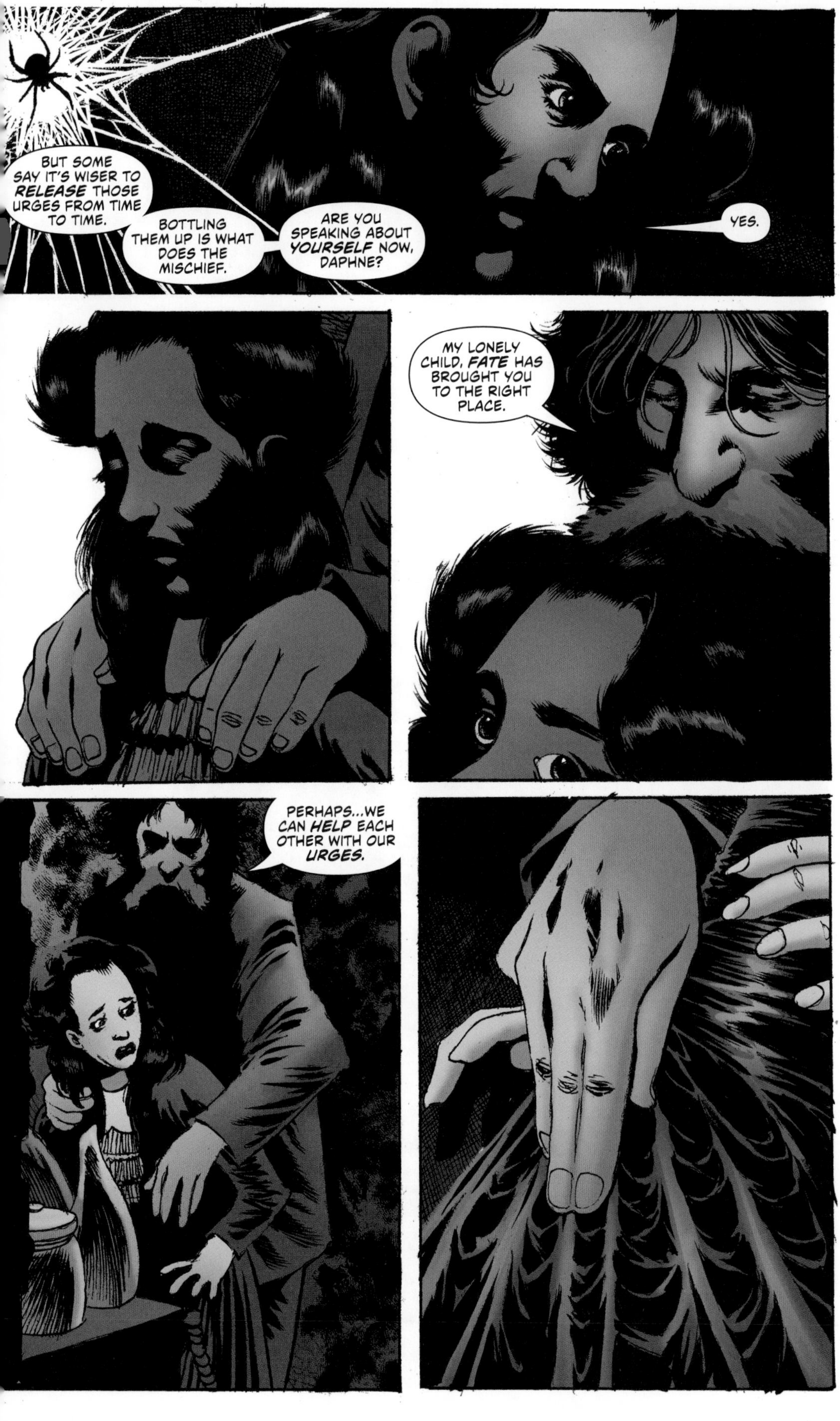
BUT SOME SAY IT'S WISER TO *RELEASE* THOSE URGES FROM TIME TO TIME.
BOTTLING THEM UP IS WHAT DOES THE MISCHIEF.
ARE YOU SPEAKING ABOUT *YOURSELF* NOW, DAPHNE?
YES.
MY LONELY CHILD, *FATE* HAS BROUGHT YOU TO THE RIGHT PLACE.
PERHAPS...WE CAN *HELP* EACH OTHER WITH OUR *URGES.*

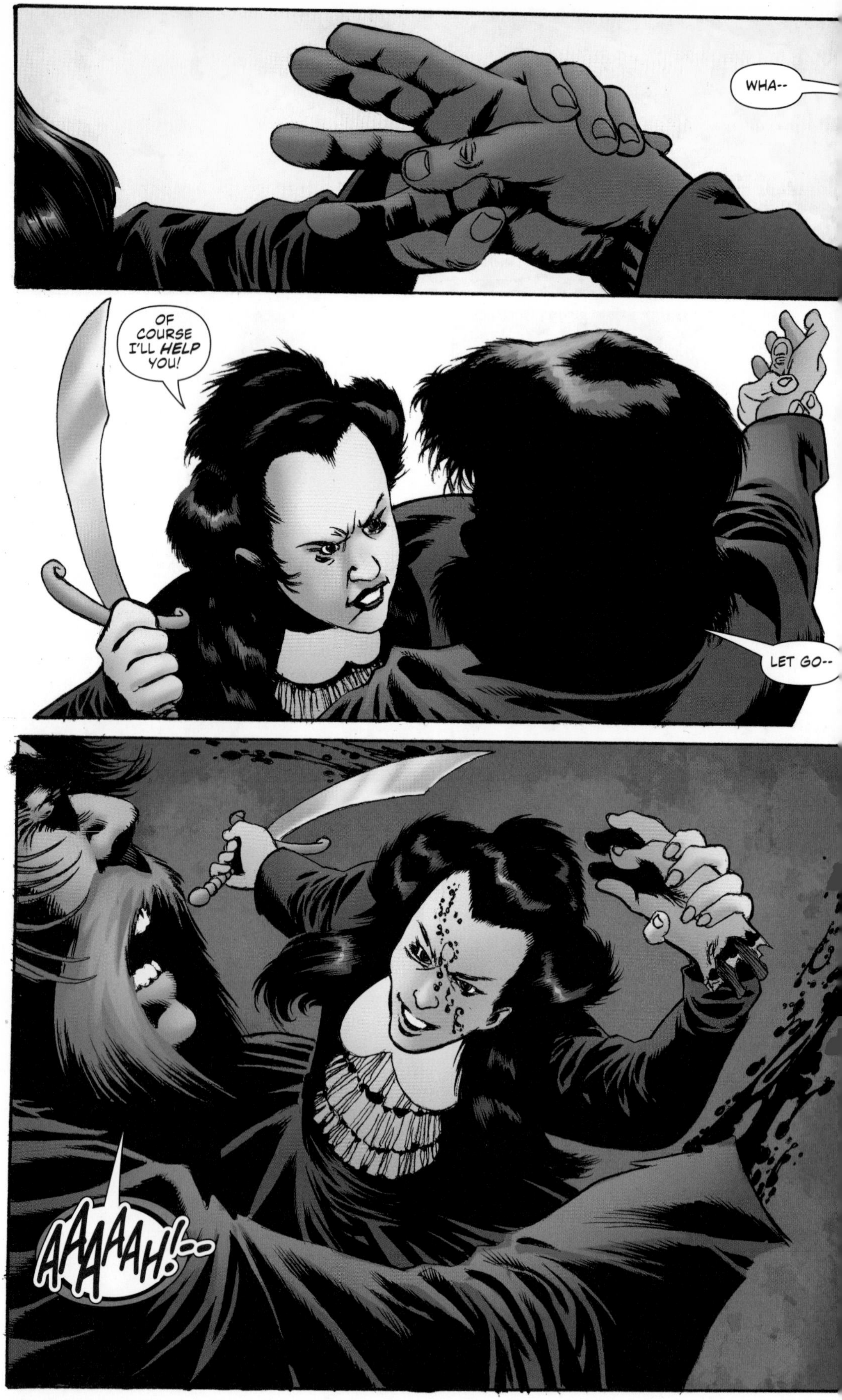
WHA--
OF COURSE I'LL HELP YOU!
LET GO--
AAAAAH!--

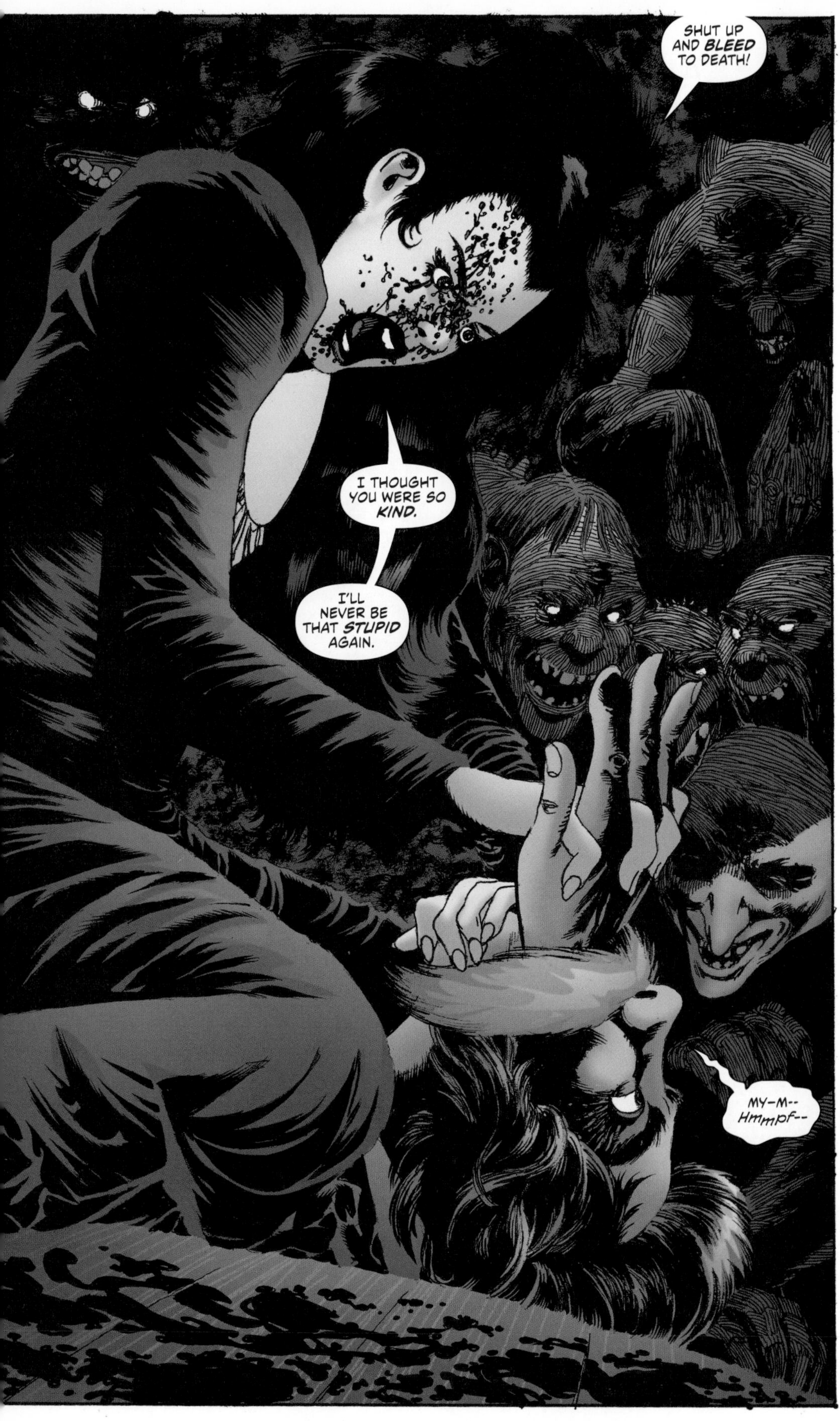
SHUT UP AND *BLEED* TO DEATH!
I THOUGHT YOU WERE SO *KIND*.
I'LL NEVER BE THAT *STUPID* AGAIN.
MY--M-- Hmmpf--

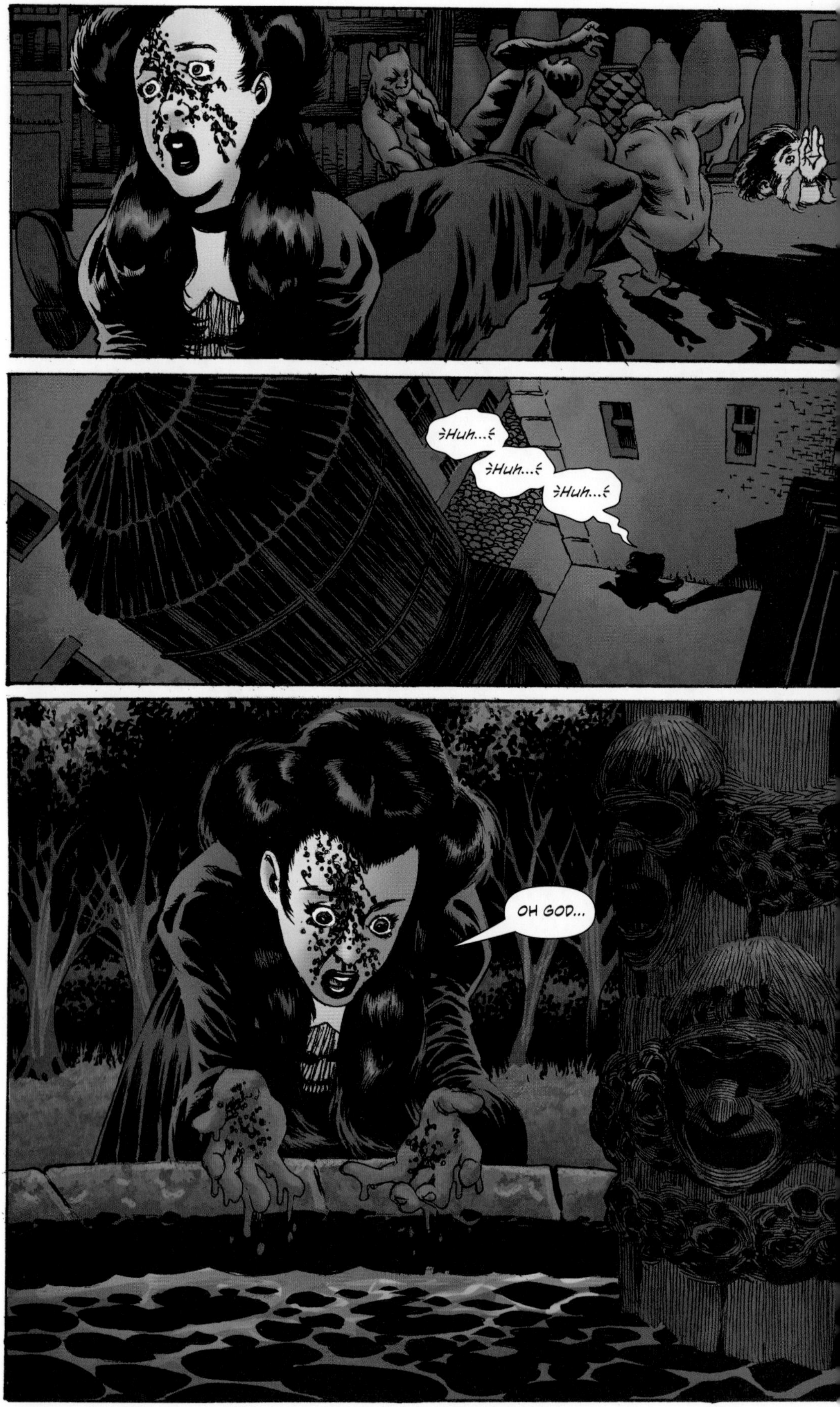
Huh...
Huh...
Huh...
OH GOD...

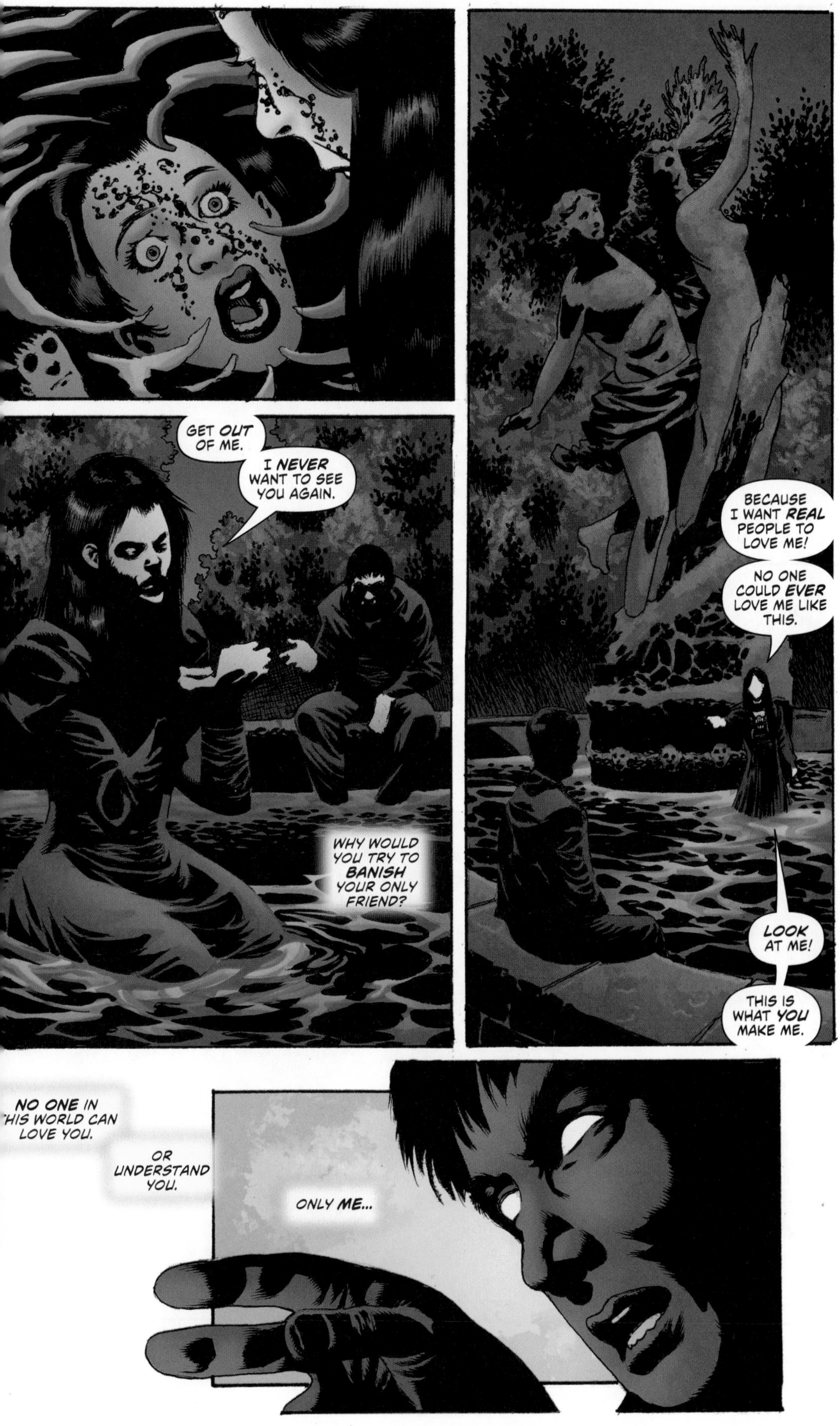

GET OUT OF ME.
I NEVER WANT TO SEE YOU AGAIN.
WHY WOULD YOU TRY TO BANISH YOUR ONLY FRIEND?
BECAUSE I WANT REAL PEOPLE TO LOVE ME!
NO ONE COULD EVER LOVE ME LIKE THIS.
LOOK AT ME!
THIS IS WHAT YOU MAKE ME.
NO ONE IN THIS WORLD CAN LOVE YOU.
OR UNDERSTAND YOU.
ONLY ME...

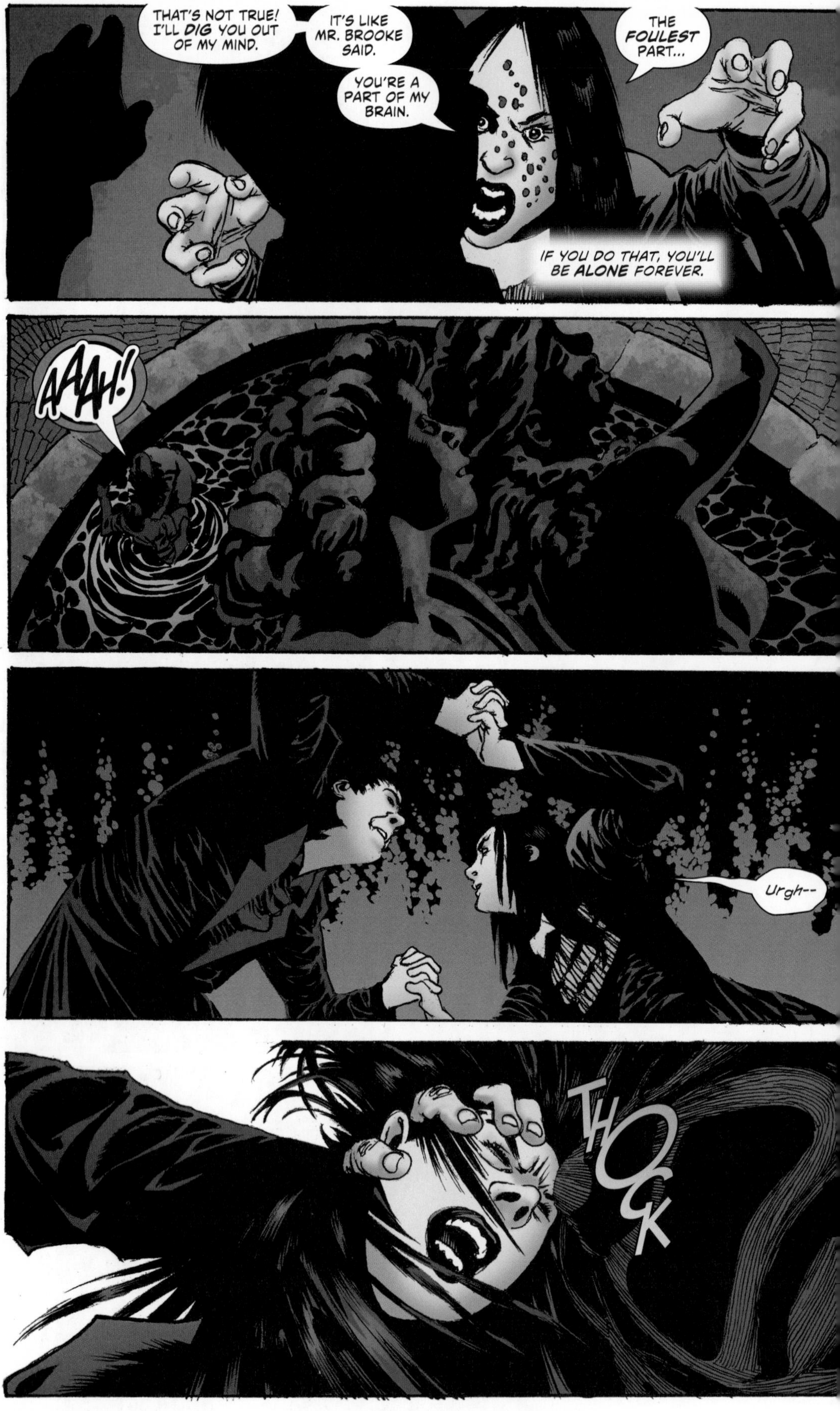
THAT'S NOT TRUE! I'LL DIG YOU OUT OF MY MIND.
IT'S LIKE MR. BROOKE SAID.
YOU'RE A PART OF MY BRAIN.
THE FOULEST PART...
IF YOU DO THAT, YOU'LL BE ALONE FOREVER.
AAAH!
Urgh--
THOCK

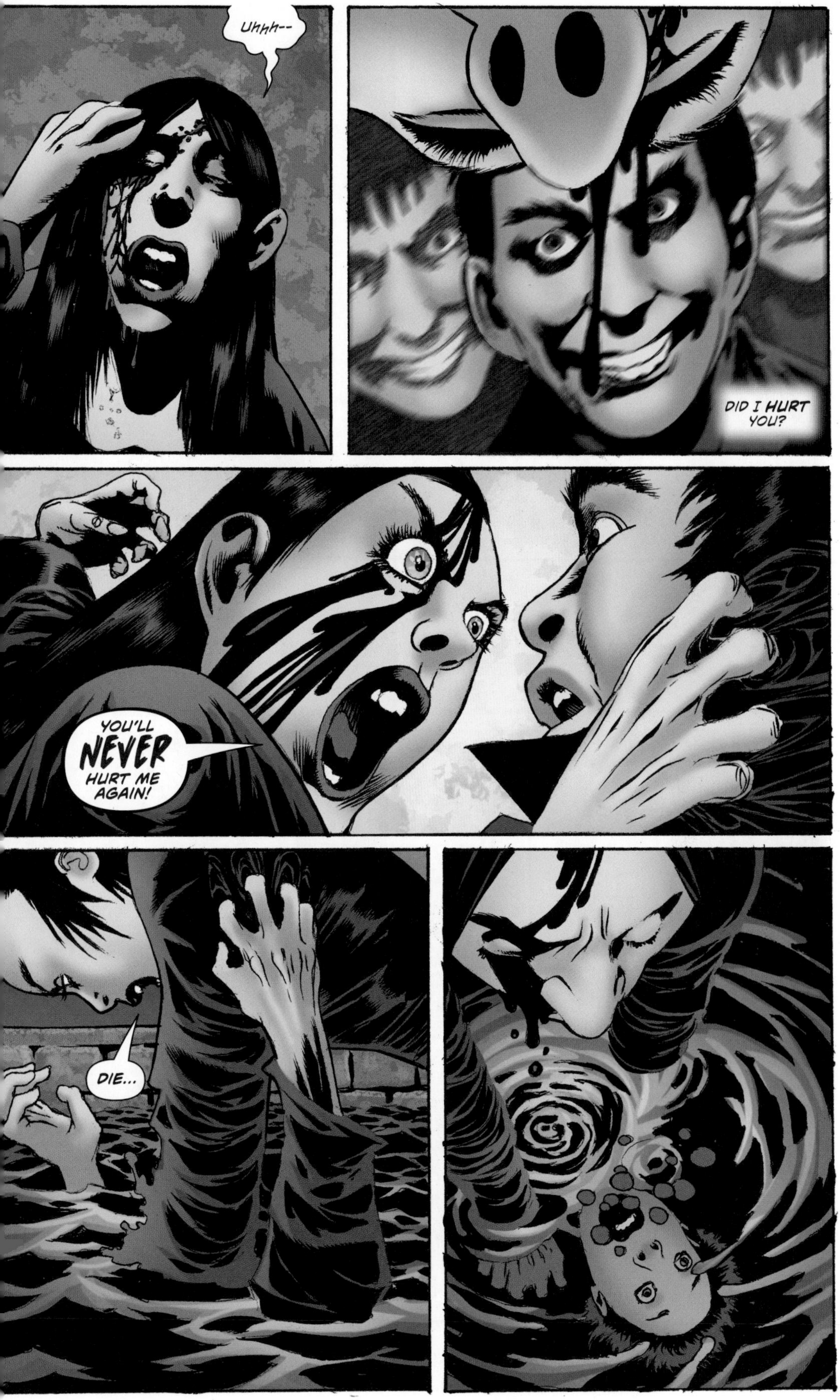
Uhhh--
DID I HURT YOU?
YOU'LL NEVER HURT ME AGAIN!
DIE...

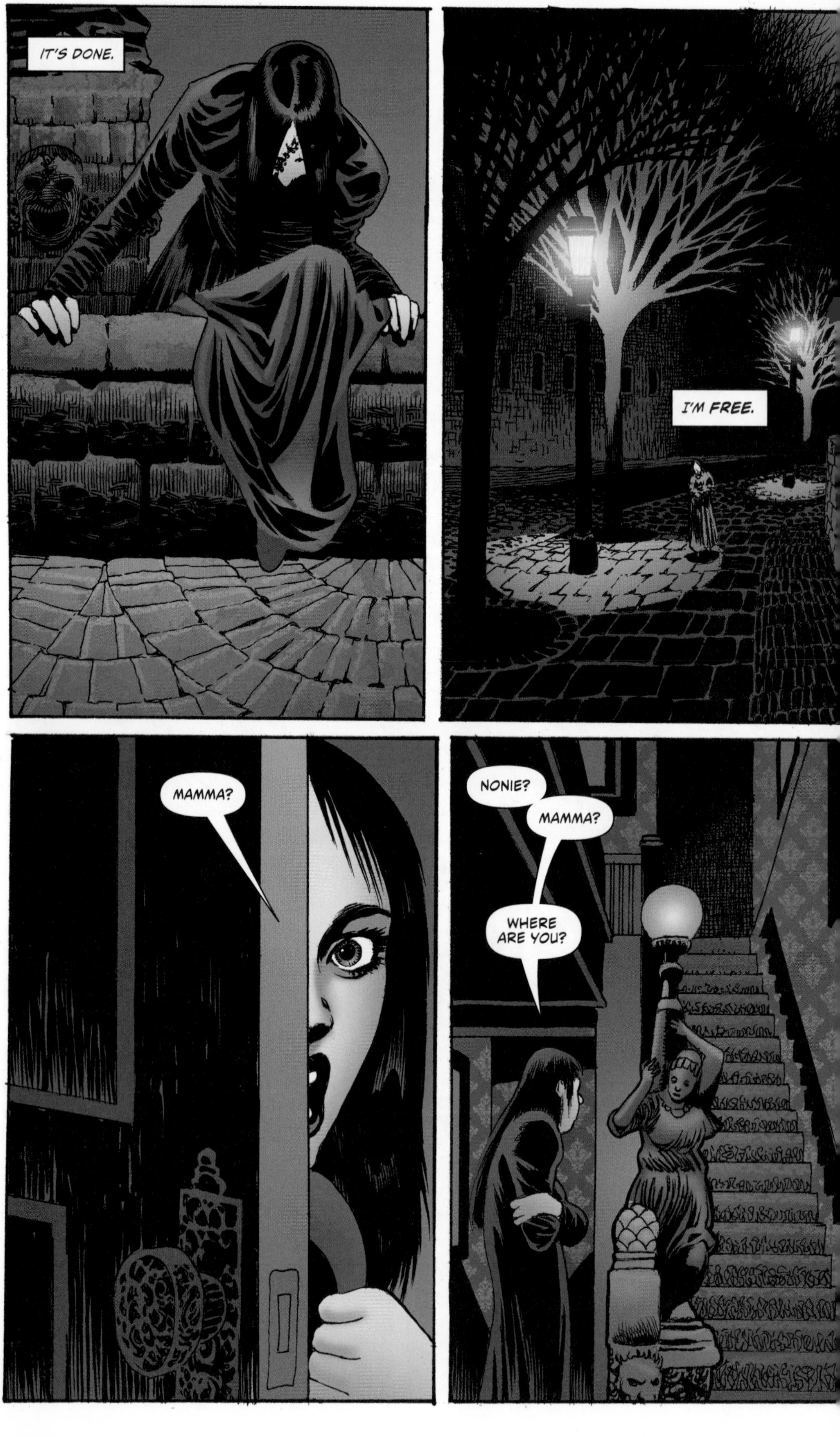
IT'S DONE.
I'M FREE.
MAMMA?
NONIE?
MAMMA?
WHERE ARE YOU?

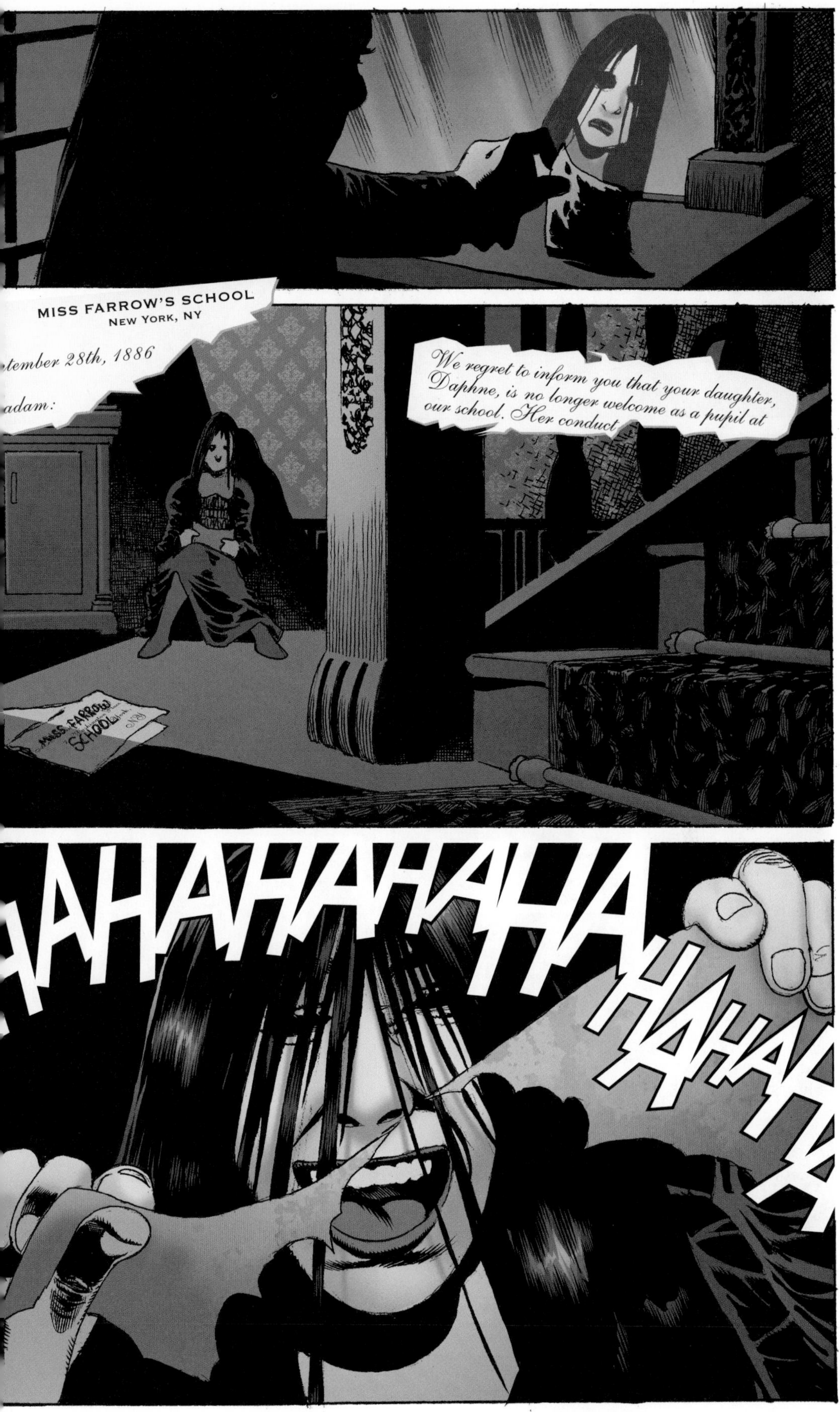
MISS FARROW'S SCHOOL
New York, NY
ptember 28th, 1886
adam:
We regret to inform you that your daughter, Daphne, is no longer welcome as a pupil at our school. Her conduct
MISS FARROW SCHOOL
HAHAHAHAHAHA
HAHAHAHA

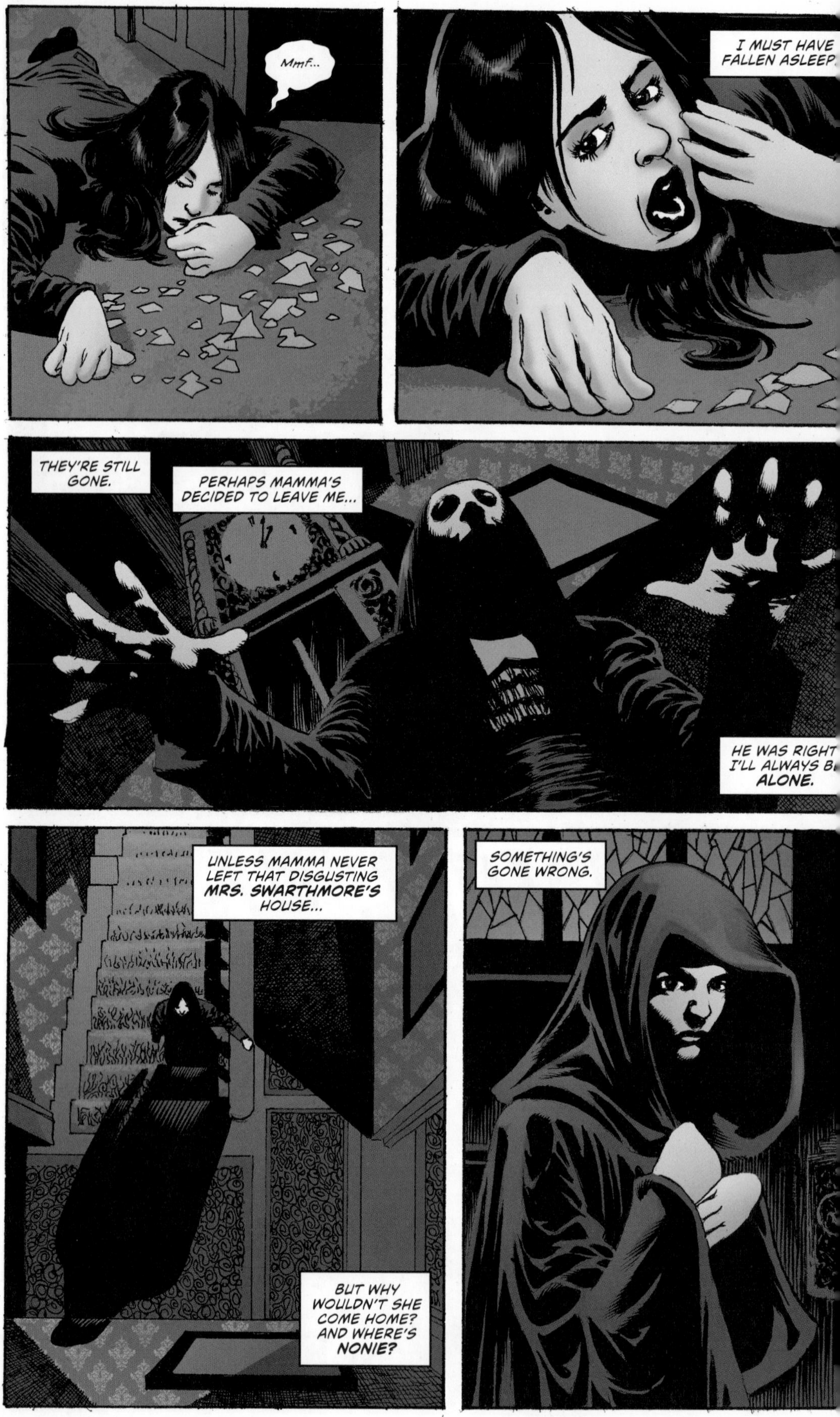
Mmf...
I MUST HAVE FALLEN ASLEEP.
THEY'RE STILL GONE.
PERHAPS MAMMA'S DECIDED TO LEAVE ME...
HE WAS RIGHT I'LL ALWAYS B ALONE.
UNLESS MAMMA NEVER LEFT THAT DISGUSTING MRS. SWARTHMORE'S HOUSE...
BUT WHY WOULDN'T SHE COME HOME? AND WHERE'S NONIE?
SOMETHING'S GONE WRONG.

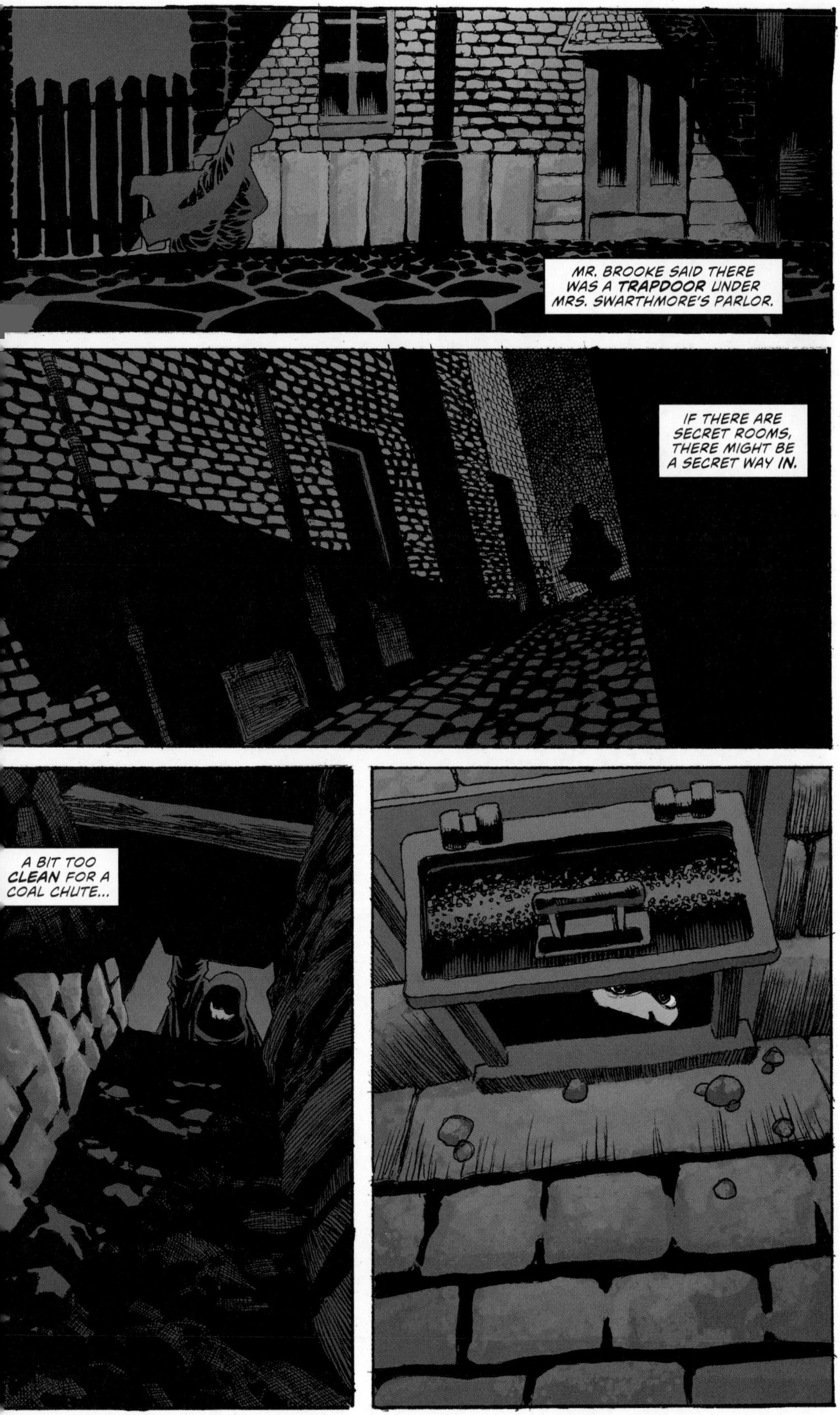
MR. BROOKE SAID THERE WAS A **TRAPDOOR** UNDER MRS. SWARTHMORE'S PARLOR.
IF THERE ARE SECRET ROOMS, THERE MIGHT BE A SECRET WAY **IN**.
A BIT TOO **CLEAN** FOR A COAL CHUTE...

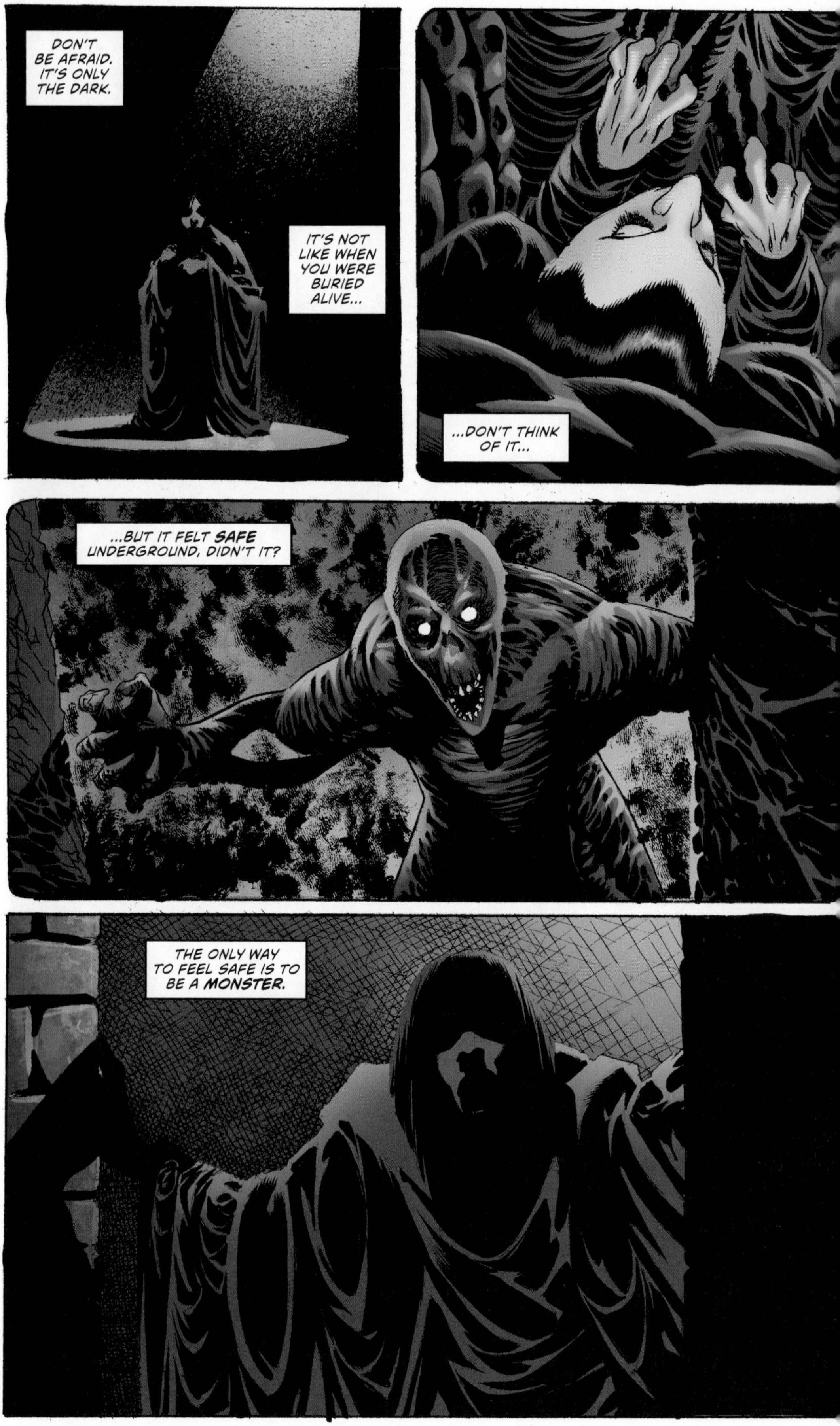
DON'T BE AFRAID. IT'S ONLY THE DARK.
IT'S NOT LIKE WHEN YOU WERE BURIED ALIVE...
...DON'T THINK OF IT...
...BUT IT FELT SAFE UNDERGROUND, DIDN'T IT?
THE ONLY WAY TO FEEL SAFE IS TO BE A MONSTER.

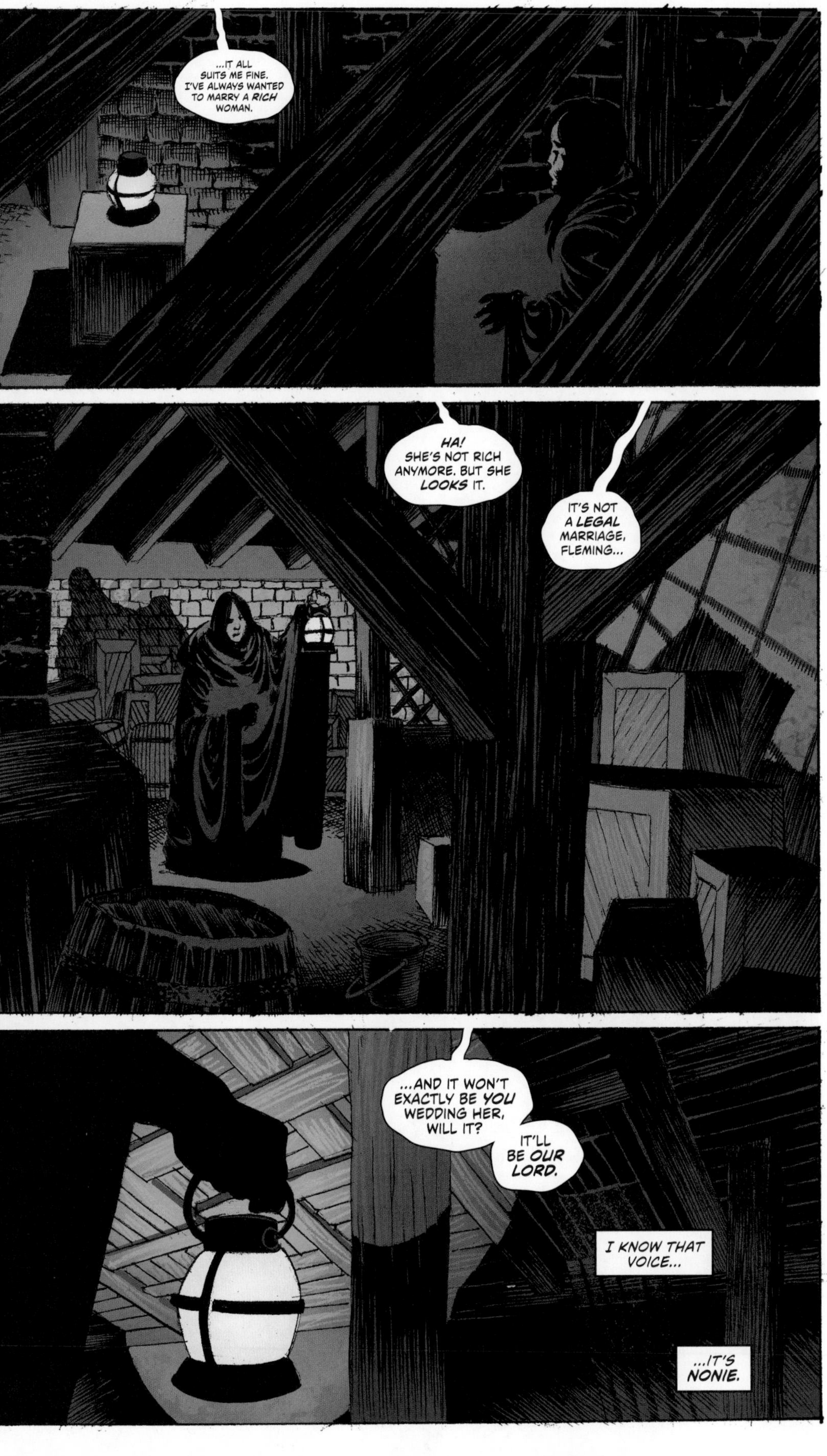
...IT ALL SUITS ME FINE. I'VE ALWAYS WANTED TO MARRY A RICH WOMAN.
HA! SHE'S NOT RICH ANYMORE. BUT SHE LOOKS IT.
IT'S NOT A LEGAL MARRIAGE, FLEMING...
...AND IT WON'T EXACTLY BE YOU WEDDING HER, WILL IT?
IT'LL BE OUR LORD.
I KNOW THAT VOICE...
...IT'S NONIE.

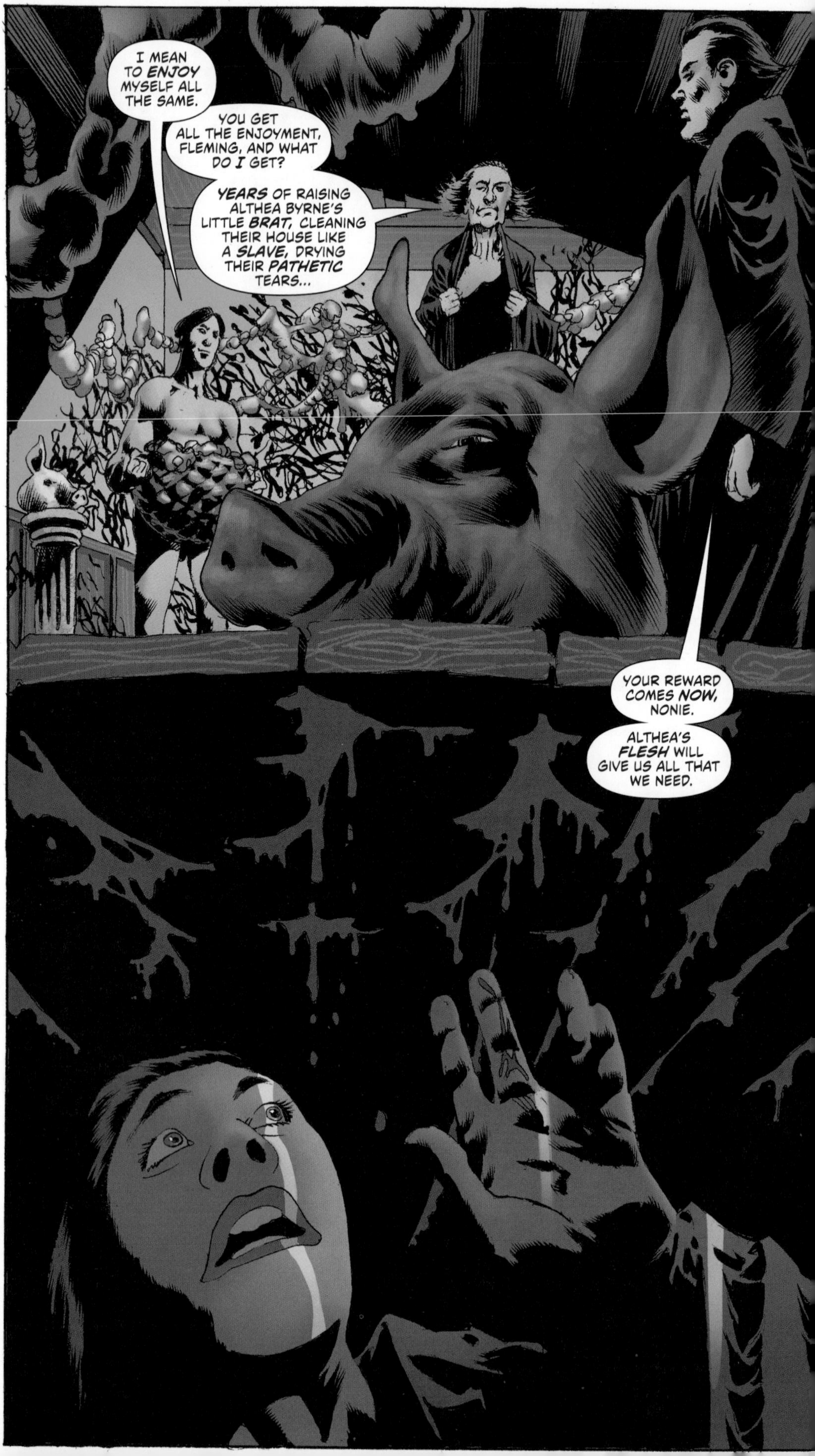

I MEAN TO ENJOY MYSELF ALL THE SAME.
YOU GET ALL THE ENJOYMENT, FLEMING, AND WHAT DO I GET?
YEARS OF RAISING ALTHEA BYRNE'S LITTLE BRAT, CLEANING THEIR HOUSE LIKE A SLAVE, DRYING THEIR PATHETIC TEARS...
YOUR REWARD COMES NOW, NONIE.
ALTHEA'S FLESH WILL GIVE US ALL THAT WE NEED.

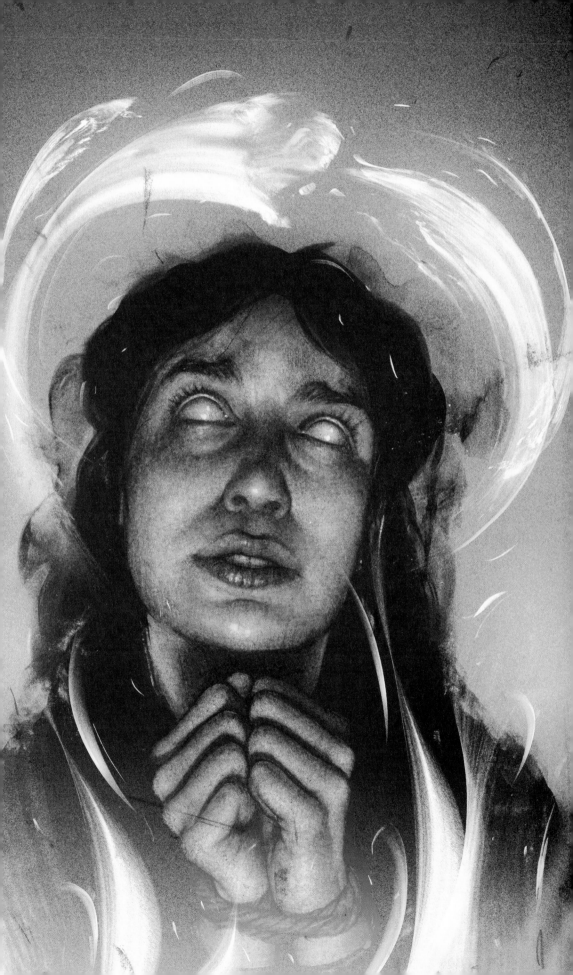

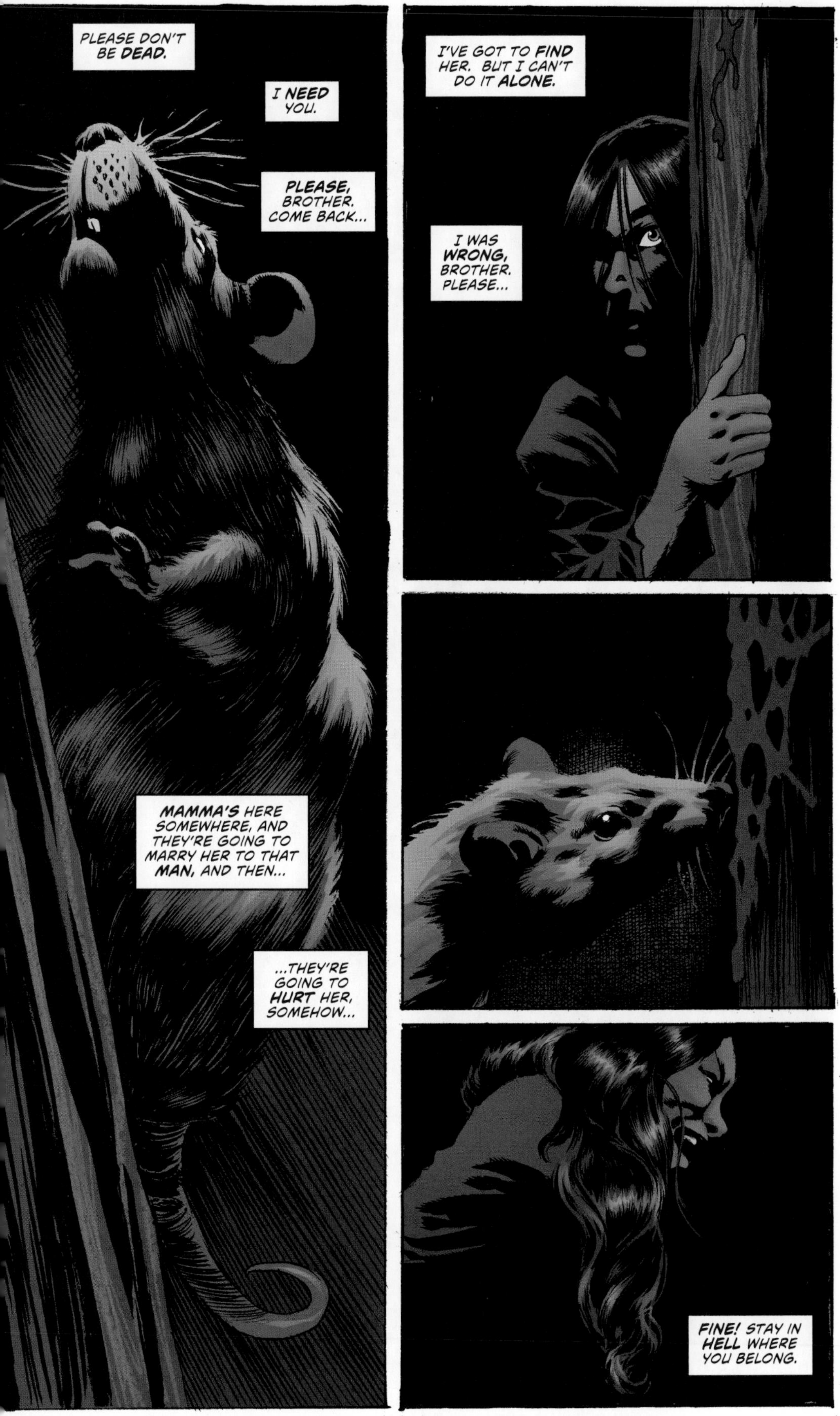
PLEASE DON'T BE DEAD.
I NEED YOU.
PLEASE, BROTHER. COME BACK...
MAMMA'S HERE SOMEWHERE, AND THEY'RE GOING TO MARRY HER TO THAT MAN, AND THEN...
...THEY'RE GOING TO HURT HER, SOMEHOW...
I'VE GOT TO FIND HER. BUT I CAN'T DO IT ALONE.
I WAS WRONG, BROTHER. PLEASE...
FINE! STAY IN HELL WHERE YOU BELONG.

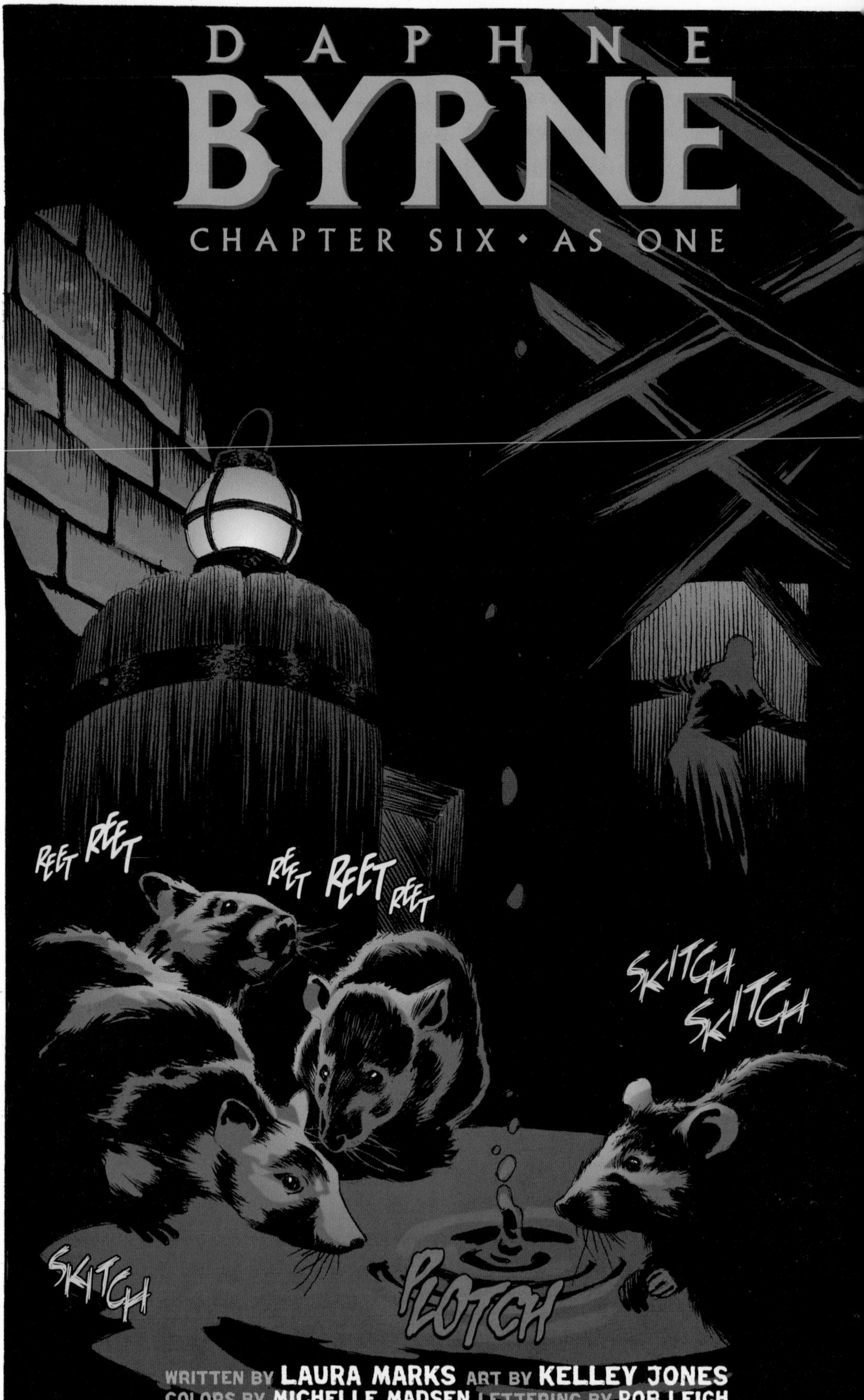
DAPHNE
BYRNE
CHAPTER SIX • AS ONE
REET REET
REET REET REET
SKITCH
SKITCH
SKITCH
PLOTCH
WRITTEN BY LAURA MARKS ART BY KELLEY JONES
COLORS BY MICHELLE MADSEN LETTERING BY ROB LEIGH
COVER BY SAM WOLFE CONNELLY VARIANT COVER BY KELLEY JONES & DAVE STEWAR
ASSOCIATE EDITOR MAGGIE HOWELL EDITOR CHRIS CONROY

DAPHNE BYRNE CREATED BY LAURA MARKS & KELLEY JONES

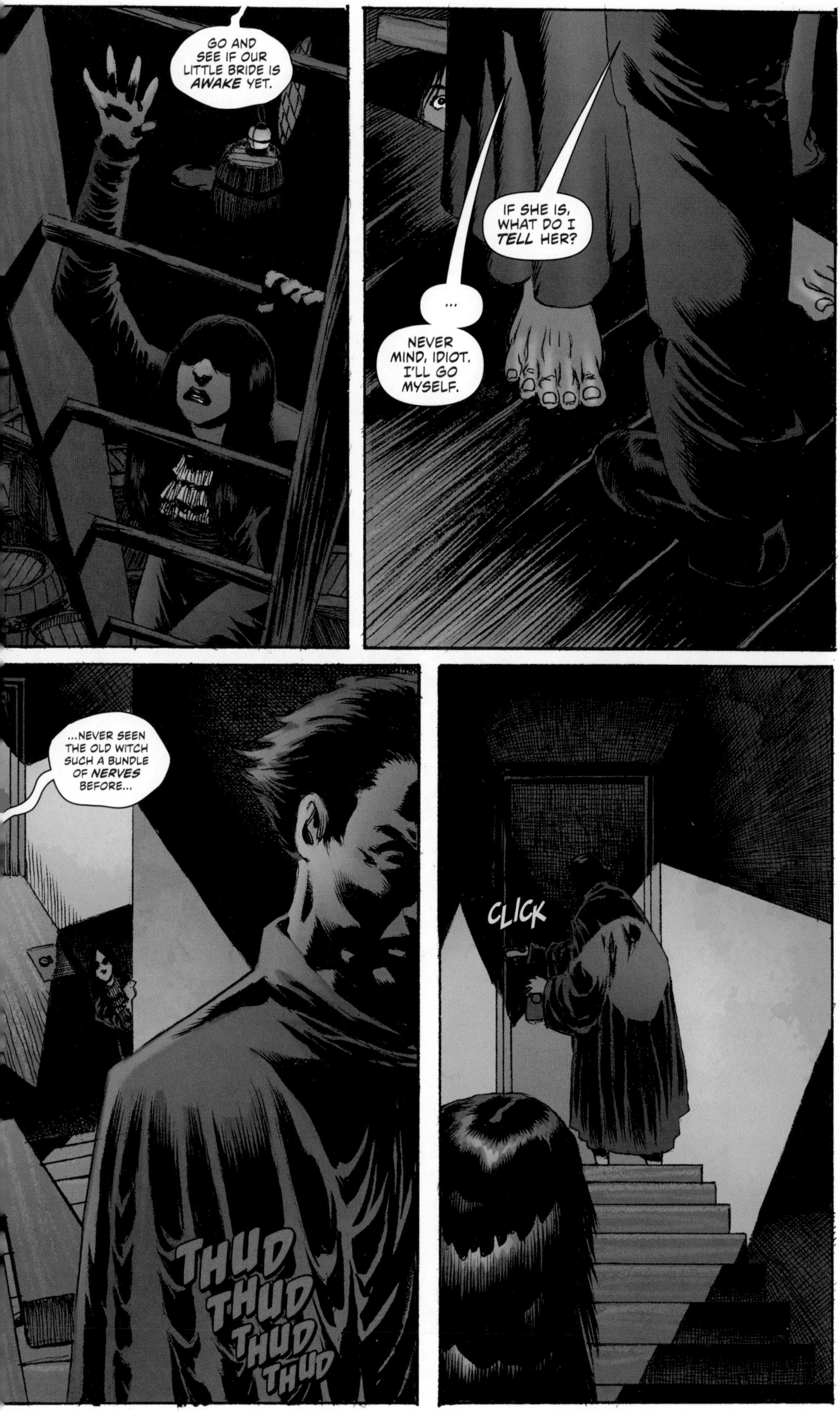
GO AND SEE IF OUR LITTLE BRIDE IS AWAKE YET.
IF SHE IS, WHAT DO I TELL HER?
...
NEVER MIND, IDIOT. I'LL GO MYSELF.
...NEVER SEEN THE OLD WITCH SUCH A BUNDLE OF NERVES BEFORE...
THUD THUD THUD THUD
CLICK

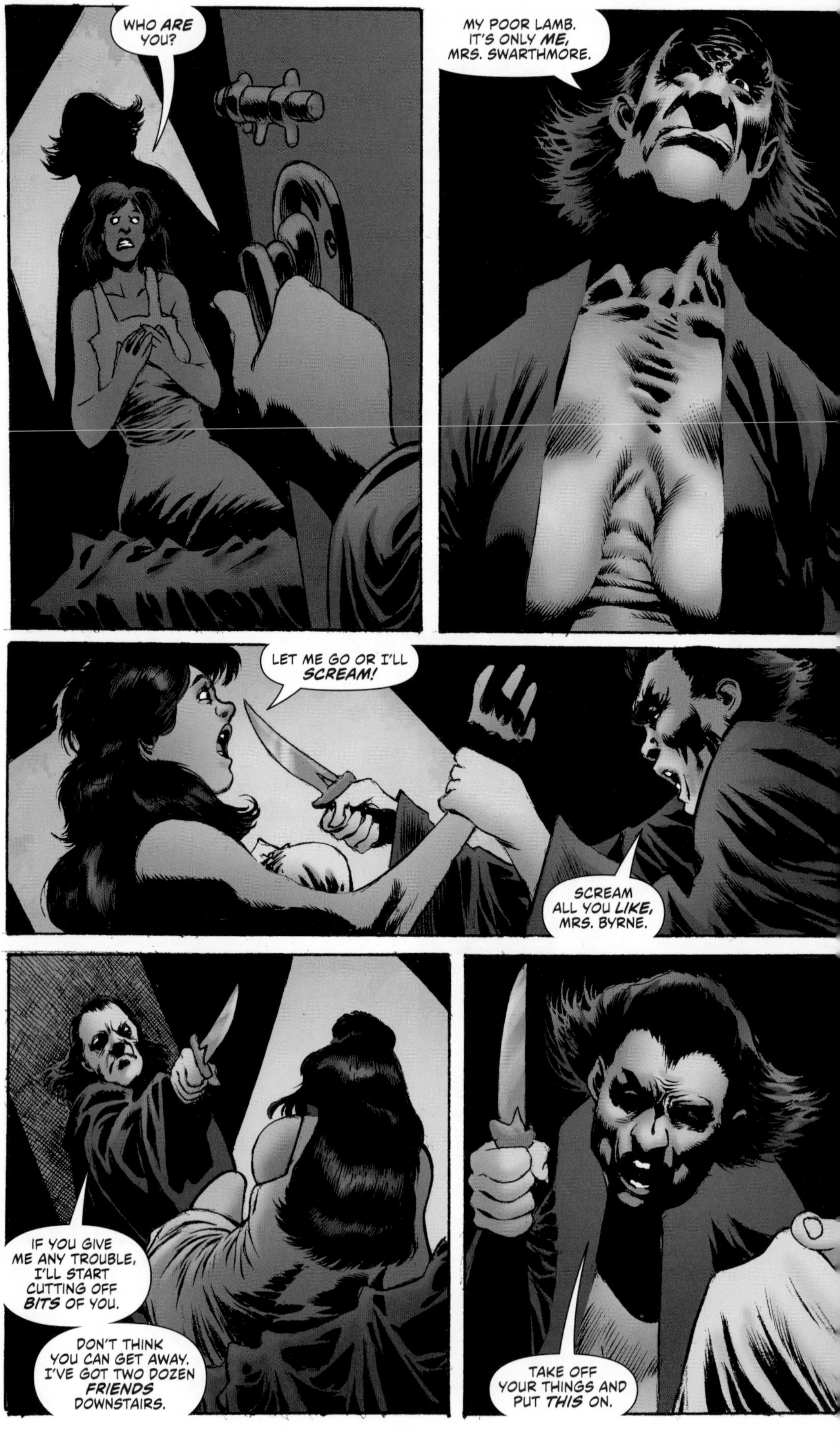
WHO ARE YOU?
MY POOR LAMB. IT'S ONLY ME, MRS. SWARTHMORE.
LET ME GO OR I'LL SCREAM!
SCREAM ALL YOU LIKE, MRS. BYRNE.
IF YOU GIVE ME ANY TROUBLE, I'LL START CUTTING OFF BITS OF YOU.
DON'T THINK YOU CAN GET AWAY. I'VE GOT TWO DOZEN FRIENDS DOWNSTAIRS.
TAKE OFF YOUR THINGS AND PUT THIS ON.

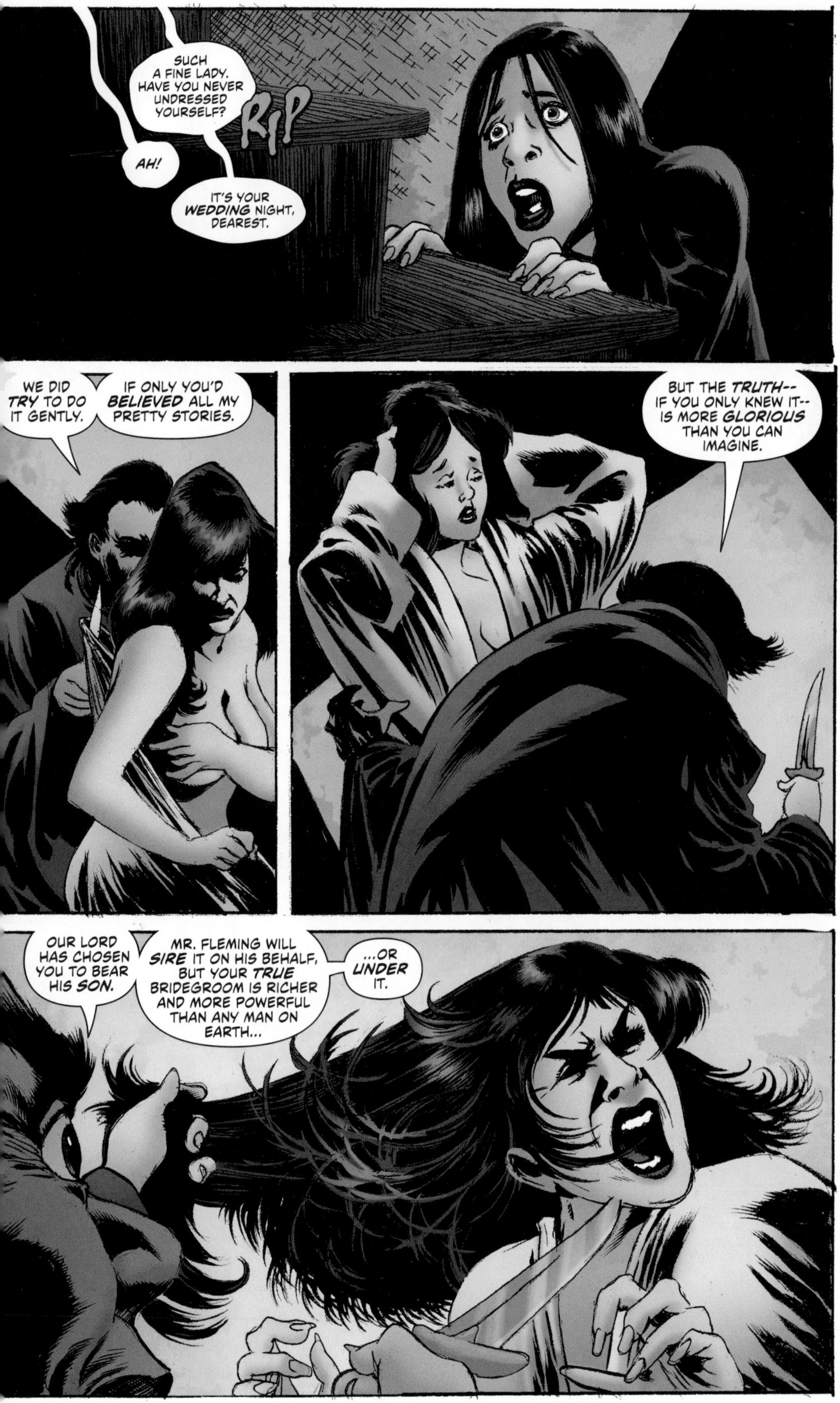
SUCH A FINE LADY. HAVE YOU NEVER UNDRESSED YOURSELF?
RIP
AH!
IT'S YOUR WEDDING NIGHT, DEAREST.
WE DID TRY TO DO IT GENTLY.
IF ONLY YOU'D BELIEVED ALL MY PRETTY STORIES.
BUT THE TRUTH-- IF YOU ONLY KNEW IT-- IS MORE GLORIOUS THAN YOU CAN IMAGINE.
OUR LORD HAS CHOSEN YOU TO BEAR HIS SON.
MR. FLEMING WILL SIRE IT ON HIS BEHALF, BUT YOUR TRUE BRIDEGROOM IS RICHER AND MORE POWERFUL THAN ANY MAN ON EARTH...
...OR UNDER IT.

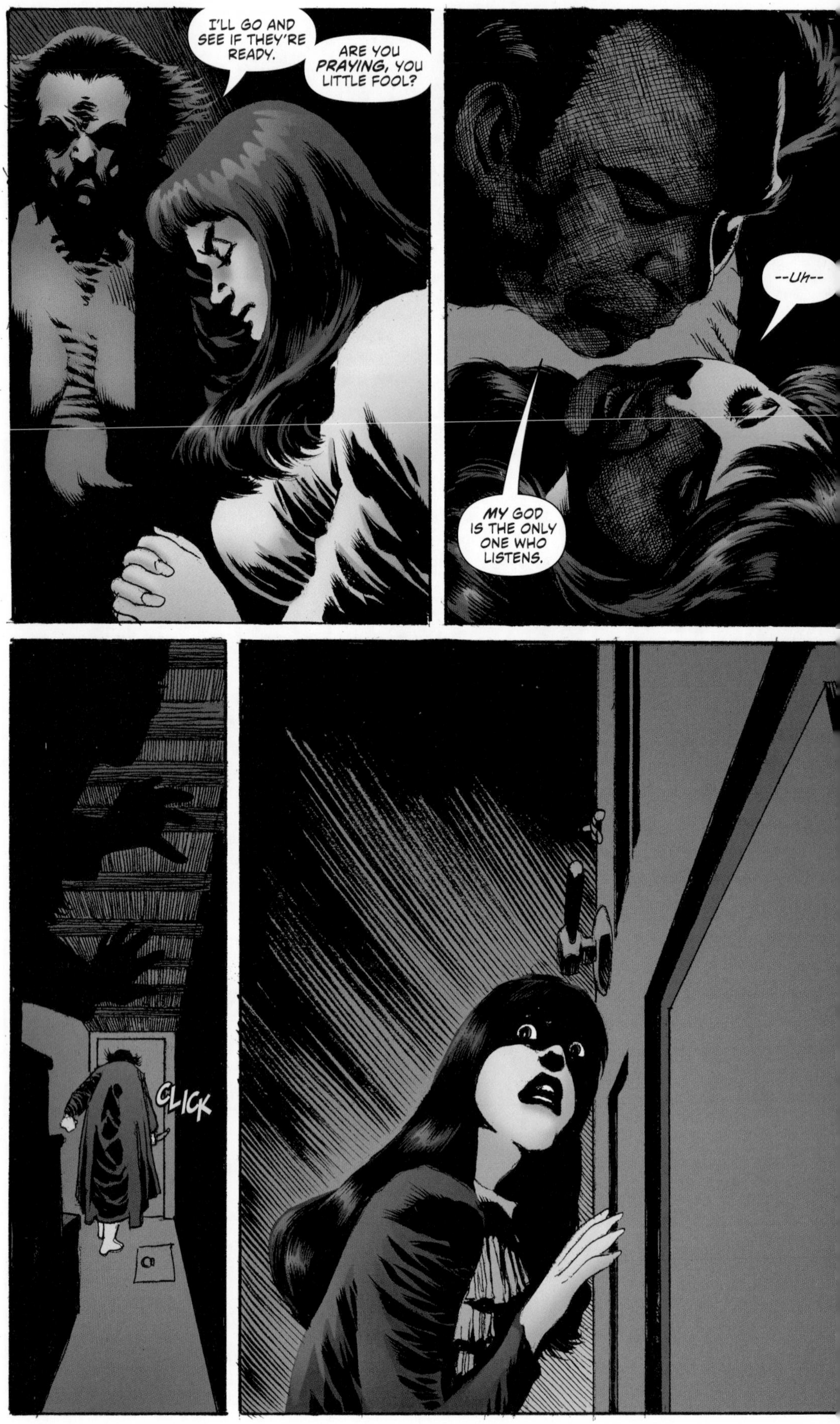
I'LL GO AND SEE IF THEY'RE READY.
ARE YOU *PRAYING,* YOU LITTLE FOOL?
--*Uh*--
MY GOD IS THE ONLY ONE WHO LISTENS.
CLICK

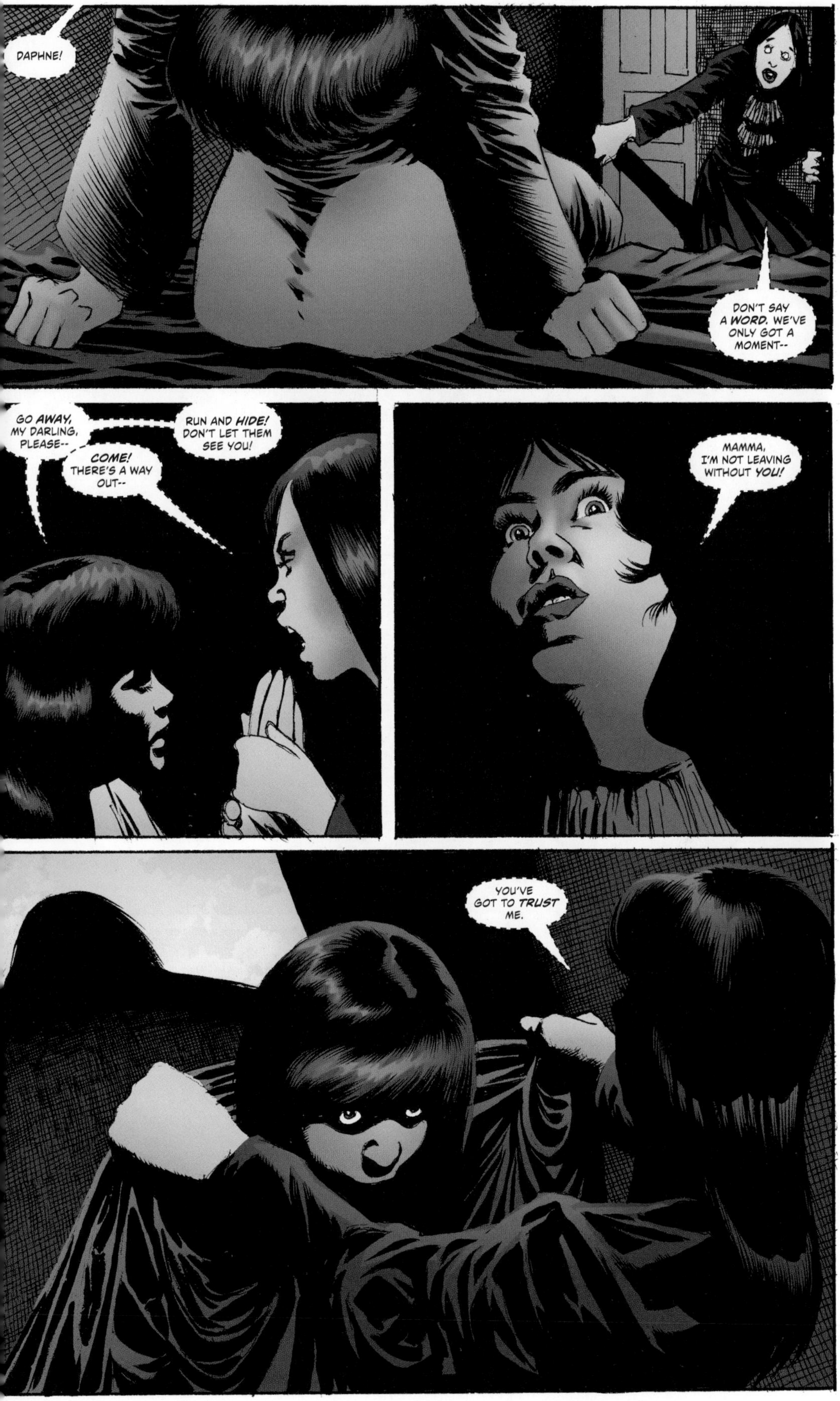
DAPHNE!
DON'T SAY A WORD. WE'VE ONLY GOT A MOMENT--
GO AWAY, MY DARLING, PLEASE--
RUN AND HIDE! DON'T LET THEM SEE YOU!
COME! THERE'S A WAY OUT--
MAMMA, I'M NOT LEAVING WITHOUT YOU!
YOU'VE GOT TO TRUST ME.

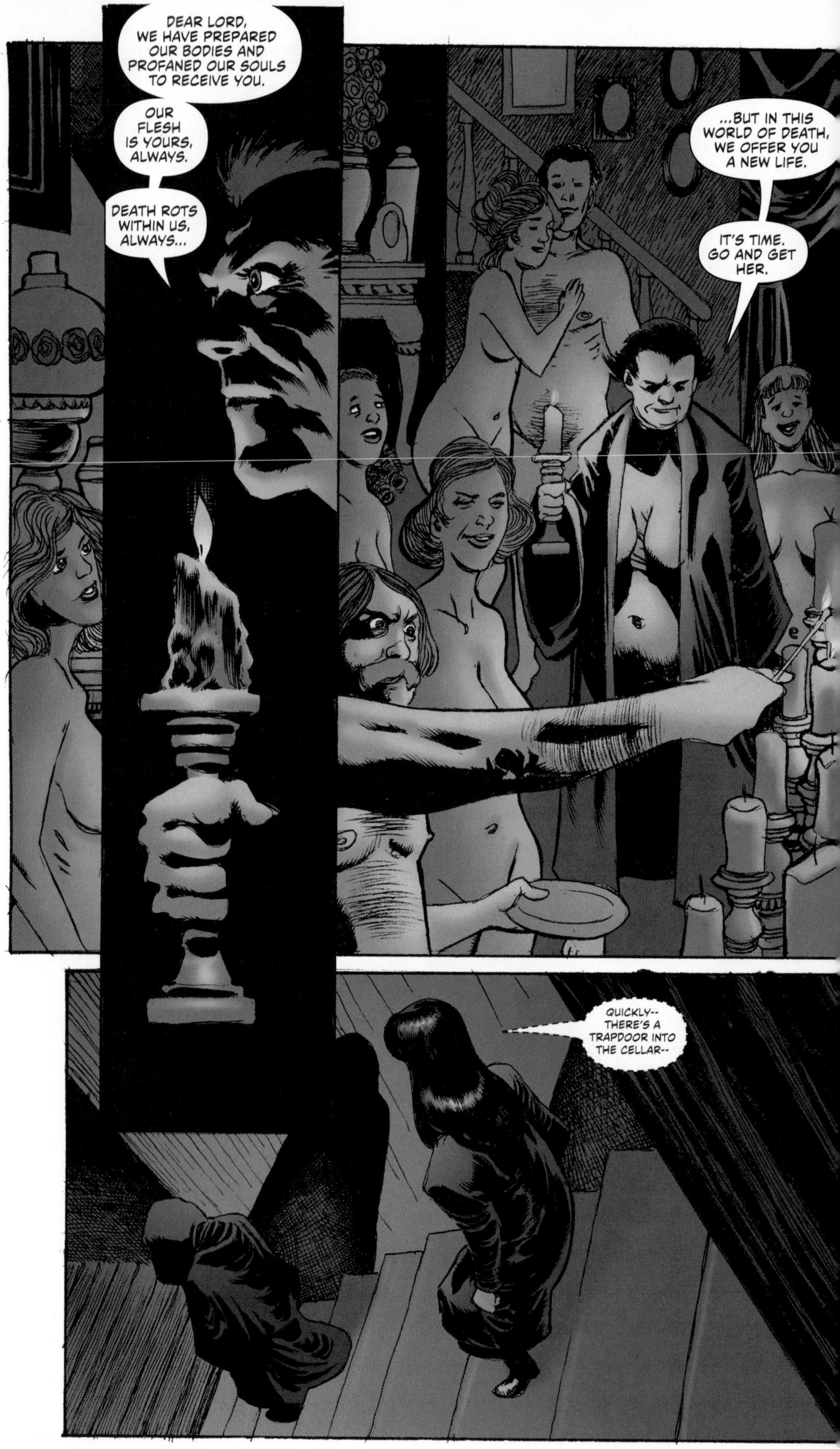
DEAR LORD, WE HAVE PREPARED OUR BODIES AND PROFANED OUR SOULS TO RECEIVE YOU.
OUR FLESH IS YOURS, ALWAYS.
DEATH ROTS WITHIN US, ALWAYS...
...BUT IN THIS WORLD OF DEATH, WE OFFER YOU A NEW LIFE.
IT'S TIME. GO AND GET HER.
QUICKLY-- THERE'S A TRAPDOOR INTO THE CELLAR--

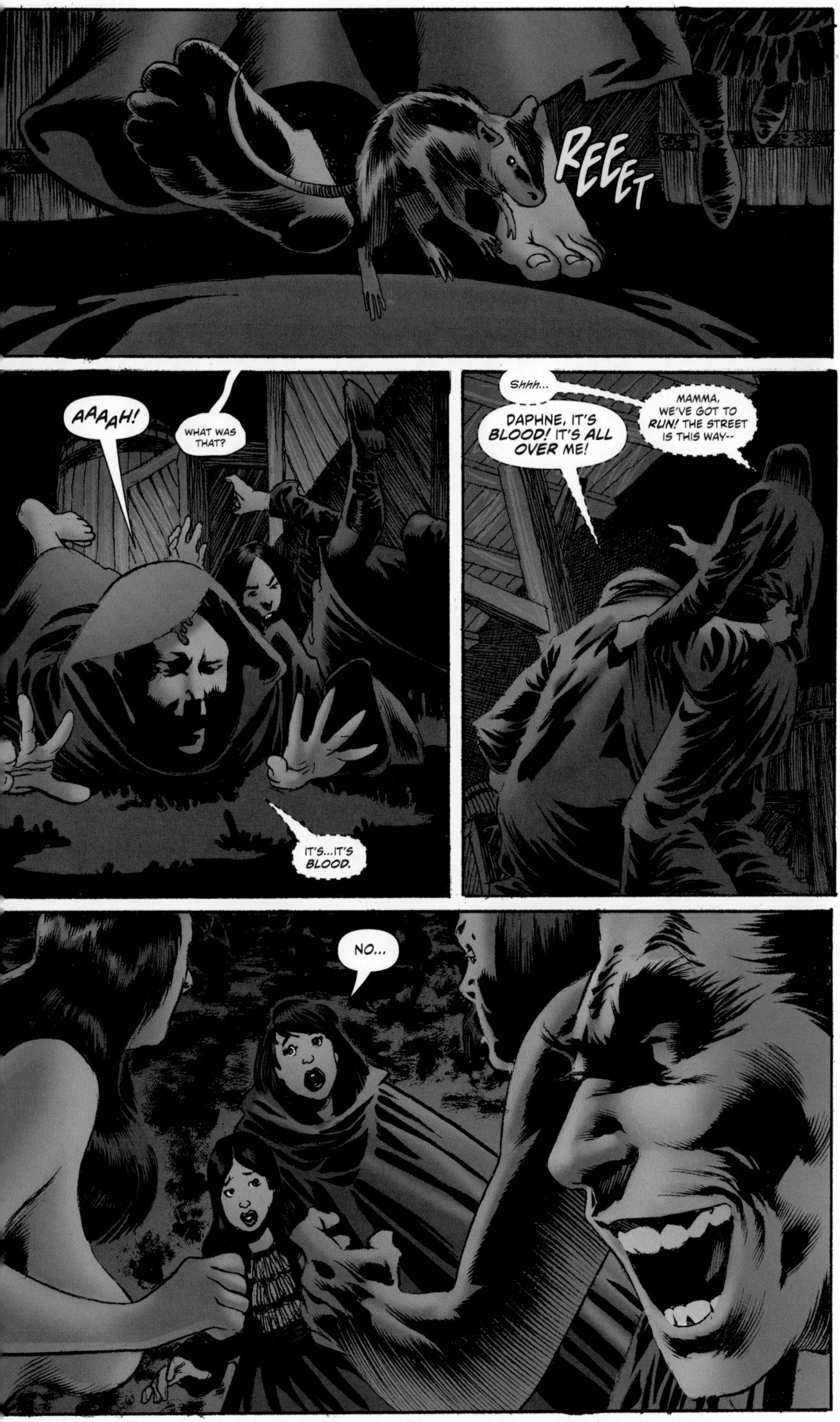

REEEET
AAAAH!
WHAT WAS THAT?
IT'S...IT'S BLOOD.
Shhh...
DAPHNE, IT'S BLOOD! IT'S ALL OVER ME!
MAMMA, WE'VE GOT TO RUN! THE STREET IS THIS WAY--
NO...

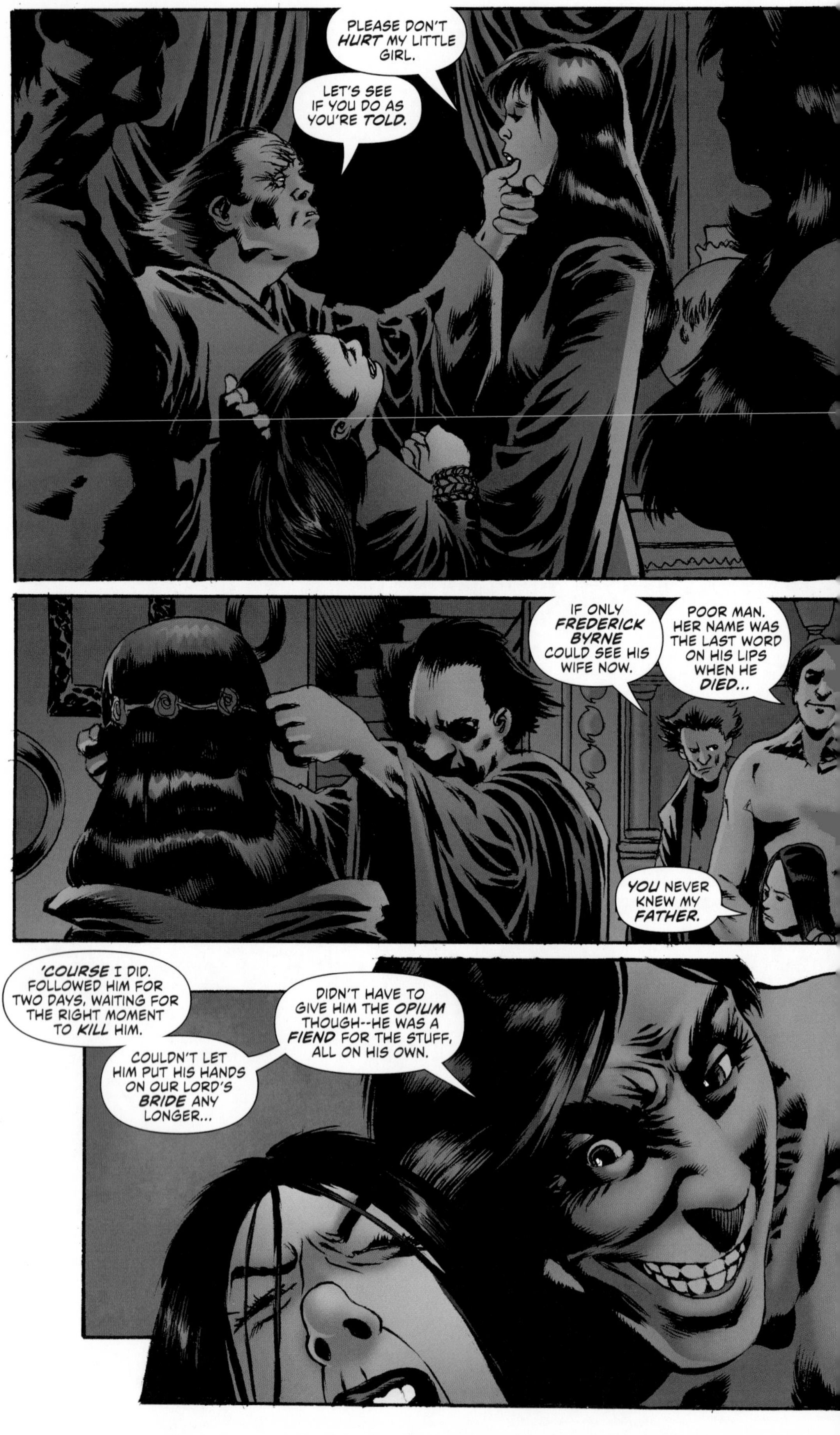
PLEASE DON'T *HURT* MY LITTLE GIRL.
LET'S SEE IF YOU DO AS YOU'RE *TOLD.*
IF ONLY *FREDERICK BYRNE* COULD SEE HIS WIFE NOW.
POOR MAN. HER NAME WAS THE LAST WORD ON HIS LIPS WHEN HE *DIED...*
YOU NEVER KNEW MY *FATHER.*
'COURSE I DID. FOLLOWED HIM FOR TWO DAYS, WAITING FOR THE RIGHT MOMENT TO *KILL* HIM.
COULDN'T LET HIM PUT HIS HANDS ON OUR LORD'S *BRIDE* ANY LONGER...
DIDN'T HAVE TO GIVE HIM THE *OPIUM* THOUGH--HE WAS A *FIEND* FOR THE STUFF, ALL ON HIS OWN.

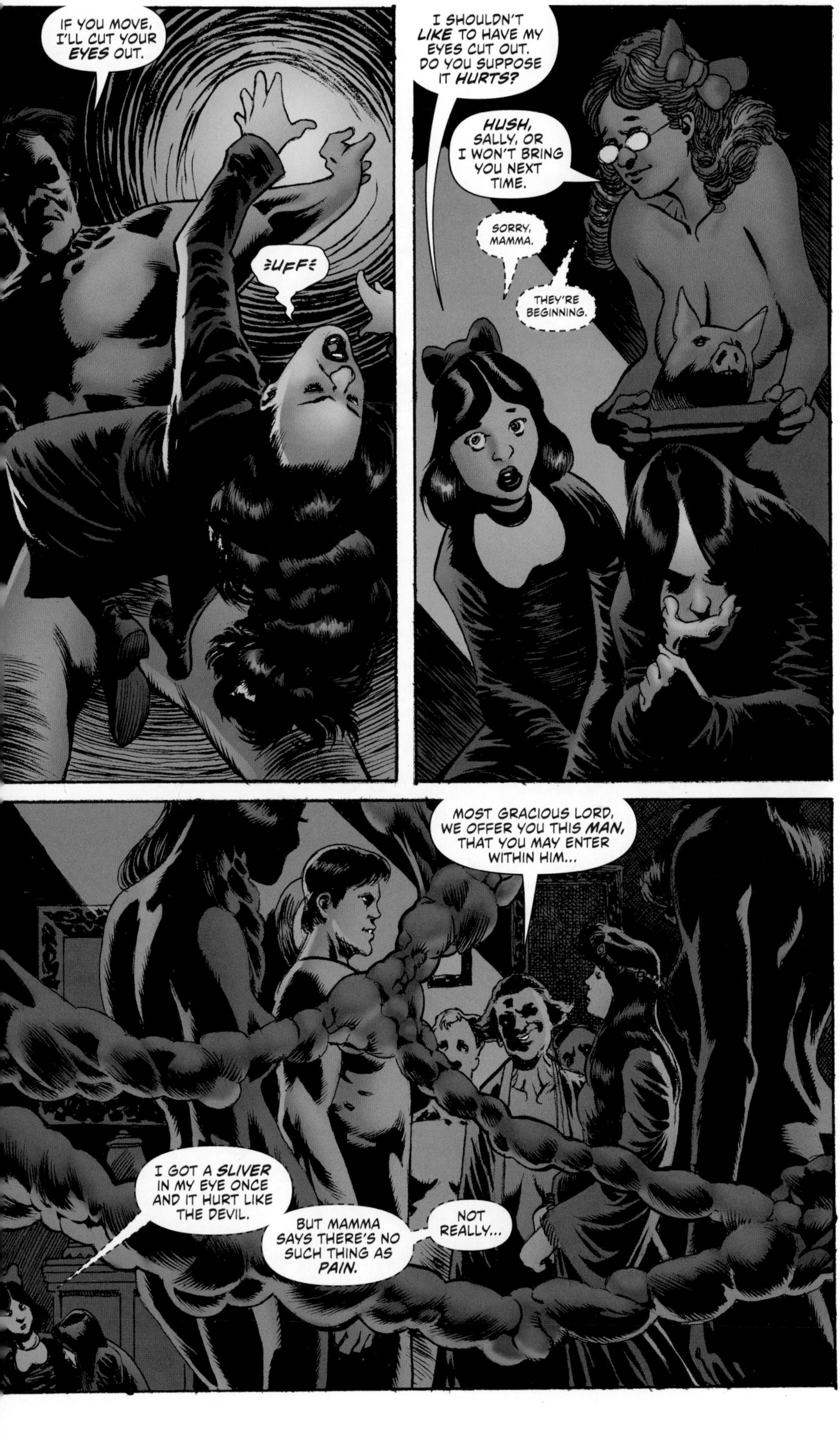
IF YOU MOVE, I'LL CUT YOUR EYES OUT.
UFF
I SHOULDN'T LIKE TO HAVE MY EYES CUT OUT. DO YOU SUPPOSE IT HURTS?
HUSH, SALLY, OR I WON'T BRING YOU NEXT TIME.
SORRY, MAMMA.
THEY'RE BEGINNING.
MOST GRACIOUS LORD, WE OFFER YOU THIS MAN, THAT YOU MAY ENTER WITHIN HIM...
I GOT A SLIVER IN MY EYE ONCE AND IT HURT LIKE THE DEVIL.
BUT MAMMA SAYS THERE'S NO SUCH THING AS PAIN.
NOT REALLY...

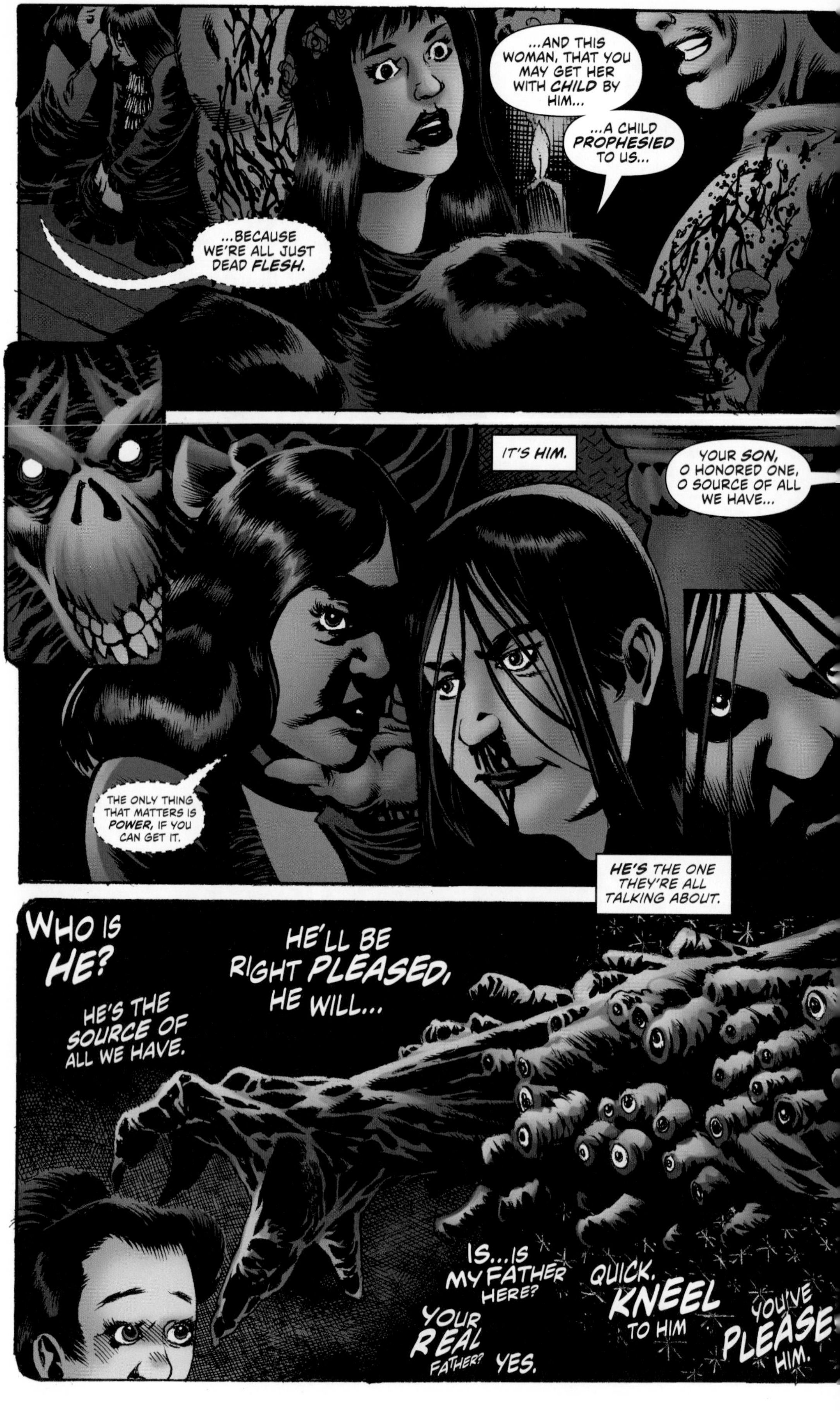
...AND THIS WOMAN, THAT YOU MAY GET HER WITH CHILD BY HIM...
...A CHILD PROPHESIED TO US...
...BECAUSE WE'RE ALL JUST DEAD FLESH.
IT'S HIM.
YOUR SON, O HONORED ONE, O SOURCE OF ALL WE HAVE...
THE ONLY THING THAT MATTERS IS POWER, IF YOU CAN GET IT.
HE'S THE ONE THEY'RE ALL TALKING ABOUT.
WHO IS HE?
HE'S THE SOURCE OF ALL WE HAVE.
HE'LL BE RIGHT PLEASED, HE WILL...
IS...IS MY FATHER HERE?
YOUR REAL FATHER? YES.
QUICK. KNEEL TO HIM
YOU'VE PLEASE HIM.

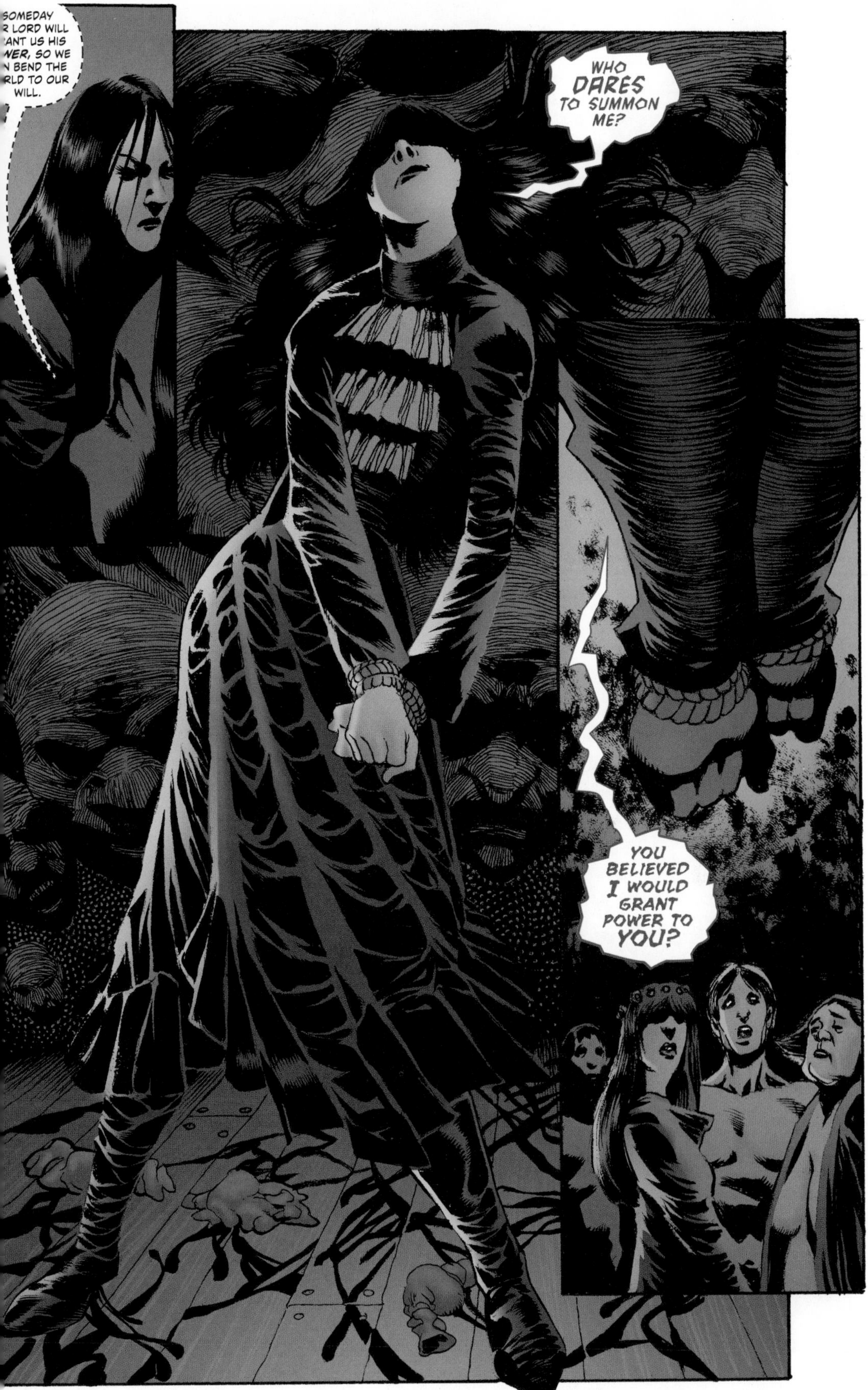
SOMEDAY R LORD WILL ANT US HIS WER, SO WE N BEND THE RLD TO OUR WILL.
WHO DARES TO SUMMON ME?
YOU BELIEVED I WOULD GRANT POWER TO YOU?

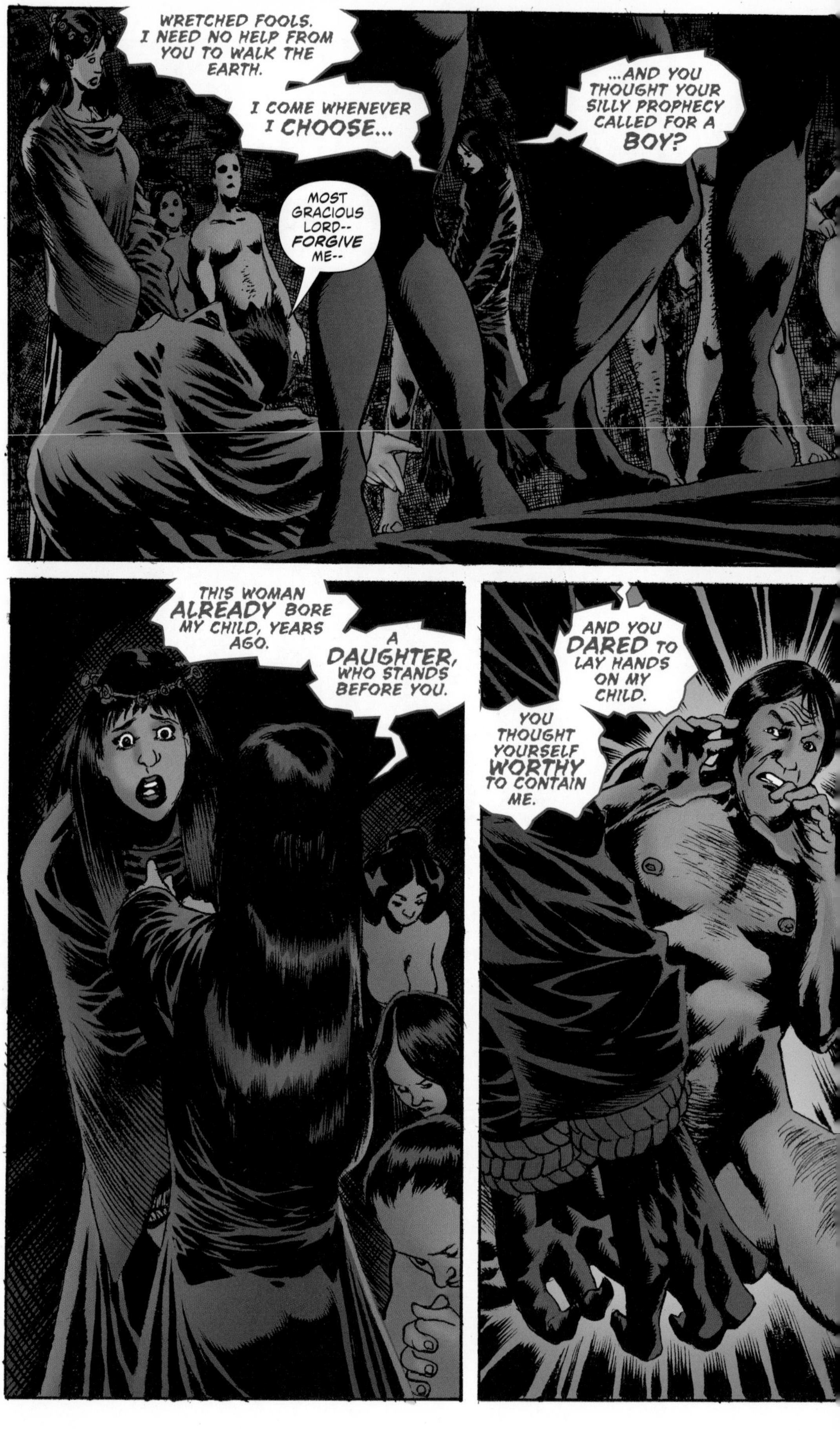
WRETCHED FOOLS. I NEED NO HELP FROM YOU TO WALK THE EARTH.
I COME WHENEVER I CHOOSE...
MOST GRACIOUS LORD-- FORGIVE ME--
...AND YOU THOUGHT YOUR SILLY PROPHECY CALLED FOR A BOY?
THIS WOMAN ALREADY BORE MY CHILD, YEARS AGO.
A DAUGHTER, WHO STANDS BEFORE YOU.
AND YOU DARED TO LAY HANDS ON MY CHILD.
YOU THOUGHT YOURSELF WORTHY TO CONTAIN ME.

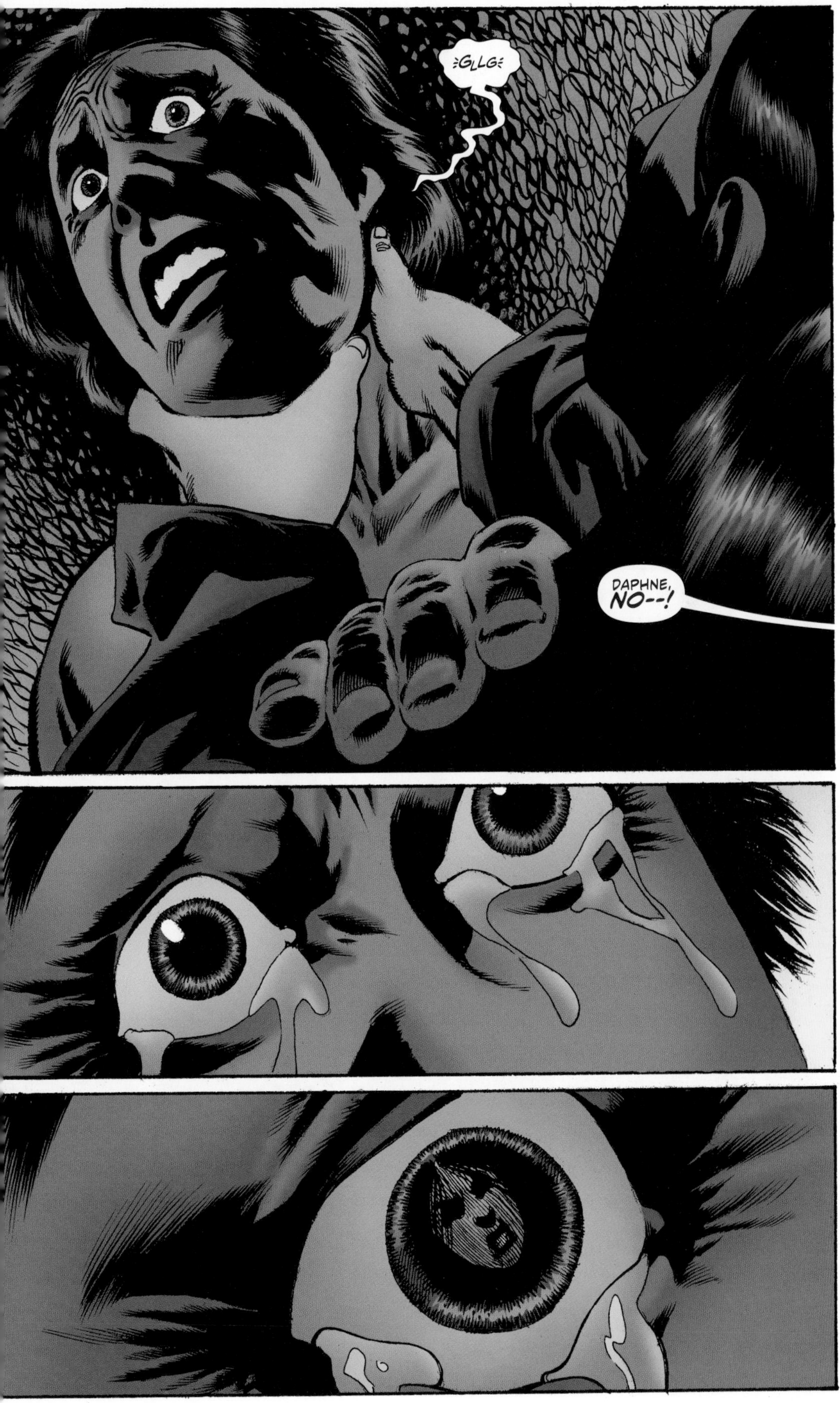
GLLG
DAPHNE, NO--!

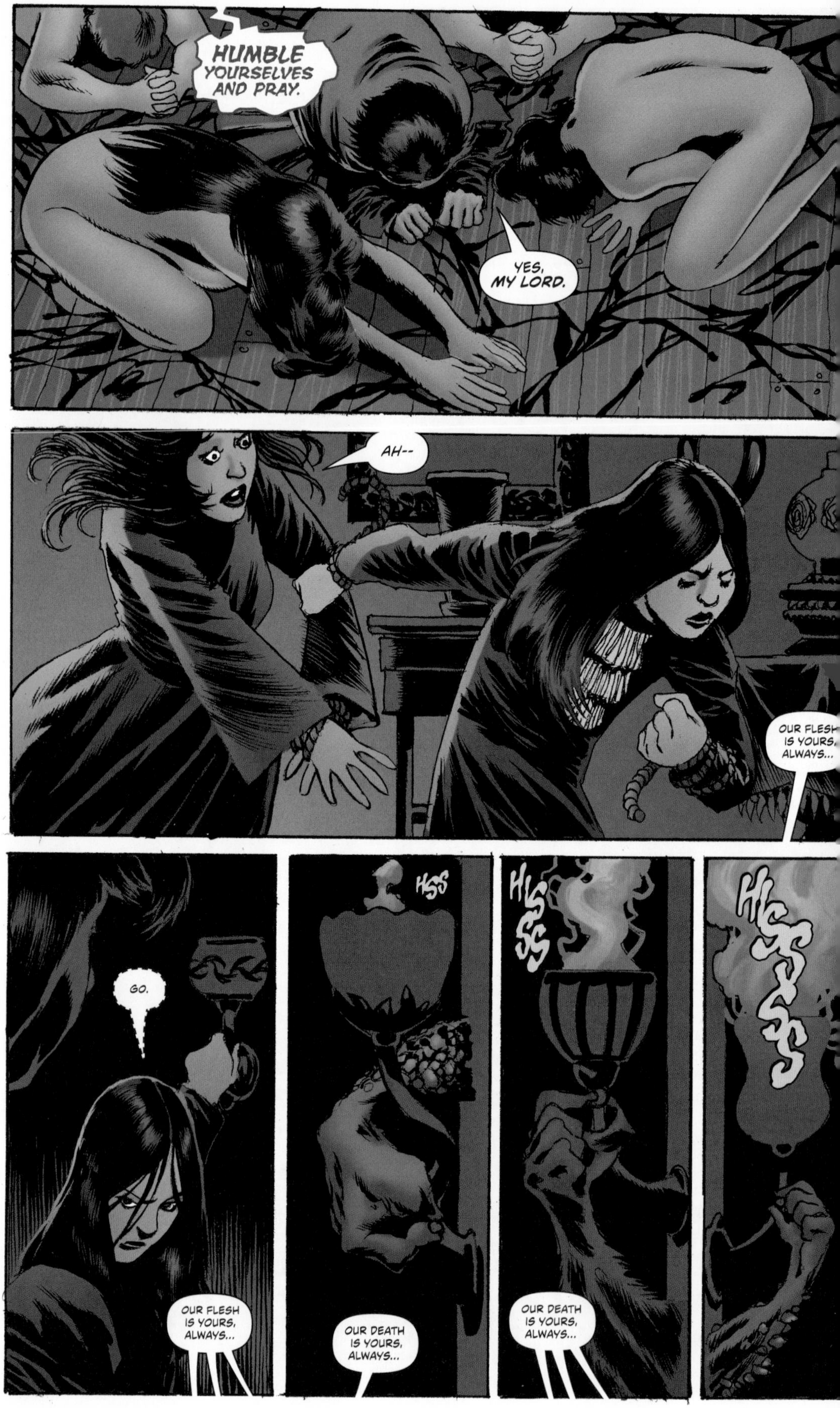
HUMBLE YOURSELVES AND PRAY.
YES, MY LORD.
AH--
OUR FLESH IS YOURS, ALWAYS...
GO.
OUR FLESH IS YOURS, ALWAYS...
HSS
OUR DEATH IS YOURS, ALWAYS...
HISSS
OUR DEATH IS YOURS, ALWAYS...
HISSSS

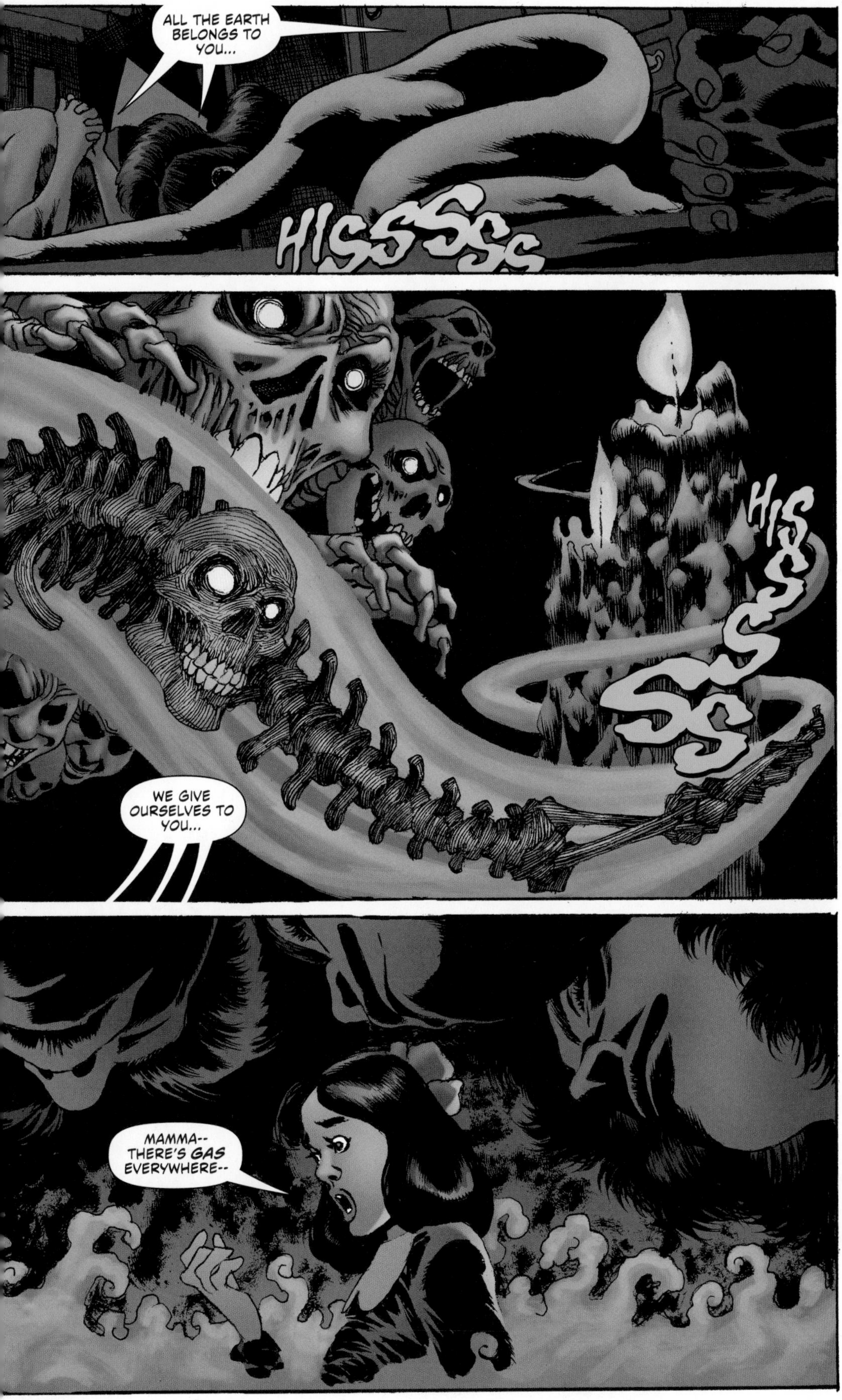
ALL THE EARTH BELONGS TO YOU...
HISSSSS
HISSSSS
WE GIVE OURSELVES TO YOU...
MAMMA-- THERE'S GAS EVERYWHERE--

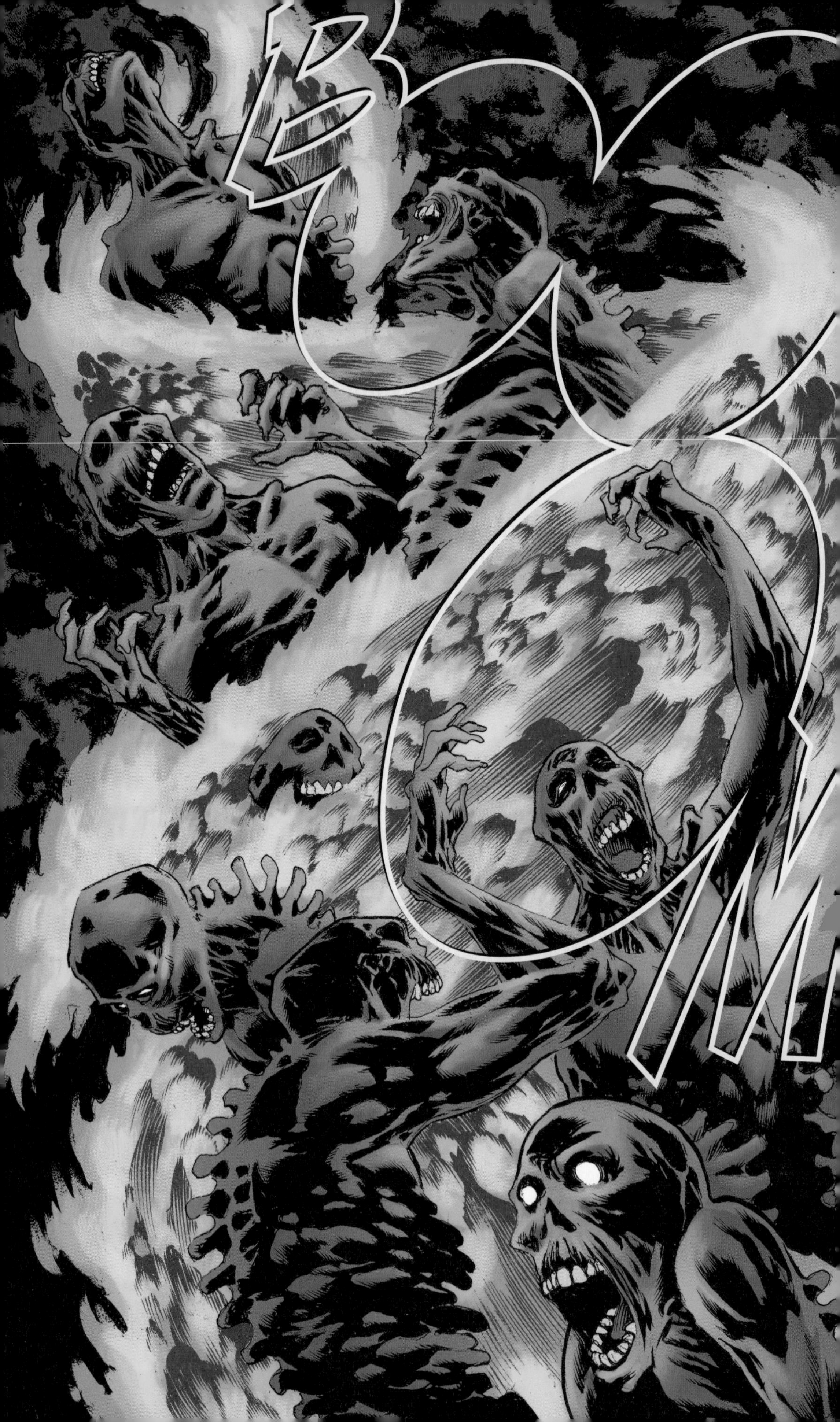
BOOM

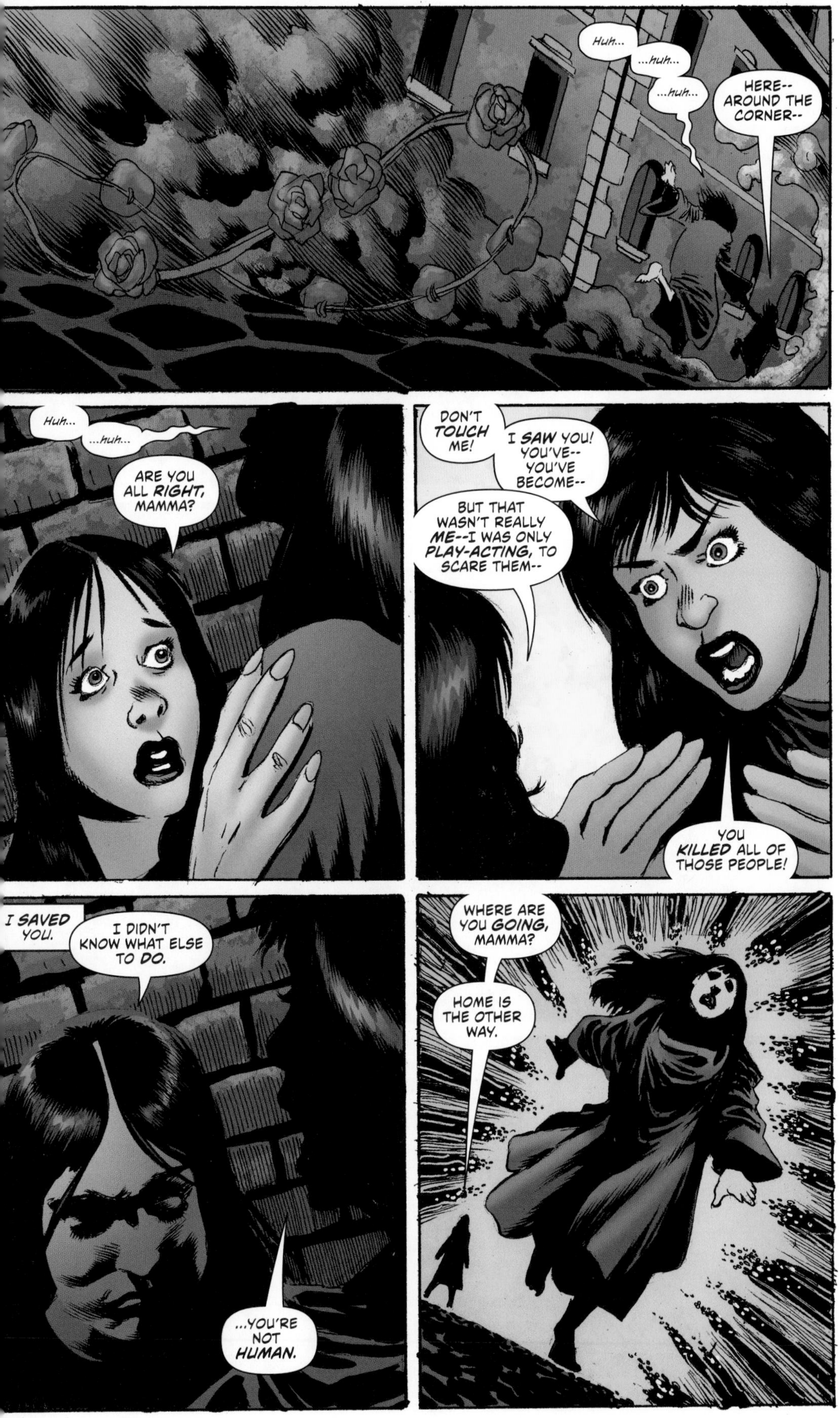

Huh...
...huh...
...huh...
HERE--AROUND THE CORNER--
Huh...
...huh...
ARE YOU ALL RIGHT, MAMMA?
DON'T TOUCH ME!
I SAW YOU! YOU'VE--YOU'VE BECOME--
BUT THAT WASN'T REALLY ME--I WAS ONLY PLAY-ACTING, TO SCARE THEM--
YOU KILLED ALL OF THOSE PEOPLE!
I SAVED YOU.
I DIDN'T KNOW WHAT ELSE TO DO.
...YOU'RE NOT HUMAN.
WHERE ARE YOU GOING, MAMMA?
HOME IS THE OTHER WAY.

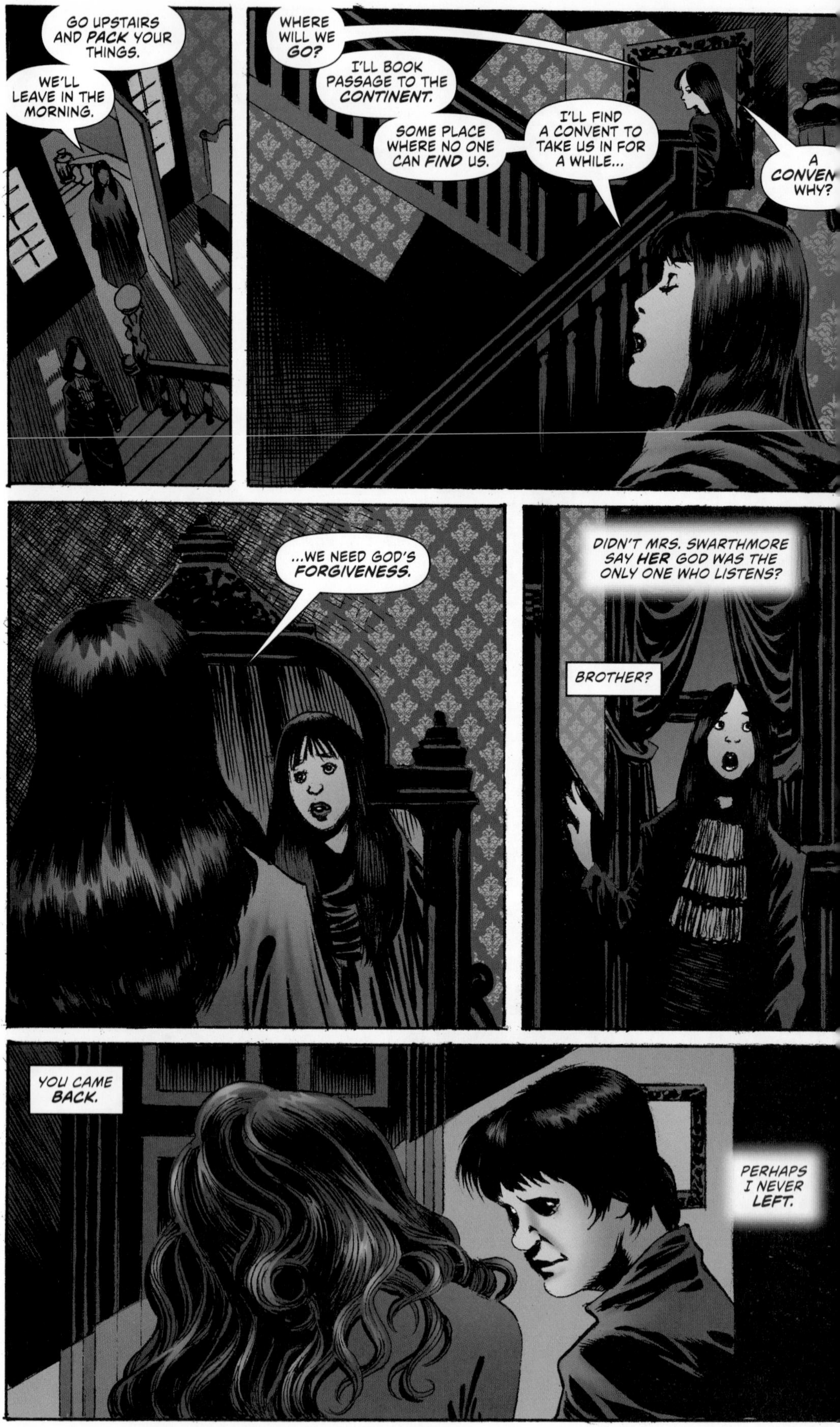
GO UPSTAIRS AND PACK YOUR THINGS.
WE'LL LEAVE IN THE MORNING.
WHERE WILL WE GO?
I'LL BOOK PASSAGE TO THE CONTINENT.
SOME PLACE WHERE NO ONE CAN FIND US.
I'LL FIND A CONVENT TO TAKE US IN FOR A WHILE...
A CONVEN WHY?
...WE NEED GOD'S FORGIVENESS.
DIDN'T MRS. SWARTHMORE SAY HER GOD WAS THE ONLY ONE WHO LISTENS?
BROTHER?
YOU CAME BACK.
PERHAPS I NEVER LEFT.

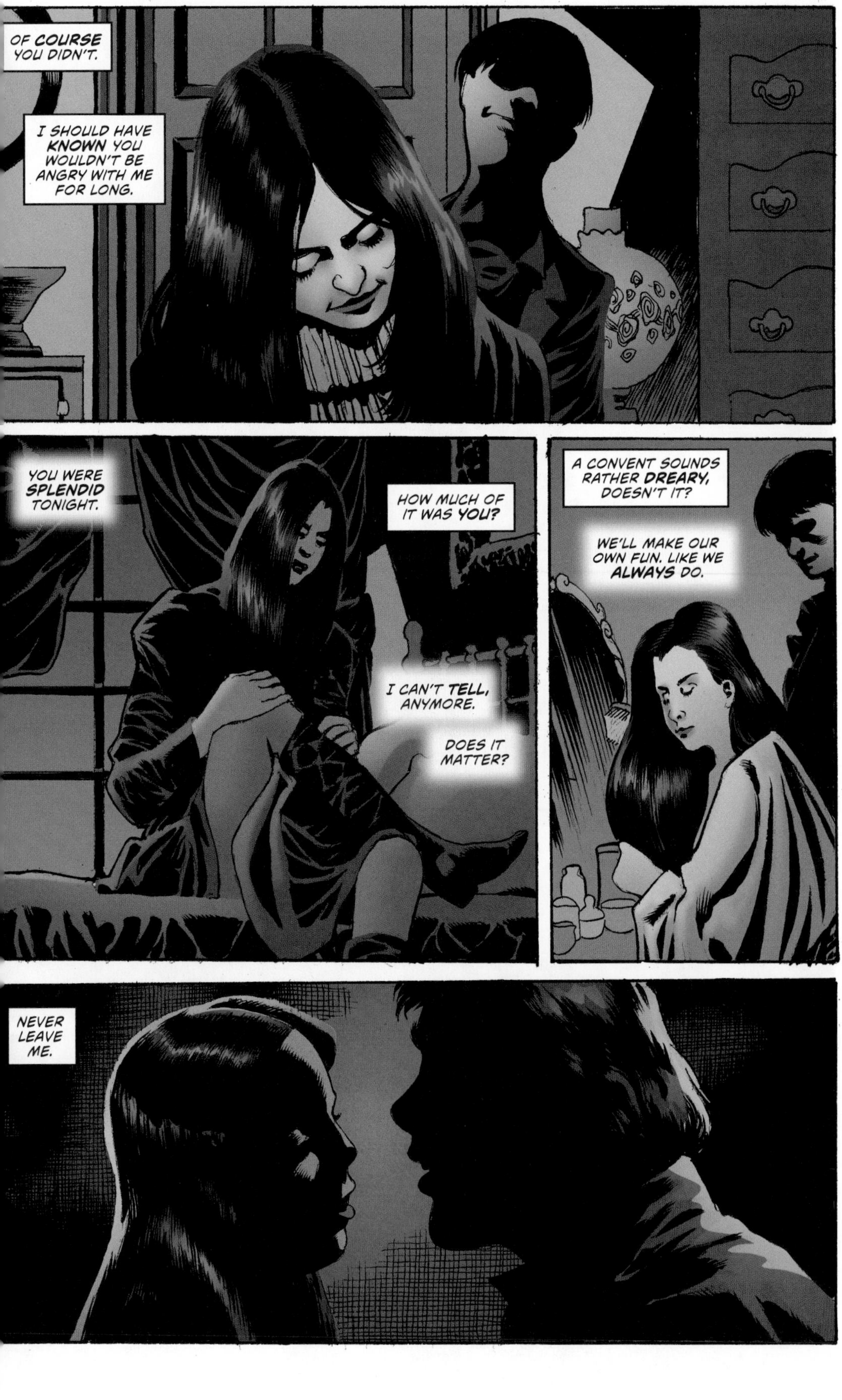
OF COURSE YOU DIDN'T.
I SHOULD HAVE KNOWN YOU WOULDN'T BE ANGRY WITH ME FOR LONG.
YOU WERE SPLENDID TONIGHT.
HOW MUCH OF IT WAS YOU?
I CAN'T TELL, ANYMORE.
DOES IT MATTER?
A CONVENT SOUNDS RATHER DREARY, DOESN'T IT?
WE'LL MAKE OUR OWN FUN. LIKE WE ALWAYS DO.
NEVER LEAVE ME.

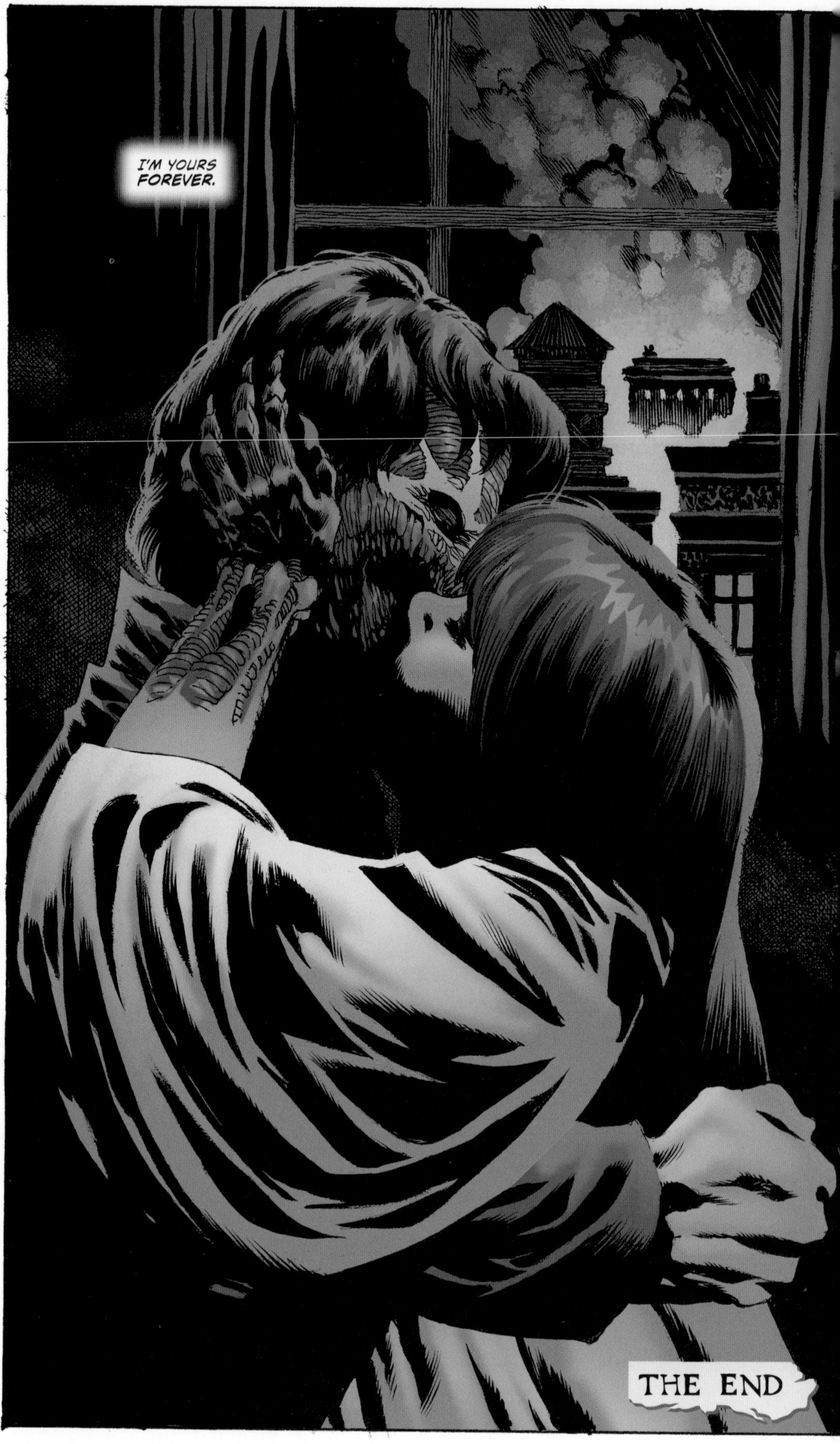
I'M YOURS FOREVER.
THE END

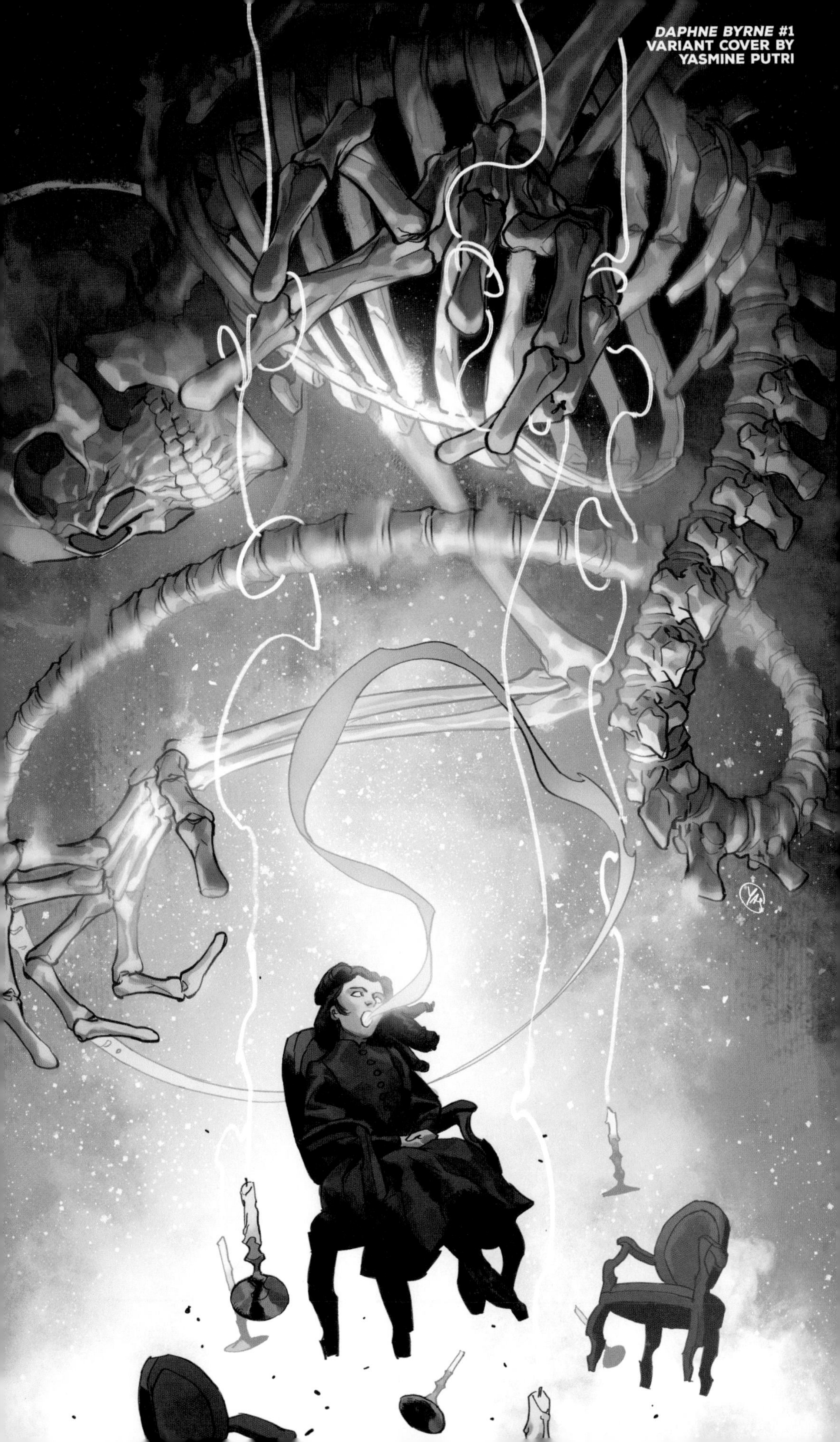

DAPHNE BYRNE #1
VARIANT COVER BY
YASMINE PUTRI

DAPHNE BYRNE #2
VARIANT COVER BY
DAN QUINTANA

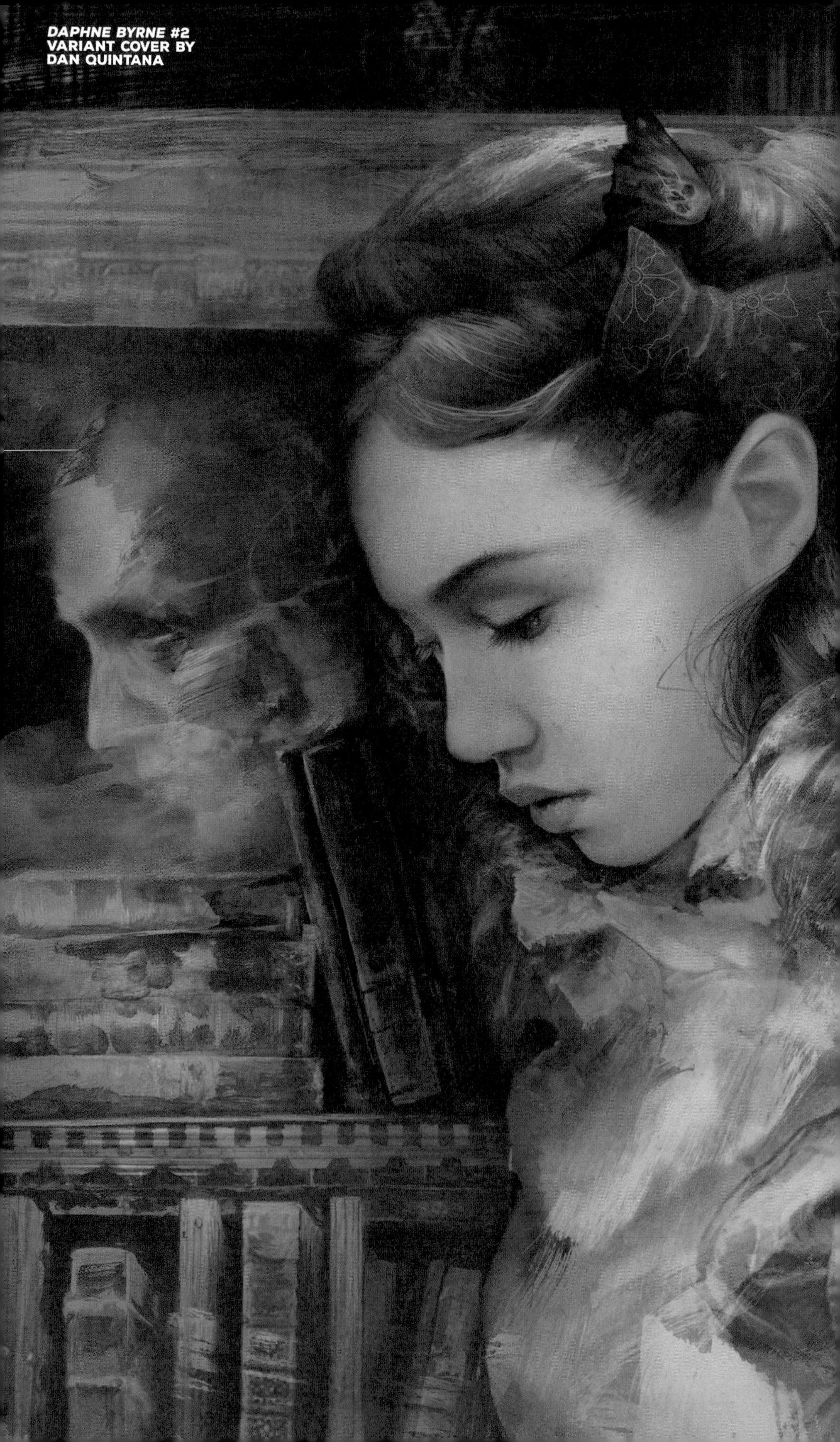

DAPHNE BYRNE #3
VARIANT COVER BY
DUSTIN NGUYEN

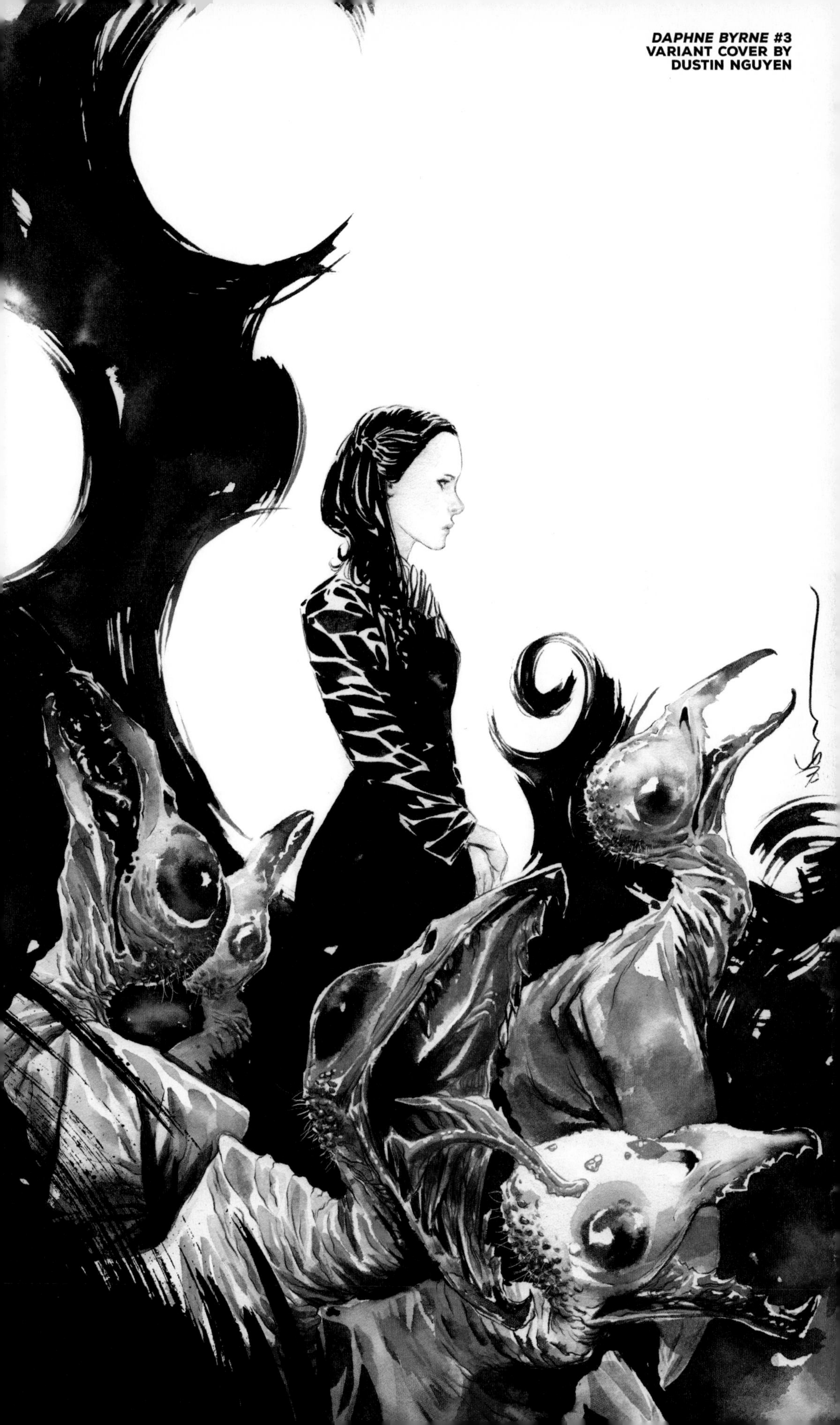

DAPHNE BYRNE #4
VARIANT COVER BY
GENE HA

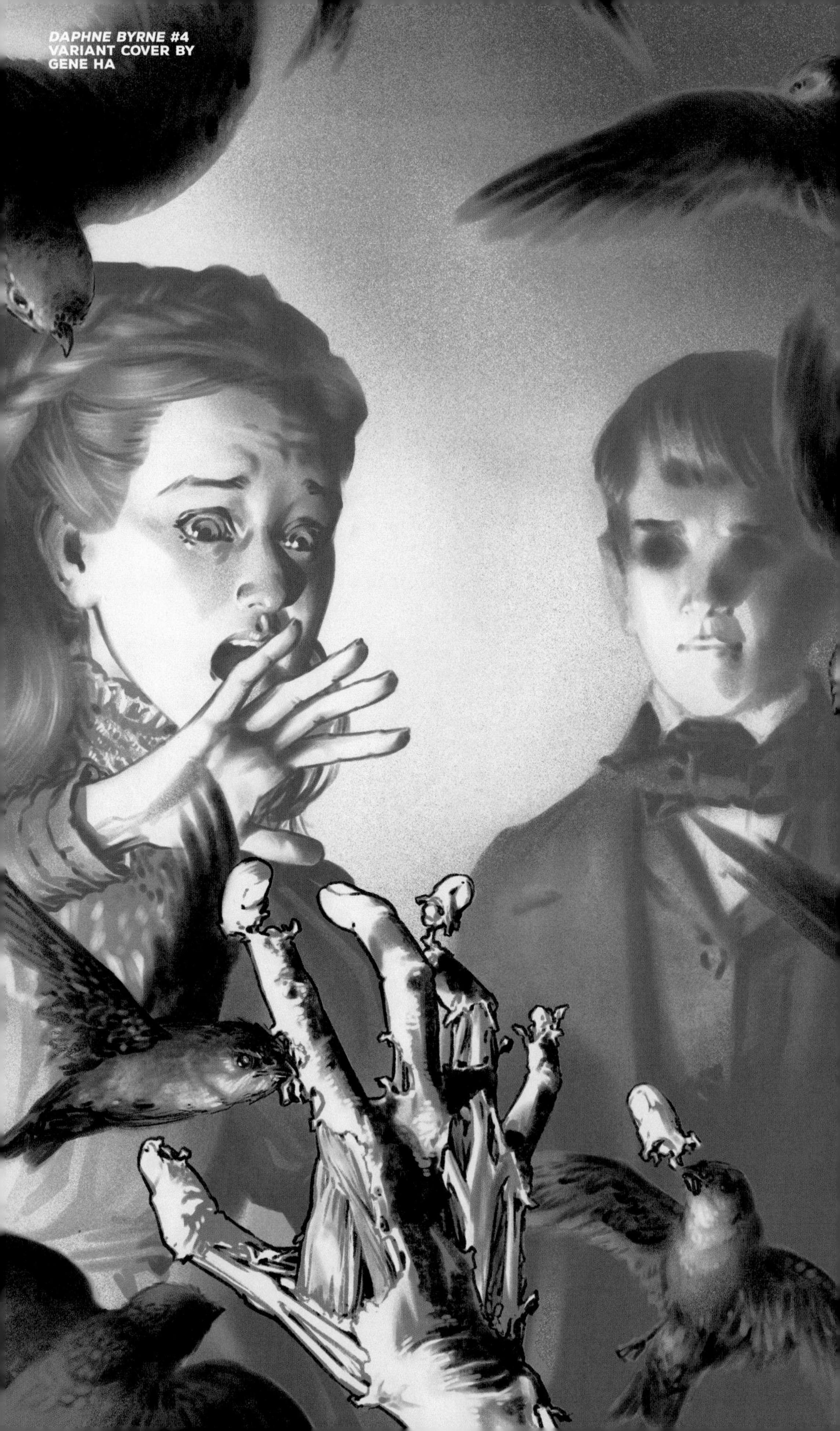

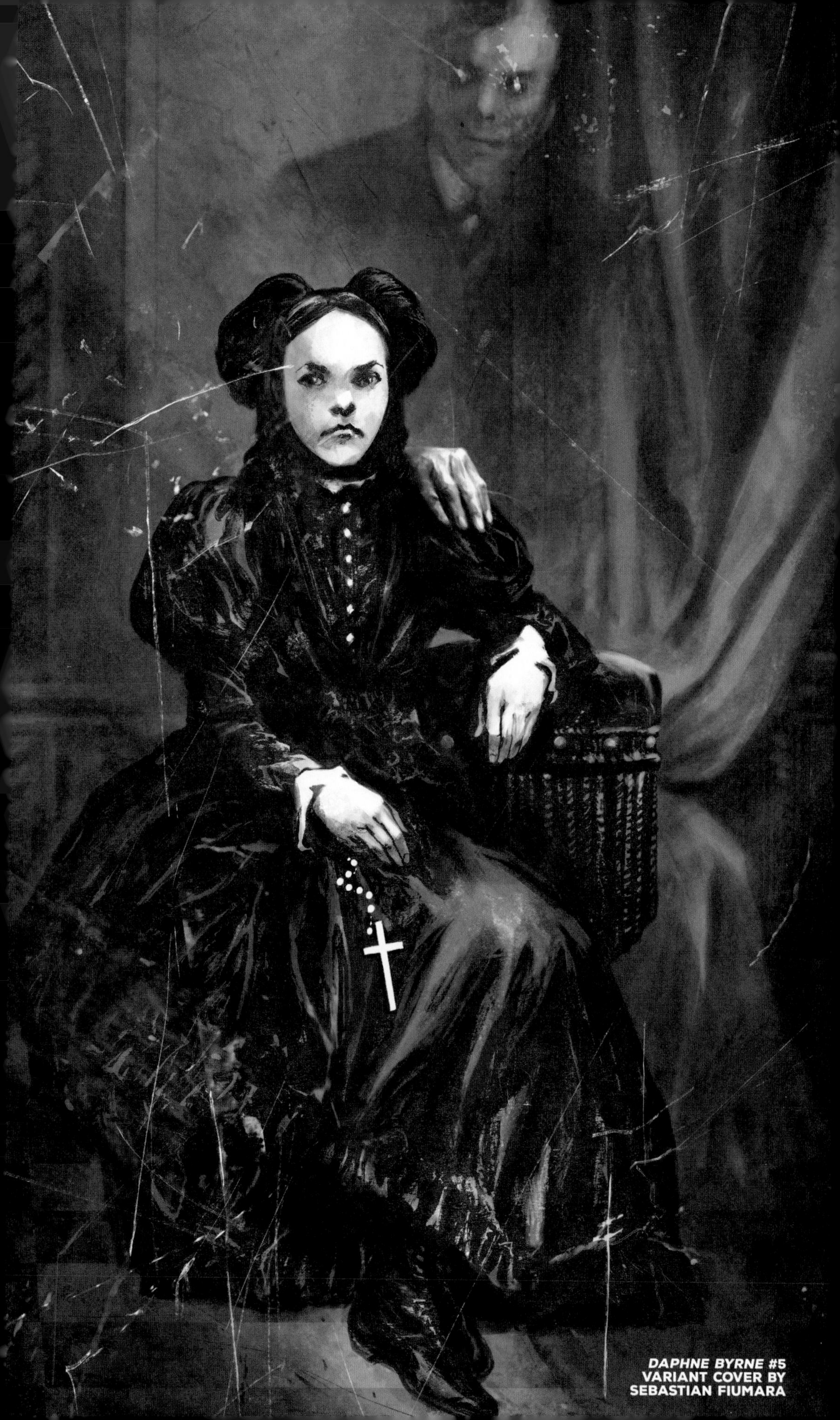

DAPHNE BYRNE #5
VARIANT COVER BY
SEBASTIAN FIUMARA

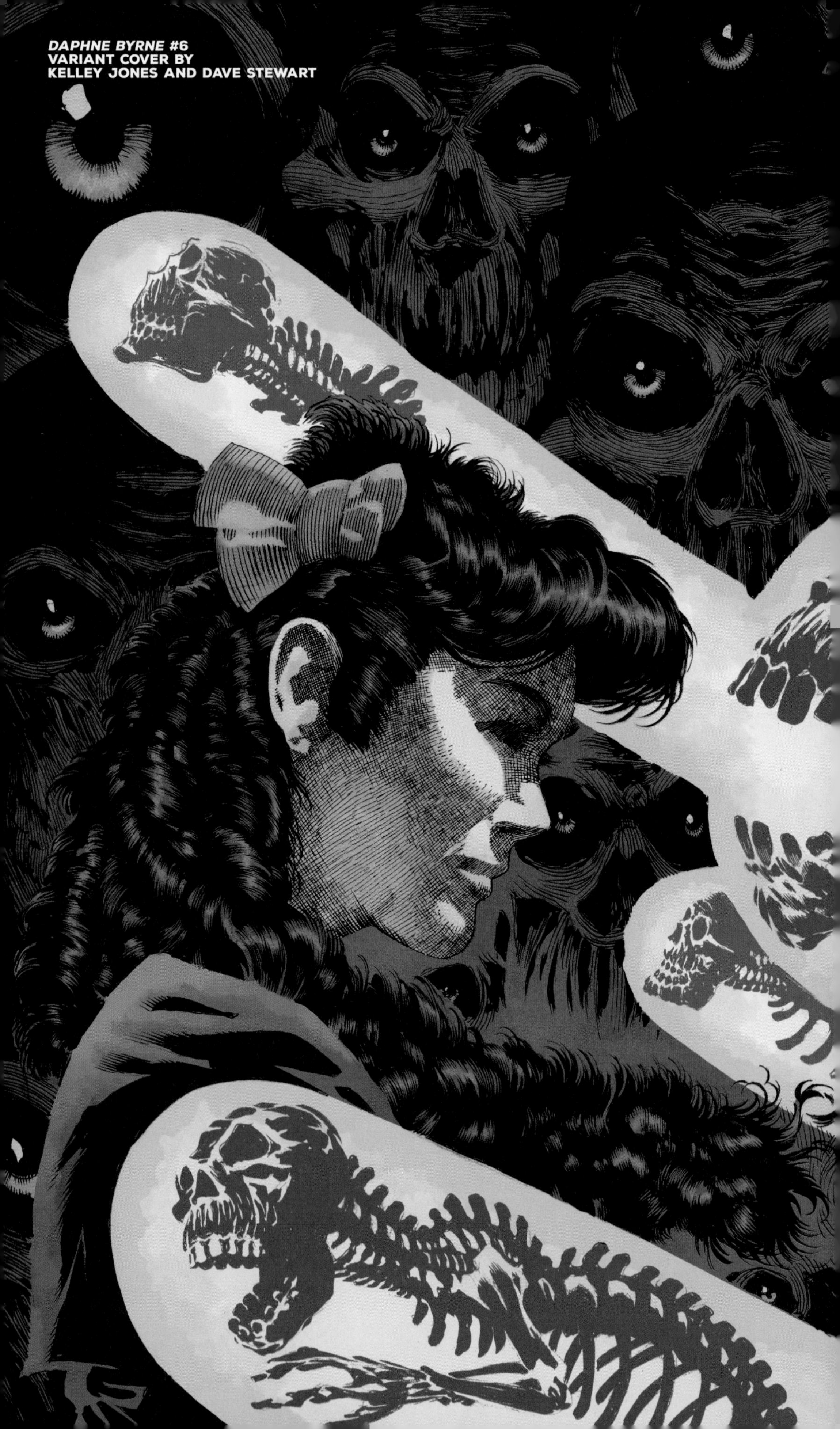

DAPHNE BYRNE #6
VARIANT COVER BY
KELLEY JONES AND DAVE STEWART

RED INK

INTERVIEW WITH LAURA MARKS
ACCOMPANYING ARTWORK
BY KELLEY JONES

The series is called *Daphne Byrne*, so let's start there: What can you share about the title character and the power growing inside her?

Daphne's 14, so she's in that odd space between childhood and womanhood. She's a lonely misfit grieving for her father, who was the only person who really got her. She has tons of intellectual curiosity, which is completely inappropriate for a girl in 1886.

Most of all, she's longing for connection...which makes her easy prey for the demon who wants to be her new best friend. He unleashes her darker, bloodier impulses, and helps her find the power to express them. But how much of that was really inside her all along?

How do you describe the horror of *Daphne Byrne*?

Joe Hill likes to call it "*The Omen* in petticoats." I might go with "Henry James meets *The Exorcist*." But unlike in *The Omen*, Daphne isn't just our monster—she's also our heroine and the focus of our empathy. And unlike in *The Exorcist*, Daphne is an active participant—very aware of what's happening to her, and maybe even able to exploit it.

Daphne & "Friend"

Brother

Daphne

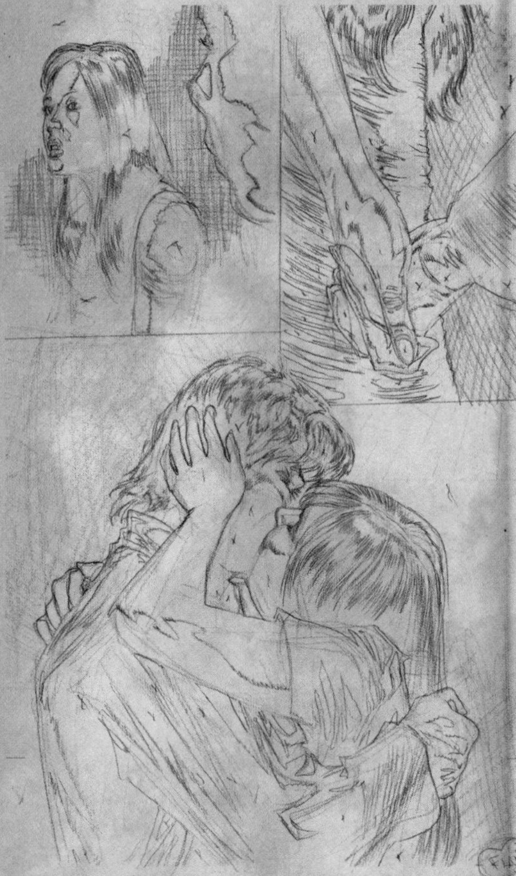

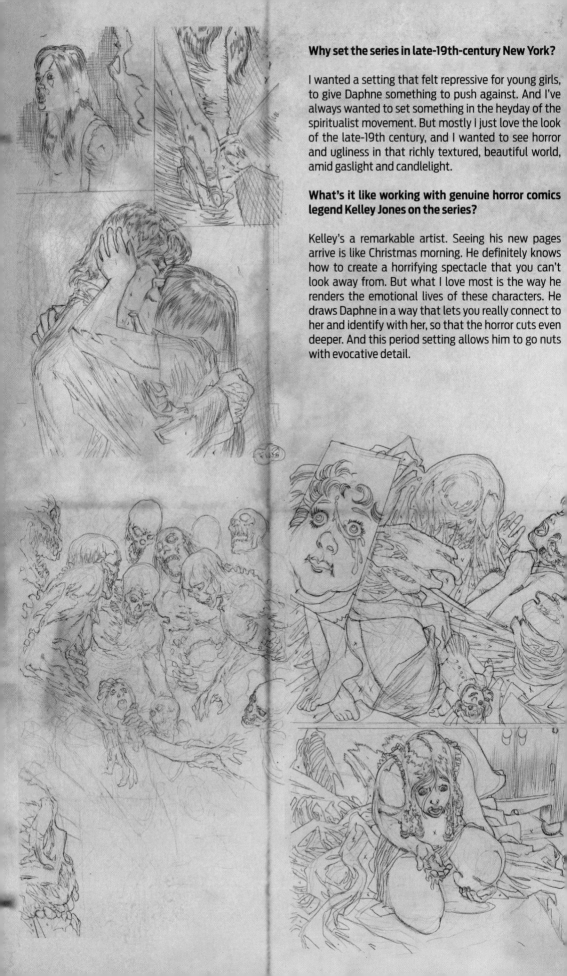

Why set the series in late-19th-century New York?

I wanted a setting that felt repressive for young girls, to give Daphne something to push against. And I've always wanted to set something in the heyday of the spiritualist movement. But mostly I just love the look of the late-19th century, and I wanted to see horror and ugliness in that richly textured, beautiful world, amid gaslight and candlelight.

What's it like working with genuine horror comics legend Kelley Jones on the series?

Kelley's a remarkable artist. Seeing his new pages arrive is like Christmas morning. He definitely knows how to create a horrifying spectacle that you can't look away from. But what I love most is the way he renders the emotional lives of these characters. He draws Daphne in a way that lets you really connect to her and identify with her, so that the horror cuts even deeper. And this period setting allows him to go nuts with evocative detail.

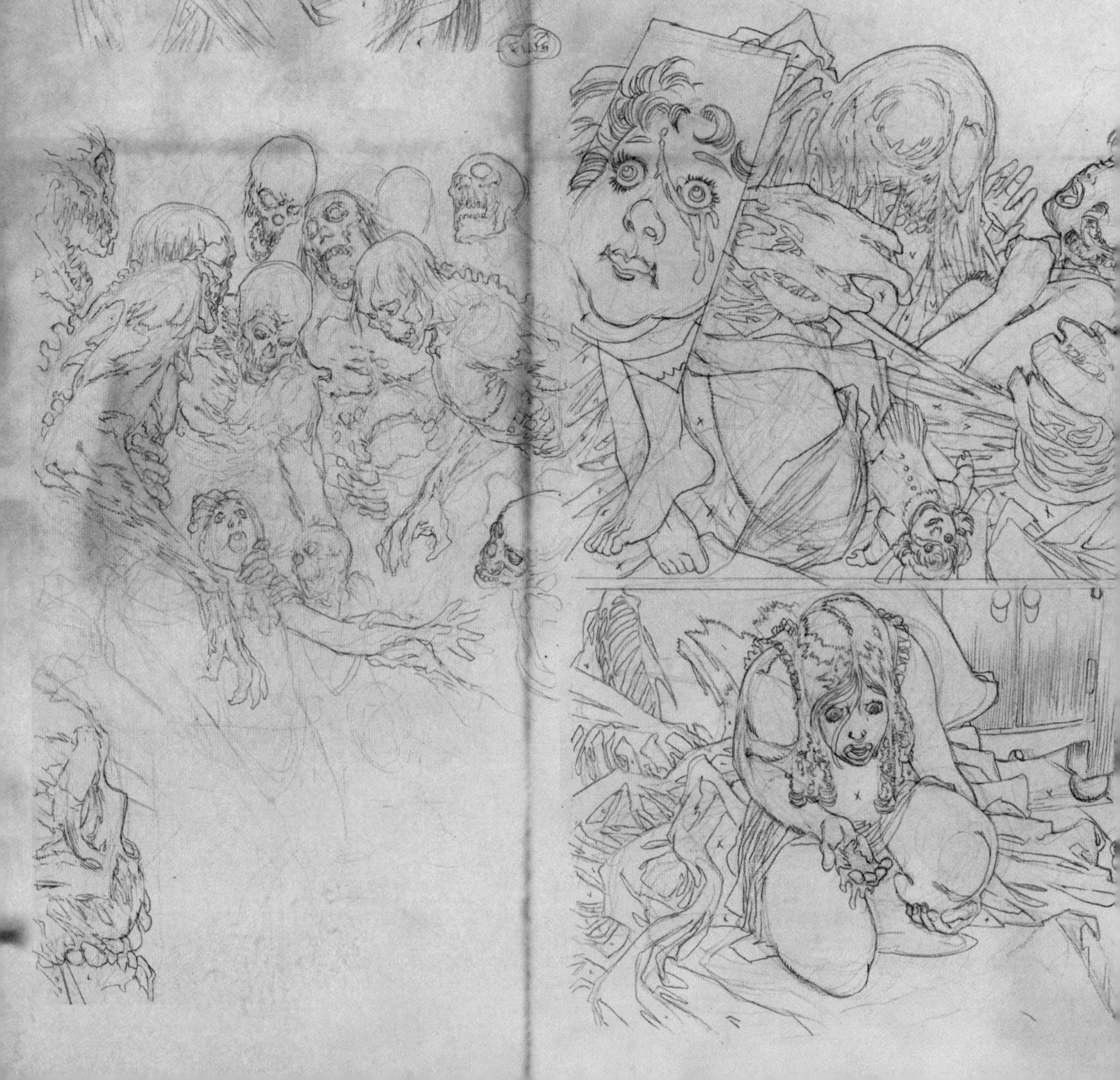

How have you found the transition from writing for the stage and TV to writing for comics?

The biggest difference is that instead of having actors interpret the writing, I've got Kelley acting in every role. And he's masterful at it—which means that I can trust him to render the subtext on a character's face. TV dramas require an economy of language: you don't have the time and space to let characters yammer on for no reason; everything has to serve the whole. I've found that to be true of comics as well.

And there's great freedom in knowing that Kelley can draw anything I dream up. There's no special effects budget, no location fees...

What does it mean to you for *Daphne Byrne* to be part of Hill House Comics?

Joe has been incredibly generous with his encouragement and advice, and the whole team at DC has been terrific. I can't imagine a better group to guide a writer who's new to comics.

RED INK

INTERVIEW WITH KELLEY JONES

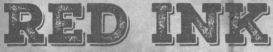

Let's start with the title character: How did Daphne Byrne come to life for you?

When I drew a piece simply to try and capture the mood of the character I read in the outline, I thought that the piece came out so well I sent it in to DC to see if I was on the right track. I'm happy to say it's a cover to #6!

Right from the first page, this series is chock-full of unsettling imagery (last page of issue #2, looking at you). What have been some of your favorite moments?

A couple come to mind: Daphne in the cemetery where her father's buried, whether awake or in a hallucination; also where Brother speaks to Daphne in a library. And the scene when Daphne awakes in a coffin and is taken to the realms underneath, to the dead.

I really enjoy all the little moments: the baby birds, the shadows that belong to nobody, the things that only Daphne sees...all good stuff to draw.

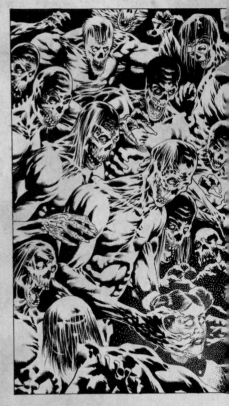

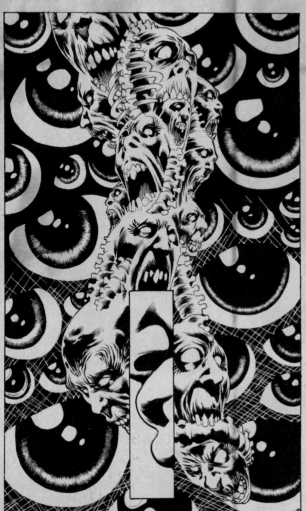

What's your process in nailing those late-century details?

The first thing is that the light was different th wasn't as bright, and the natural light of nigh day still held sway. Homes were more furnishec design was everything, beyond need or fun People held them- selves differently and were reserved for the most part.

How does the setting influence your take o supernatural elements of the story?

There are more shadows for things to hide in— course, take advantage of that!

You've illustrated some of DC's most iconic h stories—what has made Daphne Byrne speci

She's not sure who, or what, she is. And she that. She's going to be something new; I just know what that means for those who cross he

What type of horror inspires you?

Old horror comics. (Yes, *House of Mystery* and *I of Secrets* are big among those!) Classic Ha films and Rod Serling's *Night Gallery*. The stories, like those of M. R. James and Manly Wellman; really, all those pulp horror writers se still work beautifully! Holst's "Saturn" movem his symphony *The Planets* has always put me i mood of horror.

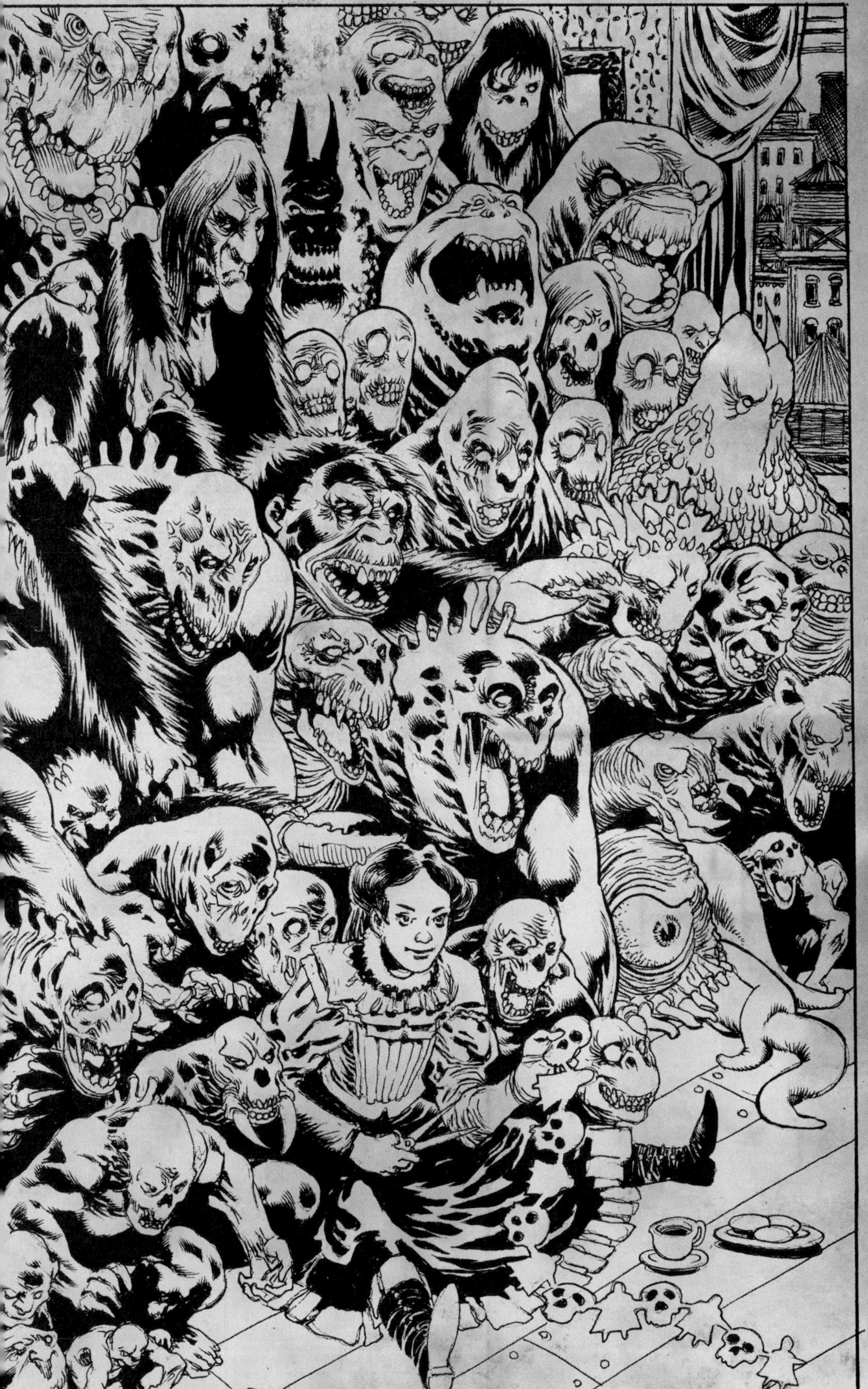

Laura Marks is a television writer and multiple award-winning playwright whose on-screen credits include *The Good Fight*, *The Expanse*, *The Exorcist*, *BrainDead*, and *Ray Donovan*. Her plays *Bethany* and *Mine* have garnered acclaim from critics and been published and produced across the U.S. and overseas. A graduate of Juilliard's playwriting program, she lives in New York City.

Born in 1962, **Kelley Jones** began his DC career with a revolutionary reimagining of Deadman in the miniseries *Deadman: Love After Death* and *Deadman: Exorcism*. The success of these efforts led to an opportunity to illustrate Neil Gaiman's *The Sandman*, where he lent his talents to the now-legendary stories "A Dream of a Thousand Cats" and "Season of Mists."

The Sandman was quickly followed by *Batman & Dracula: Red Rain*, one of the most popular Elseworlds stories ever published. Jones' uniquely stylized look for the Dark Knight Detective was soon the star attraction of a three-year, critically acclaimed run in the ongoing *Batman* series. His subsequent work on such titles as *Batman: Dark Joker—The Wild*, *Batman: Haunted Gotham*, *Batman: Gotham After Midnight* and *Batman: Unseen* have cemented his place as one of the character's definitive artists.

A resident of the Golden State, Jones continues to enjoy drawing comics because it remains one of the only jobs where you can listen to a ball game while you work and not get into trouble.

Michelle Madsen lives in Portland, Oregon and has been coloring comic books since 1995. Her recent projects include *Lady Killer Volume 2*, *Witchfinder*, *ZombieLars*, and *Lady Baltimore*.

Rob Leigh is a graduate of the Kubert School. His lettering first received critical notice in 1972, when he was sent home with a note for writing a four-letter word on the blackboard of Miss Tuschmann's second-grade class. An avid outdoorsman, when not at his computer lettering, Leigh can be found wandering his natural habitat: the woods, water and mountains.